The Feldenkrais Method for Instrumentalists

The Feldenkrais Method for Instrumentalists

....

A Guide to Awareness through Movement

Samuel H. Nelson and Elizabeth L. Blades

Illustrated by Amy Walts

ROWMAN & LITTLEFIELD
Lanham • Boulder • New York • London

Published by Rowman & Littlefield
An imprint of The Rowman & Littlefield Publishing Group, Inc.
4501 Forbes Boulevard, Suite 200, Lanham, Maryland 20706
www.rowman.com

86-90 Paul Street, London EC2A 4NE

Copyright © 2024 by The Rowman & Littlefield Publishing Group, Inc.

All rights reserved. No part of this book may be reproduced in any form or by any electronic or mechanical means, including information storage and retrieval systems, without written permission from the publisher, except by a reviewer who may quote passages in a review.

British Library Cataloguing in Publication Information Available

Library of Congress Cataloging-in-Publication Data
Names: Nelson, Samuel H., author. | Blades, Elizabeth L., author.
Title: The feldenkrais method for instrumentalists : a guide to awareness through movement / Samuel H. Nelson and Elizabeth L. Blades.
Description: Lanham : Rowman & Littlefield, 2024. | Includes bibliographical references and index.
Identifiers: LCCN 2023039600 (print) | LCCN 2023039601 (ebook) | ISBN 9781538182581 (cloth) | ISBN 9781538182598 (paperback) | ISBN 9781538182604 (ebook)
Subjects: LCSH: Music—Performance—Physiological aspects. | Music—Performance—Health aspects. | Feldenkrais method. | Musicians—Health and hygiene. | Overuse injuries—Prevention. | Perceptual-motor learning.
Classification: LCC ML3820 .N45 2024 (print) | LCC ML3820 (ebook) | DDC 784.14/3—dc23/eng/20230906
LC record available at https://lccn.loc.gov/2023039600
LC ebook record available at https://lccn.loc.gov/2023039601

Contents

Acknowledgments	ix
Online Supplement	xi

1 Overview — 1
  Relating the Feldenkrais Method to Playing a Musical Instrument — 1
  Overview of the Feldenkrais Method — 2
  Key Ideas in the Development of the Feldenkrais Method — 3
  Awareness Through Movement — 6
  Introduction to the Lessons — 6
  Mini-ATM: Freeing the Neck to Turn Easily — 9
  Audio Versions of Lessons — 9

2 Self-Image and Kinesthetic Imagination — 11
  What Is Self-Image? — 11
  Role of Kinesthetic Imagination in Playing — 12
  Enhancing Your Kinesthetic Awareness — 14
  ATM: The Broken Wing — 14
  Research and Imagination — 20
  Shifting the Focal Point — 21
  ATM: Attending to the Back of the Head — 21
  Good Side, Bad Side — 22
  Mini-ATM: Shoulders—A Thought Experiment — 23
  Reverse Mimicry — 24
  Review: Ways to Use Kinesthetic Imagination — 25

3 Physics of Easy Movement — 27
  Newtonian Mechanics — 27
  ATM: Moving Back to Reach Forward — 28
  Levers and Leverage — 32
  Potential Energy and Kinetic Energy — 33
  ATM: Sitting to Standing — 33
  Reversibility and Momentum — 35
  Tension and Function — 35

4 Neuroplasticity — 37
  The Medical "Discovery" of Neuroplasticity — 38

	How Does Neuroplasticity Work?	39
	Neuroplasticity in Action: The Visual System	41
	Movement	43
	Hearing	44
	Bimodal Stimulation	45
5	**The Cost of Choice, Intention, and the Power of Habit**	47
	Opportunity Cost Revealed	47
	Intention	48
	The Power of Habit	50
6	**The Base of Support**	53
	ATM: Balance in Standing	54
	Using the Floor	58
	ATM: The Connection of the Feet Through to the Head	58
	Leg-Length Differential	61
7	**The Pelvis**	63
	ATM: The Pelvic Clock	64
	The Pelvis in Sitting	69
	ATM: The Role of the Pelvis in Sitting Erect	70
8	**Breathing**	73
	Mechanics of Breathing	73
	ATM: Opening the Lungs	75
	Recovery from Illness	78
	ATM: Freeing the Ribs	78
9	**Upper Trunk Flexibility**	83
	The Upper Trunk	83
	ATM: Spinal Rotation	83
	The Mid-Spine	87
	ATM: Lateral Flexion	88
	Scoliosis	91
	Mini-ATM: Evening the Sides	91
	ATM: Circling the Legs	92
10	**Shoulder Girdle and Arms**	97
	Shoulders and Breath	97
	ATM: Reach and Drop	97
	ATM: Winging It	101
	Shoulder Tension	104
	ATM: Drop Your Elbow	105
11	**Head and Neck**	109
	Positioning the Head	109
	ATM: Relating Head and Pelvis	110
	Neck as Extension of the Spine	113

	ATM: Neck Turned Passively	114
	Headaches	119
	Mini-ATM: Releasing the Neck	119
12	**Hands and Mouth**	121
	ATM: Mobile Wrists, aka "Mel's Lesson"	121
	Mini-ATM: Fast Finger Release	126
	Relationship of the Hands and Tongue	127
	Mini-ATM: Clarifying the Hands	127
	Mini-ATM: Softening the Hands for Calm	129
	The Mouth	131
	ATM: Softening the Mouth	132
13	**The Eyes**	137
	Role of the Eyes in Movement	137
	Releasing Minor Neck Cricks	138
	Visual Tension	139
	ATM: Releasing the Eyes	139
	ATM: Dark Eyes	142
	Ocular Muscles and the Sinuses	145
14	**Bonus Lessons**	147
	ATM: Ankle Circles	147
	ATM: Push Me, Pull You	151
	ATM: Moving the Sternum	155
	ATM: Releasing the Neck and Arms	158
15	**Perspectives from Instrumentalists**	163
	Preamble	163
	Responses	164
	Final Thoughts for Everyone	186

APPENDIX A: FUNCTIONAL INTEGRATION	189
APPENDIX B: ATM LESSONS AND AREAS OF MAJOR IMPACT	191
INDEX	199
ABOUT THE AUTHORS	207

Acknowledgments

Many thanks to:

- Christine Moss, who once more put up with me (Sam Nelson) through the creation of yet another book and, amazingly, still wants to spend time with me.
- All the students who have taken my classes over the years, especially those in my Zoom classes. I've learned more from them than I can say. Not only were they beta testers for the Awareness Through Movement lessons in this book, but also proved that, with technology, a room can expand to span continents.
- Betsy Blades, whose upbeat presence has been a joy to work with on these books.
- Sam Nelson (Betsy here) who opened an amazing, new, life-changing way of being to me thirty-five years ago.
- Amy Walts, who not only provided all the illuminating illustrations, but also urged us to write this book.
- Michael Tan, whose encouragement, patience, and abiding faith in this project we hope we have rewarded.

Online Supplement

This book features an online supplement courtesy of Samuel Nelson. Visit the following link to discover audio recordings of guided walk-throughs of certain lessons in the book:

https://on.soundcloud.com/NouE4

CHAPTER 1

Overview

RELATING THE FELDENKRAIS METHOD TO PLAYING A MUSICAL INSTRUMENT

Every musician is an athlete. Athletes hone their bodies, coordinate their reflexes, and train their minds, seeking to perfect a balance of strength, skill, and agility.

Instrumentalists seek to excel at their particular "sport" as well. Complicated, demanding, and repetitive movements often result in unnatural and difficult positions which put the instrumentalist at risk of injury and disability. It is not uncommon to find musicians, like athletes, "playing damaged" with performance-related injuries. This environment of tension and misalignment increases the potential for permanent damage.

When injury occurs, the athlete-musician may naturally focus on the primary, that is, the area that is injured. However, the actual cause or source of the injury may be elsewhere, related, but not obvious.

Dr. Blades has taught a number of music education majors who are also dedicated instrumentalists. Marcy Jones, a college senior and serious saxophonist, was juggling a full-time class schedule, a heavy practice regimen, participation in a number of instrumental ensembles, *and* caring for a home and husband. When Dr. Nelson came to campus to conduct Feldenkrais workshops, Marcy approached him with a request: could he help her sore wrist? She related that not only was she in pain while playing her sax, she nearly had a serious kitchen accident the night before when she picked up a hot frying pan and almost dropped it. Her wrist injury was having a dire impact on her musical and personal life.

Dr. Nelson met with Marcy for a Functional Integration session. Imagine Marcy's surprise when he worked primarily with her shoulder, *not* the wrist! Tension, misalignment, and overuse in her shoulder had resulted in strain, stress, and pain in her wrist. Had Dr. Nelson applied Feldenkrais work directly to the wrist, further damage may very well have occurred. Marcy was very pleased with the resulting improvement.

Every instrument presents its own particular set of physical challenges. To hold and play an instrument stresses several groups of muscles, tendons, and ligaments over a sustained period of time. String players strain arms, shoulders, neck, and back muscle groups, in addition to hands, wrists, and fingers. Keyboardists work the hands, arms, shoulders, and back vigorously while at the same time using the buttocks, legs, and feet for support. Ask any organist how demanding it is to have both feet in motion while trying to maintain balance on the console bench! Every brass and woodwind instrumentalist is required to carry out a complicated range of lip, tongue, jaw, head, and neck movements while supporting their instrument in sometimes exaggerated and uncomfortable positions. The list goes on . . .

When movement and task are coordinated, well and freely, the athlete-instrumentalist finds themselves in "the zone," or "the flow," a magical place where art and athleticism meet. Musicians who choose to employ techniques to reduce tension and imbalance reduce the potential for misuse, overuse, and abuse. Unfortunately, it is our nature as humans to worry less about taking care of ourselves until an injury occurs. Then we tend to be more proactive about our health and our jobs. This message of proactivity has substantial benefits. It helps to prevent injury recurrence and establish balance. More important, whole and healthy self-use releases the artist to express their musicality rather than be concerned only with technique, thereby empowering the instrumentalist to realize full potential. It is with this in mind that we have written this "care and repair" manual which utilizes the Feldenkrais Method.

OVERVIEW OF THE FELDENKRAIS METHOD

The Feldenkrais Method is a self-discovery process using movement. Its aim is to produce an individual organized to perform with minimum effort and maximum efficiency. Efficient organization is developed using the "organic" learning style of our early childhood, the way we learned to hold up our head, crawl, and so on. As such, it is an open-ended developmental learning process, which, like making music, offers infinite possibilities for refinement. The movements used are simple, gentle, pleasant, exploratory, and fun. They are usually repeated a number of times to clarify and enhance performance. The focus is always on the how-to of the movement, not the how much, how fast, or how hard. The movement always starts where the person is now. People are asked only to perform what they can do comfortably. They are actively discouraged from moving outside their comfort range.

The Feldenkrais Method has two aspects: Awareness Through Movement (ATM), a guided group movement lesson; and Functional Integration (FI), a hands-on session with a practitioner. The two are interrelated so that many lessons may be transposed from one to the other, much as a piece of music can be transposed from violin to piano. The work we will be presenting will, for obvious reasons, consist of only ATM. For a short explanation of FI, see appendix A.

In applying the Feldenkrais Method, individuals are led through movement sequences designed to introduce or clarify a function (e.g., sitting, breathing, reaching forward, or a more complicated function). They are thus led to "discover" a better way to perform this function, a way that involves more of themselves than their habitual way. Because, for the most part, this discovery involves the part of the nervous system that controls movement, as opposed to conceptual consciousness or "thinking," changes tend to be retained and often amplified. Typically, the changes in functional capacity are accompanied by greater pleasure in movement and often (for adults) an enhanced joie de vivre.

Our inefficient movement patterns are a result of our humanness. Unlike animals, such as dogs and horses, we are born knowing virtually nothing about movement. Thus, while it takes a foal perhaps five minutes after birth to get up and move around, it takes a normal human child about half a year to start crawling. Instead of inborn knowledge, we have an enormously powerful brain that is highly adept at learning. So, as infants we learn how to roll over, sit, crawl, stand, and walk. Some of this learning is done by trial and error and some by imitation. Because our learning is spotty, we learn some movements well, others poorly, and some not at all; over time, problems arise. We develop aches and pains or find ourselves unnecessarily restricted. In addition, injuries can cause problems both immediately and years later. Some individuals have problems that are caused by structural difficulties, for example, curvature of the spine (scoliosis). The Feldenkrais Method, by helping to reprogram the functioning of our nervous system, facilitates our overcoming many of the problems arising from faulty initial learning, injuries, and structural problems.

The Feldenkrais Method is named after its originator, Moshe Feldenkrais, D.Sc. Feldenkrais developed the method to prevent being wheelchair bound by knee problems. In his twenties, he severely injured one knee playing soccer. While hobbling around with this "bad" knee, he injured the other one. Eventually, the knee problems disappeared, and he went to the Sorbonne to study physics and electrical engineering. While there, he earned his doctorate, worked with Dr. Frederic Joliot-Curie, and met Dr. J. Kano, the founder of judo. This meeting spurred him to a serious study of judo, which led him to be the first resident European to earn a black belt.

When his knee problems resurfaced in the 1940s and threatened his walking, he asked the surgeons two questions: What are the odds of success? What does failure mean? He was told that the expectation of success was 50 percent and that failure could mean a wheelchair. He then determined that delay would not change the odds of a successful operation and decided to see what he could do for himself. Thus began a painstaking investigation of how he organized himself to move. In this investigation he used his knowledge of movement from judo, mechanics from physics, and what he proceeded to learn of anatomy, kinesiology, and physiology. A key question in this process was, "If I take one hundred steps and, on only one does my knee give out, what did I do differently that one time?" The result of this investigation, beyond recovery of walking, was minute attention to the details of function—how one sits, stands, bends to the side, and rotates. It was this attention to function that led Feldenkrais to originate his method.

KEY IDEAS IN THE DEVELOPMENT OF THE FELDENKRAIS METHOD

There are five key ideas involved in the development of the Feldenkrais Method: (1) life as a process, (2) involvement of the whole self as necessary for effective movement, (3) learning as the key activity of humans, (4) the necessity of choice, and (5) the logic of human development. That life is a process should be self-evident. No one is truly the same person they were ten years ago, nor will they be the same next year as they are now. This time period can be very short, and the statement will remain true. As we approach a day, an hour, a minute, the difference becomes so small as to be nonexistent for practical purposes. In a similar vein, each time a piece of music is approached, it seems a little different, as one perceives different aspects of the same piece. The dynamics of process embedded in the Feldenkrais Method are much the same as this musical experience. The names of the two components reveal this: ATM illustrates that it is the awareness of what we are doing that is intended, and in FI the intent is to integrate our being around a function—sitting, breathing, reaching—in such a way that performance of that function (and related functioning) is altered. This process orientation means that, although it may be helpful to know about the structure or the static situation of the individual, it is not necessary for successful work with the Feldenkrais Method.

Any action, to be completely efficient and effective, must involve the whole self. That is, all parts of the organism must support and enhance the act. When this is not the case, some areas either are not involved or are acting counter to the intended act, or both. This invariably leads to a greater energy requirement to perform any action than when all of oneself is involved, for if any areas are not involved, some effort must be expended to prevent their moving, whether the person is aware of this or not. For example, bend your wrist downward. Did you notice that you curved your fingers? Now keep the fingers straight as you bend your wrist. Can you feel the difference? If not, try both again, slowly. Did you feel how much more effort is required when the fingers do not participate? The excess energy required either is dissipated as heat from excess friction or results in excessive muscular tension (friction per se is necessary to life, for without it walking, among other things, is impossible) It is the wear and tear of this excess friction and muscular tension that causes so many movement-related problems, such as backaches, carpal tunnel syndrome, and many arthritic conditions. Finding ways to approximate more closely the ideal of using the entire self in each act underlies the Feldenkrais work.

Of all living creatures on Earth, human beings are the furthest from adult-level functioning at birth. Accordingly, they must learn more than any other animal. Indeed, for the first few years of life we are insatiable learners, nor does learning stop at adulthood. Rather, it goes on throughout life as we adjust to external and internal changes.

> In short, we may say that the human brain is such as to make learning, or acquisition of new responses, a normal and suitable activity. It is as if it were capable of functioning with any possible combination of nervous interconnections until individual experience forms the one that will be preferred and active. The actual pattern of doing is, therefore, essentially personal and fortuitous....
>
> This great ability to form individual nervous paths and muscular patterns makes it possible for a faulty functioning to be learned. The earlier the fault occurs, the more ingrained it appears, and is. Faulty behavior will appear in the executive motor mechanisms which will seem later, when the nervous system has grown fitted to the undesirable motility, to be inherent in the person and unalterable. It will remain largely so unless the nervous paths producing the undesirable pattern of motility are undone and reshuffled into a better configuration.[1]

What Feldenkrais developed was a superior way to use movement to perform this reshuffling, a way that can help anyone function better. Indeed, Feldenkrais believed that our movement was sufficiently imperfect that a person with "no problems" could use an FI for each year of age and could benefit from ATM ad infinitum. Humans are particularly constituted so that learning is possible and pleasurable throughout their lifetime.

A person who has no choices in actions is considered compulsive. This is not a desirable state. Feldenkrais believed that it was not a fully human state. If there are only two choices, the situation is not much different. We advance to being mechanical, always choosing either A or B. All of us exhibit some movement and learning areas in which we are either compulsive or mechanical. They are generally not important to us, either because the matter is itself minor or because we structure our life so that it is minor. Dr. Nelson, for example, knows only one way to knot a tie. So either he wears a tie and ties it that way or he does not wear a tie. It is a mechanical decision. If he had a bow tie or a bolo, he would have a third option and could truly exercise choice. Although having even more options is desirable, it is the creation of the third option that makes effective choice possible. It is at this point that the organism ceases to be locked into responding compulsively or mechanically and becomes alive and human. It is, therefore, the intent of Feldenkrais practitioners to help their students create appropriate options for themselves. This is done by presenting alternatives during each lesson that allow the nervous system to choose better ways to accomplish a function.

In helping a person increase functionality, it is important to follow the logic of human development. You cannot expect someone to run who cannot walk. For example, consider the brain of a damaged child. The first step is to ascertain where they are in their development, then what would normally come next, and finally find a means to evoke this normal development. The same type of thinking is used in other problems, only the question now becomes either, what is the logical development to re-establish effective action? or, what seemingly unrelated problem is involved? *The Case of Nora: Body Awareness as Healing Therapy*[2] relates Feldenkrais's use of this style of thinking to help a woman recover from the damage caused by a brain hemorrhage. Although she was able to walk and hold an intelligent conversation, she had lost the ability to read and write and had difficulty locating doors, often walking into them. After several years, she was brought to Feldenkrais as a last hope before placement in a nursing home. He found that she had no concept of left and right. Therefore, he proceeded to help her reestablish her frame of reference. With considerable difficulty, they reestablished her frame of reference while she was lying on her back. When she had learned left and right on her back, she was turned over. In this position she had to learn it all over again. In other words, these concepts are not internalized but are related to external objects such as the couch. It took about two months to internalize her frame of reference completely.

An essential ingredient of human development used with Nora was reducing tension, thereby increasing sensitivity and allowing the organism to sense and respond to small changes. This stimulates our childlike learning capacity. Because children's attention is directed by curiosity, they do not exercise like adults but rather repeat a movement for the sheer pleasure of it. Moving in this way is free of tension and maximizes the potential for growth and learning. Also, because children are much weaker than adults, they are incapable of tensing their muscles as powerfully. As sensitivity decreases with effort, this automatically makes them more sensitive than adults. Thus, by attracting our curiosity once more to movement and reducing tonus (muscle tone), we evoke again the child's style of learning.

These then are the principal ideas that underlie the efficacy of the Feldenkrais Method.

AWARENESS THROUGH MOVEMENT

ATM is usually done in a group. In ATM, students are verbally guided through movement sequences designed to clarify a function, such as side-bending or turning. This allows a superior form of functioning to be adopted. Emphasis is on the learning process, the "how" of doing. Movements are typically gentle and slow. Sensitivity to what you do is most important. According to Weber-Fechner's law, the ability to detect a change in a stimulus varies inversely with the intensity of the stimulus.[3] Put more simply, effort and sensitivity are inversely related. Therefore, to maximize sensitivity, one must reduce effort. Movements are intended to be within the individual's comfort range; the production of pain or discomfort is avoided, as it is a bar to learning and increased awareness. Students are often asked to notice what they do and how they do it throughout their entire self. For example, what does the lower spine do when the head is lifted? Because learning is a highly individual matter, ATM is not competitive. Students are encouraged to proceed and learn at their own pace.

Because of the central role sensitivity plays in learning about oneself, in a typical ATM class most lessons are done lying on the floor. Since sensitivity is inversely related to effort, the least effortful position to perform a particular lesson is usually the best for learning. Because of the special needs of musicians, we have created a series of lessons, most of which can be performed in chairs. Working through them will increase your kinesthetic image (see chapter 2) and provide a sense of ease and grace. The lessons have been modularized so that they may also be used as warm-ups.

INTRODUCTION TO THE LESSONS

The lessons have been divided into short, seven- to ten-minute modules. If you have the time to do the lesson in one sitting, that is preferable. The effects are more noticeable and more lasting. However, in today's hectic life, that is not always possible. Modularizing the lesson makes it possible to gain almost as much benefit, only spread out over more time. This is particularly true if you work through one lesson at a time and can do at least one module a day until you really have the feel of the entire lesson. Another advantage of the modules is that they are an appropriate length for warm-ups.

The lessons can be performed with only modest preparations. Unless otherwise specified, please take off your shoes, if possible, before beginning the lesson. Also, make sure you have a reasonably comfortable chair to sit in, that is, a chair where your feet reach the floor with your knees bent. If you are quite short, get a book or two to place beneath your feet. If you are over six feet tall, most chairs are too short. Therefore, sit on a cushion or some books so that the chair is comfortable. *Whenever possible, modify your environment to suit yourself.* Try to avoid forcing yourself to conform to an uncomfortable situation. However, be clear that comfort is also a function of habit, and if your habitual way of being is injurious, some temporary discomfort may be desirable. For example, many teenagers slouch when they sit. This posture will eventually cause trouble, and, of course, even with the young and supple, it impairs the ability to effectively play their instrument. However, until one learns to sit upright comfortably—that is, with the spine carrying the weight—the upright position is often forced and, therefore, uncomfortable. Just ask anyone whose mother told them to "Sit up straight" how comfortable a forced upright position is!

All the movements in the lessons should be done slowly and attentively. Take as long between separate movements as it takes to do the movement. If there is any pain, stop *immediately*. If you grow fatigued, *stop*. In both these cases, you can kinesthetically imagine doing the movement. That is, imagine what it feels like to do the movement. For example, imagine making a fist. Did you *feel* the contractions of the muscles? Try it a few more times to get clearer about *feeling what it is you are imagining*. We shall go further with this concept in a later chapter.

Please remember that *how you do what you do* is what is of value in this play/work. Thus, two or three repetitions done with attention, where the system has the chance to observe what it is doing and learn, are far more valuable than ten or twenty or more movements done mechanically. Also, the movements should, in some sense, be *enjoyable*. If they are done as a chore or to accomplish some external goal, they become vastly less effective. This is especially true if you override feelings of pain or discomfort. In such a case, the continued movements can be *harmful*. Thus, allowing yourself the time to make the movements pleasant is crucial. If you are short on time, do fewer repetitions and do them slowly. Do not try to make the movements faster.

It is very common to feel that you are not doing a lesson correctly. If this is the case, *do not panic*. Instead, reread the directions, then repeat the lesson as you now understand it. If you still feel that what you are doing is not correct, there are two possibilities.

First, you could be wrong, and what you are doing is a correct interpretation of the instructions. However, if it feels wrong to you because it is currently very difficult or impossible, don't worry. Learning sometimes entails doing that which is difficult. During a Feldenkrais training program, every participant will experience this difficulty or feeling of impossibility more than once. However, when you persist, magical things happen. Sometimes you suddenly find yourself able to do the movement. Or the next day, or the next time you do the lesson, you may discover that the impossible has become doable, and the doable pleasant.

Second, you could be right. You could be making the wrong movement. However, if you do this movement in a careful attentive way that avoids pain and discomfort, the worst that can happen is nothing. In all likelihood, you will learn something about your movement. And quite possibly the next time you try the lesson, the "right" movement will come to you.

Also, please realize there is no absolute right way. Each person is different. Therefore, we must each discover our own present best way. These lessons will enable you to do that. Further, please realize that the "worse" you are at the start, the more benefit you will get from a lesson. Thus, do not focus on someone else's "accomplishment" or skill, but on improving your own kinesthetic awareness and abilities.

You should, when possible, repeat a movement many times until you feel it to be easy (or at least easy by comparison with your first attempt). Often, twenty repetitions are useful. Take the suggested number of repetitions in these lessons as minimums. If you feel the value of doing more, by all means do so. Each time you repeat a movement, notice what is different as you refine it. Do not worry about doing the movement badly. Doing badly is merely a part of learning. If we only acted when we did things well, we would do very little!

At the end of a module, you will be asked to notice differences. See what has changed, not only with the movement, but also with other aspects of yourself: What is your mind state like now? What other sensations do you notice? Also notice changes as you get up and move around.

A short, simple lesson to give you a feel for what these lessons are like follows. It involves freeing the neck in turning. Before beginning, be sure to read the "grammatical" and movement rules for doing all the lessons in the book.

Grammatical Rules

- All movement directions are in **bold** type.
- All guidance, questions, and repetition numbers are in standard type.

Movement Rules

- If you feel pain, ***stop***. Then change either the speed, range, or size of the movement. If this doesn't work, *imagine how it feels to do the movement*.
- Go slowly, do not hurry or become mechanical; you want to *feel* what you are doing.
- Let go of the idea that *trying harder* helps. It doesn't. Especially in a learning situation, extra effort gets in the way of feeling what you are doing.
- The number of repetitions suggested is a minimum the first time you do a lesson. Where possible do fifteen to twenty slowly, unless it is a checking movement at the end of a module.
- The pauses are as important as the actions. Do not skip over them.
- As you do the lessons, periodically recollect that if you can't smile while you're doing this you are working too hard.
- You are interested in doing the lesson attentively, not "right"; you're interested in learning at the most primal level. If you are doing that, whatever you're doing is "right"!

Ending a Lesson or Module

We strongly recommend standing for a brief moment and then walking for about a minute at the end of a lesson, or if only doing a module or two at the end of your session.

Alternatively, you could play a short piece or run a scale before and after you play with these lessons. Either approach will help you retain the changes you value.

The illustrations usually follow the first direction to which they apply. Wait until you have read that direction before looking at and using the illustration. A few illustrations apply to more than one set of directions. In this case, the large illustration is for the first direction and the inset is for a later direction. If this is confusing, ignore the illustration.

Where there are black and gray arrows, black indicates where the force is applied and gray represents movement in response to that force.

MINI-ATM: FREEING THE NECK TO TURN EASILY

1. Stand comfortably with your feet shoulder width apart. **Slowly turn your head left and right several times.** Notice how far, how easily, and how smoothly it moves in each direction.
2. **Move your head and shoulders to look to the left and back to the center.**
3. Do this four to six times. Remember to do this slowly and gently.
4. Slowly turn just your shoulders toward the left and back to the center, leaving your head facing forward. **Do this four to six times.**
5. **Fix your eyes on a point in front of you. Now turn your head to the left and back to the center, leaving your eyes fixed on that point.** Slowly repeat this motion. Move gently so you avoid eye strain.
6. **Now turn your head left and right slowly.** Compare the ease and distance of your movements to the left to those of your movements to the right. Also compare them to the movements you made when you began.
7. To balance yourself, repeat steps two through four on the right side.

AUDIO VERSIONS OF LESSONS

We have included links to audio recordings of Sam (Dr. Nelson) teaching some of the lessons. These are recordings of actual classes he taught using the lesson as a template. Sometimes there are minor deviations to accommodate class members. Occasionally there will be questions asked and answered. This is intended to help use the lessons and is especially to help those unfamiliar with ATM prior to using this book.

Video lessons are not included. The primary reason is that, if you watch someone else, you are apt to copy them. But remember, these lessons are all about what you're learning and figuring out. Furthermore, people's physiognomies differ. What works for someone else may not work for you. Finally, by using a model, you deprive yourself of that "AHA" moment, when the second, third, fourth time, etc., that you do a lesson, you suddenly realize, "OH, that is what is meant!"

Redoing a Lesson

If you wish to redo a lesson, remember to go slowly and attentively. If you do so, you may reduce the number of repetitions to 3 or 4 (and 3 or 4 movements done well are worth dozens done mechanically).

NOTES

1. Feldenkrais, Moshe. 1949. *Body and Mature Behavior: A Study of Anxiety, Sex, Gravitation, and Learning* (New York: International Universities Press).
2. Feldenkrais, Moshe. 1977. *The Case of Nora: Body Awareness as Healing Therapy* (Berkeley, CA: Frog, Ltd. and Somatic Resources).
3. Shafarman, Steven. 1997. *Awareness Heals: The Feldenkrais Method for Dynamic Health* (Reading, MA: Addison-Wesley).

CHAPTER 2

Self-Image and Kinesthetic Imagination

WHAT IS SELF-IMAGE?

What you can do you can imagine, and what you can imagine you can do.
—M. Feldenkrais

Kinesthesia: a sense mediated by receptors located in muscles, tendons, and joints and stimulated by bodily movements and tensions; also: sensory experience derived from this sense.
—Merriam-Webster

How good is your self-image? Not in the usual sense of how well do you think of yourself, but, rather, can you sense yourself? That is, how accurately can you sense yourself both statically and in movement? For example, if you think of your hands, do you represent them equally well, or do you have a greater sense of your dominant hand? Now lean forward. How much of yourself did you feel was involved in this movement? You probably felt the involvement of your back muscles. But did you also sense the shift in the thigh muscles? What about your buttocks? In truth, none of us accurately represents ourselves to ourselves at all times. Most people do not even attempt this. It is this representation of ourselves that is known as the kinesthetic image (or felt sense).

Developing a more accurate kinesthetic image is immensely valuable because it allows you to know more completely what you are doing. Otherwise, you may not be doing what you think you are doing or you may inadvertently introduce tension into your system. The equestrian world provides a good example of not doing what you think you're doing. The effective way to signal a horse to turn is to shift weight in that direction. However, some riders always have their weight off to one side, even though that feels straight to them. Thus, no matter what they do with the reins, a horse will always want to go that way. A more accurate kinesthetic image also allows you to notice excess tension before it becomes a major problem. Any tension beyond the minimum necessary is both wasteful and harmful. Fortunately, humans have repair mechanisms, since no one can operate perfectly efficiently. Of necessity, living involves some damage and repair. Unfortunately, these repair mechanisms diminish with age. What one can get by with as a youth becomes problematic in middle age and can be painful as an old person. Hence, a well-developed kinesthetic image can make one more comfortable and effective. Finally, one can make performance-enhancing changes by using kinesthetic imagination to develop a more accurate self-image.

ROLE OF KINESTHETIC IMAGINATION IN PLAYING

There are a number of ways kinesthetic imagination can be used to help any musician play better. In this section, we will go over the ones we found. Perhaps you will think of others.

Transfer Sense of Ease

One simple way to use kinesthetic imagination is to play a piece you have really mastered and pay attention to your sense of ease. Then see if you can recreate that sense of ease while playing the troublesome piece. If that doesn't work, go back and reimagine playing this piece with the sense of ease, and then see what it is like to actually play it.

Extend Practice

Many musicians injure themselves needlessly because they cannot feel what they are doing until too late and/or they often practice for far too long at one time. Overlong practice usually involves excessive tension if there is difficulty with a piece. The usual approach is to keep practicing, even though this may be frustrating. In this situation, all too often, not only does one become fatigued, which is when most injuries occur, but often the error becomes embedded. By using kinesthetic imagination, it is possible both to shorten the learning time and to find ways to achieve the desired sound, dramatically reducing the likelihood of injury. This may be why the noted pianist Glenn Gould relied largely on mental practice when preparing to record a piece of music toward the end of his career. Further, when recovering from an injury, kinesthetic imagination allows you to practice when you are not able and to extend practice time when it is limited.

Change the Pattern of Error

Practice makes perfect. However, if you practice something incorrectly, you perfect your errors. This is why it is so very difficult to change one's way of performing. Indeed, the internal image for "correct" performance becomes this wrong way of doing. It is this difficulty that often results in failure to get it right despite hours of practice. Because, in effect, the wrong way has become habitual. Kinesthetic imagination is the ideal tool for this situation. It allows you to change the internal image that is the basis of the problem. In short, if you can change the internal program, the performance problem disappears, almost like magic.

If one continually makes the same error, it becomes ingrained. You have, in effect, perfected the problem and wired it in. Practicing more only makes this worse. Another approach is needed. This, as the following shows, is an area where kinesthetic imagination, by shifting the focus, shines. Dr. Nelson worked extensively with a young violinist at the Eastman School of Music. One time she arrived with a piece she was learning, unable to complete a passage without running out of bow. She picked up her bow and played the piece and, as usual, ran out of bow during the passage. He asked her to kinesthetically imagine playing the piece. When she came to the difficulty, she broke into a big smile. Even without the instrument, she had run out of bow! So the problem was clearly in her internal organization of the section. She was asked to imagine playing the section with the bow being long enough. After she could do this three times, Dr. Nelson asked her to pick up her violin and play. This time, there was plenty of bow. Now when she practiced the piece, she could perfect it instead of perfecting her error.

Speed Recovery from Injury

Another advantage is speeding recovery from injury. With some injuries, an area becomes or is immobilized to facilitate healing. The classic example is being casted for a bone break. If you adapt fully to a cast, once the cast is removed, you have to relearn proper movement. However, if you imagine the full proper movement of the impacted area, once freed from its "cast," normal movement is much more rapidly regained. There are two reasons for this: most important, you retain the "correct" movement pattern and, interestingly, you also keep some muscular tone that would otherwise be lost.

As you recover and begin playing, kinesthetic imagination allows you to extend practice time by alternating periods of actual playing with imagining, or playing and then imagining, or having periods of imagining.

Feel the Sound

Kinesthetic imagination can also be used to reinforce playing or learning a piece by associating the sound with the feel. Once you get the sound you wish, you can then sense what it feels like. Once you have that in hand, you can then imagine the feel that gives you the sound you want. To some extent this is the inverse to the above of using kinesthetic imagination when you've mastered the mistake.

Silent Practice

A final advantage for musicians of kinesthetic imagination is the ability to practice noiselessly. There are many times when you otherwise cannot practice: when you are with someone who is asleep, when no practice room is available, and when you are on a public conveyance. In these situations and many others, unless you learn to practice noiselessly, you will not be able to practice.

ENHANCING YOUR KINESTHETIC AWARENESS

Helping you develop your kinesthetic imagination is one of the major objectives of this book. It follows naturally from doing the lessons, for they increase your kinesthetic awareness. But it is a skill that must be developed. Accordingly, some lessons call for you to imagine a movement and then to do it. You may also use this practice when doing any lesson or activity. Slowly and gently do a simple movement, such as opening your mouth or lifting your foot. Choose a movement you are comfortable with. Notice how you do this movement as you do it. Now imagine the same movement. Then do the movement again. Notice how completely you represented this movement in your imagination. Then imagine it a few more times including something you missed the last time you imagined it. Alternate between imagining and doing it several more times. The last time you imagine, you will find that there is far more to the movement than what you first imagined. You will also notice that you cannot imagine a movement without actually doing it (at a reduced level). For example, imagine moving your right shoulder forward. Can you feel the subtle movement forward of the shoulder muscles? A close observer would actually see this very slight movement. Because our imagination and actuation (kinesthetically) are fundamentally the same, this approach allows us to bypass obstacles that we did not realize we had put in our own way.

The following lesson provides an opportunity to practice kinesthetic imagination. It will also allow you to experience firsthand just its potency.

ATM: THE BROKEN WING

This lesson can be done sitting in a chair, sitting on the floor, or standing up. If you have the time to do the entire lesson, it will be even more effective and dramatic if you first do numbers 1, 2, 5, 6, 9, 10, 13, and 14 and then go back to the beginning and do the others.

1. **Sit comfortably and raise your right arm so that the arm points in front of you. Move your arm to the right as far as it can go. Pause your arm movement and look and see where your arm points to on the wall behind you.** Put your arm down and rest a minute.

   Now raise your left arm so that the arm points in front of you. Move your arm to the left as far as it can go. Pause your arm movement and look and see where your arm points to on the wall behind you. Put your arm down and rest a minute.

   Raise your right arm so the forearm is parallel with your chest (the arm is bent at the elbow) and the right hand points to the left. Move your right arm to the left and back four to six inches. Repeat this seven to ten times. See if you can make this easier each time. But do not follow the movement with your head and eyes. Put your arm down and rest a minute.

2. **Raise your right arm so the forearm is parallel with your chest and the right hand points to the left. Move your right arm to the left four to six inches and**

back. Follow this movement with your head and eyes. Repeat this seven to ten times. Put your arm down and rest a minute.

Raise your right arm so that the arm points in front of you. Move your arm to the right as far as it can go. Pause your arm movement and look and see where your arm points to on the wall behind you. Compare this with how far it went the first time you did this. Put your arm down and rest a minute.

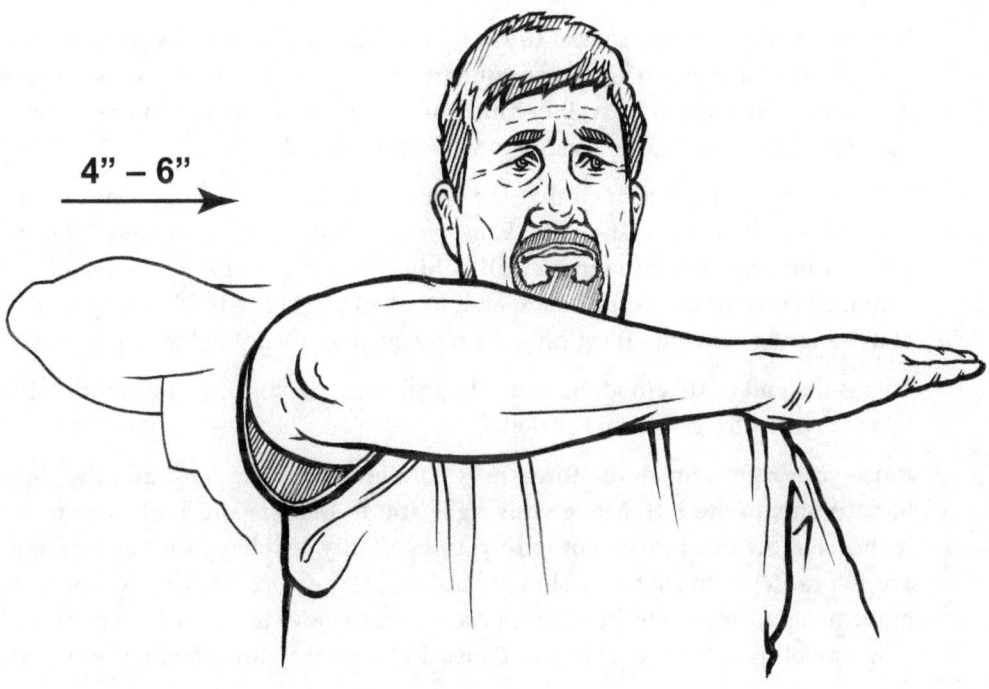

3. **Raise your left arm so the forearm is parallel with your chest and the left hand points to the right. Move your left arm to the right and back four to six inches once.** You may leave the arm in place and put it down. *Continue this movement in your imagination only.* This means you imagine feeling what it is like to move the arm to the right. Do you notice a slight movement as you imagine initiating this movement? Imagine making the movement four or five times. **Actually do the movement once or twice.** Do you notice anything in the movement that you left out of the imagining? *Resume doing the movement in your imagination.* Repeat this two or three times, seeing if you can incorporate into your imagination something you noticed you left out the last time. Pause. **Actually do this movement one more time noticing its quality.** Pause and rest.

4. **Raise your left arm so the forearm is parallel with your chest and the left hand points to the right. Move your left arm to the right four to six inches once or twice. Follow this movement with your head and eyes.** Pause. *Continue this movement in your imagination only.* This means you imagine feeling what it is like to move the arm, head, and eyes to the right and back. Imagine making

this movement four to six times. Did you notice any slight actual movements as you do this? You probably do, since it is not possible to do something you can't imagine, nor is it possible to imagine something (kinesthetically) that you can't do. Do you notice anything in the movement that you left out of the imagining? *Resume doing the movement in your imagination.* Repeat this two or three times seeing if you can incorporate into your imagination something you noticed you left out the last time. Pause. *Actually do this movement one more time noticing the quality of the movement.* Pause and rest.

Now raise your left arm so that the arm points in front of you. Move your arm to the left as far as it can go. Pause your arm movement and look and see where your arm points to on the wall behind you. Put your arm down and rest a minute. How far did you go compared to when you started?

Now raise your right arm so that the arm points in front of you. Move your arm to the right as far as it can go. Pause your arm movement and look and see where your arm points to on the wall behind you. Put your arm down and rest a minute. How far did you go compared to when you started? Did you get more of a change from mostly imagining the movement or by doing the movement?

This is the end of this module. It is a logical place to stop if you cannot do the lesson in one sitting. Resume at step 5.

5. **Raise your right arm so the forearm is parallel with your chest and the right hand points to the left. Move your right arm to the left and back four to six inches. Follow this movement with your eyes only, leaving your head stationary.** Repeat seven to ten times, slowly, pausing to take a breath every two or three movements. Can you feel how your head wants to move as you move your eyes? How smoothly do your eyes move? **Pause.** Put your arm down and rest a minute.

6. **Raise your right arm so the forearm is parallel with your chest and the right hand points to the left. Move your right arm to the left and back four to six inches. Follow this movement with your head and eyes, but when you get as far as you go to the left, pause. Now only return your arm to neutral. Then continue to make the movement of both head and arm, only now the head goes center as the arm goes left and vice versa.** Repeat eight to twelve times. Each time see if you can make this movement smoother and easier. **Pause.** Put your arm down and rest a minute.

Now raise your right arm so that the arm points in front of you. Move your arm to the right as far as it can go. Pause your arm movement and see where your arm points to on the wall behind you. Put your arm down and rest a minute. How far did you go compared to when you started?

Now raise your left arm so that the arm points in front of you. Move your arm to the left as far as it can go. Pause your arm movement and see where your arm points to on the wall behind you. Put your arm down and rest a minute. Recall how far and how easily it moved.

7. **Raise your left arm so the forearm is parallel with your chest and the left hand points to the right. Move your left arm to the right and back four to six inches once or twice. Follow this movement with your eyes only, leaving your head stationary.** Repeat this one more time and notice how you do what you are doing. Pause. *Continue this movement in your imagination only.* Imagine making this movement three to five times. Does the movement become clearer each time you imagine it? Pause. **Actually perform the movement one or two times checking to see how well you had imagined it.** Pause. *Once more do this movement in your imagination.* Repeat two to three times. Were you able to add any you left out? **Actually do this movement one more time noticing the quality of the movement.** Pause and rest a minute.

8. **Raise your left arm so the forearm is parallel with your chest and the left hand points to the right. Move your left arm to the right and back four to six inches. Follow this movement with your head and eyes, but when you get as far as you go to the right, pause. Now only return your arm to neutral. Then continue to make the movement of both head and arm, only now the head goes center as the arm goes right and vice versa.** Repeat this three or four times to get the pattern firmly established. Pause. *Continue this movement in your imagination only.* How well are you able to do this movement in your imagination? No matter how poorly you feel you are doing, continue to imagine making this movement three to five times. See if, as you continue, it becomes clearer. Pause. **Actually perform the movement.** Repeat four to six times. Was it easier to actually do this movement after imagining it? Was something about the movement clarified? Pause and rest.

   Now raise your left arm so that the arm points in front of you. Move your arm to the left as far as it can go. Pause your arm movement and look and see where your arm points to on the wall behind you. Put your arm down and rest a minute. Recall how far and how easily it moved.

   Now raise your right arm so that the arm points in front of you. Move your arm to the right as far as it can go. Pause your arm movement and look and see where your arm points to on the wall behind you. Put your arm down and rest a minute. How far did you go compared to when you started?

   This is the end of this module. It is a logical place to stop if you cannot do the lesson in one sitting. Resume at step 9.

9. **Move your left ear toward your left shoulder and return to neutral. This is not a matter of turning the head but is, rather, a tipping movement of the head and neck.** Repeat this seven to ten times going only so far as you can go comfortably. How far into the back can you feel this movement? Pause and rest a minute.

   Slowly move your left shoulder toward your left ear and down to neutral. Repeat this six to eight times. Avoid straining in the shoulder or neck. See how comfortably and smoothly you can make this movement. Pause and rest a minute.

10. **Move your left ear toward your left shoulder as you move your left shoulder toward your left ear.** Repeat nine to eleven times. Have a sense of luxuriant lengthening as you move the ear and shoulder away from each other. See if you can keep that sense as you move the shoulder and ear toward each other. Pause and rest a minute.

    Now raise your right arm so that the arm points in front of you. Move your arm to the right as far as it can go. Look and see where your arm points to on the wall behind you. Put your arm down and rest a minute. How far did you go compared to when you started?

11. **Move (tip) your right ear toward your right shoulder and return.** Repeat this seven to ten times. Go only as far as you can go comfortably. Is it easier than moving the left ear to the left shoulder? How far into the back can you feel this movement on this side? Pause and rest a minute.

    Slowly move your right shoulder toward your right ear and back twice. How comfortably and smoothly can you make this movement? **Now imagine the movement three or four times.** Can you let go of any strain you feel in the shoulder or neck? **Do the movement again, twice.** Were you able to reduce any felt sense of strain? Pause and rest a minute.

12. **Move your right ear toward your right shoulder as you move your right shoulder toward your right ear.** Repeat once. **Now imagine the movement three or four times.** Each time you imagine the movement can you allow it to be lighter? Pause. **Now do the movement again once or twice.** Notice anything you left out in your imagination. Pause and rest a minute.

    Now raise your left arm so that the arm points in front of you. Move your arm to the left as far as it can go. Look and see where your arm points to on the wall behind you. Put your arm down and rest a minute. Recall how far and how easily it moved.

    Now raise your right arm so that the arm points in front of you. Move your arm to the right as far as it can go. Pause your arm movement and look and see where your arm points to on the wall behind you. Put your arm down and rest a minute. How far did you go compared to when you started?

    This is the end of this module. It is a logical place to stop if you cannot do the lesson in one sitting. Resume at step *13*.

13. **Raise your right arm so the forearm is parallel with your chest and the right hand points to the left. Move your right arm to the left and back four to six inches. At the same time move your left ear toward your left shoulder.** Repeat seven to ten times. See if you can coordinate this movement better as you make more repetitions. Can you make the movement of the head and arm equally gentle? Pause, put your arm down, and rest a minute.

    Raise your right arm so the forearm is parallel with your chest and the right hand points to the left. Move your right arm to the left and back four to six inches. Simultaneously move your left shoulder toward your left ear. Repeat six to eight times. How well can you coordinate this movement? Is this movement as gentle as the last one? Pause, put your arm down, and rest.

14. **Raise your right arm so the forearm is parallel with your chest and the right hand points to the left. Move your right arm to the left and back four to six inches. At the same time move your left ear toward your left shoulder while moving your left shoulder toward your left ear.** Repeat seven to ten times. Does moving the head and shoulder at the same time reduce your ability to keep the movement gentle? Can you find ways to soften this movement? Pause, and rest a minute.

15. **Raise your left arm so the forearm is parallel with your chest and the left hand points to the right. Move your left arm to the right and back four to six inches. At the same time move your right ear toward your right shoulder.** Make this movement once or twice. Now imagine making this movement three or four times. Pause. **Resume actually making the movement.** Repeat four or five times. What changes did you find yourself making in this movement from imagining it? Pause, and rest a minute.

    Raise your left arm so the forearm is parallel with your chest and the left hand points to the right. Move your left arm to the right and back four to six inches. At the same time move your right shoulder toward your right ear. Repeat three or four times. Now imagine this movement twice. Pause. **Resume making the movement once or twice.** What movement did you sense having left out of your imagination when you resumed actually doing the movement? Pause, and rest a minute.

16. **Raise your left arm so the forearm is parallel with your chest and the left hand points to the right. Move your left arm to the right and back four to six inches. At the same time move your right ear toward your right shoulder. As your arm returns to center and your head to the middle, move your right shoulder toward your right ear.** Repeat this movement six to eight times. Can you keep the movement soft and gentle as the right shoulder and ear alternately move up and down? Pause and rest a minute.

    Now raise your left arm so that the arm points in front of you. Move your arm to the left as far as it can go. Pause your arm movement and look and see where your arm points to on the wall behind you. Put your arm down and rest a minute. Compare this movement with how it was the first and last times you made it.

Now raise your right arm so that the arm points in front of you. Move your arm to the right as far as it can go. Look and see where your arm points to on the wall behind you. Put your arm down and rest a minute. How far did you go compared to when you started?

Stand and walk around for a minute. Notice what walking feels like now.

End of lesson

RESEARCH AND IMAGINATION

In the last quarter century, as interest in neuroplasticity has risen, there has been research into the role of imagination in taking action. The following are two of the more intriguing findings. The interested reader can find more in the references and resources, where we list books on neuroplasticity written for the general public.

Alvaro Pascual Leone, MD, PhD, a neurologist, is a researcher in brain mapping at Beth Israel Deaconess Medical Center. As reported in Norman Doidge's book, *The Brain That Changes Itself*,[1] Pascual Leone taught a sequence of notes to two groups of people who had never studied piano, showing them which fingers to move and letting them hear the notes as they were played. The members of the "mental practice" group sat in front of an electric piano keyboard, two hours a day, for five days, and imagined playing the piano and hearing it played. The second "physical practice" group actually played the music two hours a day for five days. Both groups had their brains mapped before the experiment, each day during it, and afterward. Then both groups were asked to play the sequence as a computer measured the accuracy of their performances.

Pascual Leone found that both groups learned to play the sequence and both showed similar brain map changes. Remarkably, mental practice alone produced the same physical changes in the motor system as actually playing the piece. By the end of the fifth day, the changes in motor signals to the muscles were the same in both groups, and the imagining players were as accurate as the actual players on the third day.

The level of improvement at five days in the mental practice group, however substantial, was not as great as in those who did physical practice. But when the mental practice group finished its mental training and was given a single two-hour physical practice session, its overall performance improved to the level of the physical practice group's performance at five days.[2]

Even more surprising, at first, is that imagining one is using one's muscles actually strengthens them. Drs. Guang Yhe and Kelly Cole performed a study with two groups, one that did physical exercise and the other that imagined doing exercise. Both groups exercised a finger muscle, Monday through Friday, for four weeks. The physical group did trials of fifteen maximal contractions, with a twenty-second rest between each. The mental group merely imagined doing fifteen maximal contractions, with a twenty-second rest between each, while also imagining a voice shouting at them, "Harder! Harder! Harder!" At the end of the study the subjects who had done physical exercise increased their muscular strength by 30 percent. Those who only imagined doing the exercise, for the same period, increased their muscle strength by 22 percent. The explanation lies in the motor neurons of the brain that "program" movements. During these imaginary contractions, the neurons responsible for stringing together sequences of instructions for movements are activated and strengthened, resulting in increased strength when the muscles are contracted.[3]

SHIFTING THE FOCAL POINT

An interesting variant of kinesthetic imagination is to shift one's focal point. Humans are highly visual creatures. As such, we typically pay most of our attention to what we see. Hence, to kinesthetize is already a shift from our habitual way of being. Unless we are blind, our vision is the dominant sense. This leads us to be head and front centric. If you were asked where you were, you would most likely say you were in your head (in one sense, because this is where the brain is, this is true). Not just in your head, but most likely the forehead. But just as it is possible, and valuable, to approach a work from different perspectives, it is possible to sense the world from different internal vantage points.

Just as visiting a new place leads to intriguing possibilities, new possibilities can happen when we shift our focal point. The following short lesson is designed to provide a glimpse of the possibilities that arise from shifting the focal point.

ATM: ATTENDING TO THE BACK OF THE HEAD

1. Sit forward in a comfortable chair. Take several breaths and notice first how you're breathing and then where you notice yourself breathing. **Then turn your head left and right two or three times.** Notice how far you go and where you sense yourself turning from, that is neck, mid-back, or all the way to the sacrum. Pause.
2. **Tip your head back and return to neutral four times.** Focus on the occipital region, the area below the base of your skull as you make this movement. Pause.

    Now tip your head back six times and return to neutral, but as you do this, focus on the back of the head. That is the region of the skull above the occipital region that fits nicely into the palm of your hand. Pause and rest.
3. **Tip your head forward and return to neutral eight times, focusing on the back of the head.** Do you sense it going skyward as your face drops toward the floor? Pause and rest.
4. **Breathing slowly, take eight to ten breaths focusing on the back of the head.** Notice if this makes breathing into the back more accessible or brings it more into your awareness. Pause.
5. **Tip your head back and forth (up and down) seven to eight times focusing on the back of the head as you make this movement.** Where do you sense your center as you make this movement? Pause. Notice how you are breathing.

    Turn your head left and right. What changes do you notice from before? Pause.

This is the end of this module. It is a logical place to stop if you cannot do all of this lesson at one sitting. Resume at step **6**.

6. **Turn your head left and right several times.** How easy was it to turn? How far did you go? Pause. **Turn the back of your head to the left about two inches and then back to neutral.** Repeat this six to eight times. Breath normally, with arms hanging by your sides, for a minute or so and notice what this is like. Pause.

7. **Turn the back of your head to the right about two inches and then back to neutral.** Repeat this six to eight times. Pause. Notice what your breathing is like now. Where is your sense of yourself?

8. **Turn the back of your head left and right about two inches in each direction.** Go slowly and remember to pause between movements. Repeat this about ten times. Do you have a better sense of the back of your head as you continue this movement? And see if you can find ways to make the movement easier. Pause.

9. **Tip your head forward and back a couple of times.** Pause. What, if anything, has changed from before? Breathe normally for a minute or so. What do you notice?

   Turn your head left and right three times. What changes do you notice?

End of lesson

GOOD SIDE, BAD SIDE

Humans are bilateral creatures. However, virtually every movement we make we will have a preferred side with which we perform. For important movements like starting to walk or run or raising an arm for defense, not having a preference is especially dysfunctional. After all, if being chased, you are at a disadvantage that can be fatal if you have to think "which leg do I start off with?" or "what hand do I raise to defend myself?" This is why perfectly ambidextrous people are extraordinarily rare. Yes, there are many people who are "ambidextrous," but they will have a preferred hand for any given movement. Dr. Nelson once heard of a man who was close to perfectly ambidextrous and the informant stated that he was extraordinarily clumsy because he had to think first before making many movements.

So, it is the nature of being functional that one side is "better" able to perform certain tasks. This happens without any injury but simply because it is more efficient to wire the brain this way. We can use kinesthetic imagination in a couple of ways to reduce the difference between our sides. One way is to actually make the movement on the better-performing side and then imagine the movement on the other side working as well as on the better side. The following short lesson/thought experiment gives you a chance to experience this way to use kinesthetic imagination. The second way is to reverse this and have the better side perform like the lesser side. More about this a little later.

MINI-ATM: SHOULDERS—A THOUGHT EXPERIMENT

If at any time you feel there is a switch between which arm moves better, then, on the next segment, switch the preferred arm.

1. Sit in a comfortable flat-seated chair. **Alternately raise your arms forward and up in the direction of the ceiling.** Decide which arm feels or moves better currently.

   Now put that hand on your leg. Gently slide your hand along the leg toward your knee and then back. Pause for at least two full breaths and then repeat this movement three or four times, always pausing for several breaths between movements. Pause. Put your arms down by your sides and compare sides.

   Now put your other hand on its leg. Make the sliding movement once, just to get the feel. Pause. Now imagine this movement being performed as well as the other side. Repeat four or five times again taking several breaths in between. Pause. Put your arms down by your sides and compare sides. Rest.

   What do you notice now?

   Alternately raise your arms forward and up in the direction of the ceiling. What changes do you notice?

2. **Make a fist with your "better" hand. Gently raise your shoulder straight up in the direction of the ceiling. Only go as far as you can without any skips, or other discontinuities. Then slowly let your arm down, opening your hand as you do so.** Pause for at least two full breaths and then repeat this movement three or four times. Pause, open your hand, rest, and compare sides.

   Now make a fist with your other hand. Imagine gently raising your shoulder straight up in the direction of the ceiling. As you do so, imagine a smooth continuous movement. Repeat three or four times. Then actually make the movement once. Pause. Put your arms down by your sides and compare sides. Rest. What do you notice now?

   Alternately raise your arms forward and up in the direction of the ceiling. What changes do you notice?

3. **Put your better hand behind your head. Slowly and easily move your elbow forward and back. Stay within your range of comfort and ease.** Pause for at least two full breaths and then repeat this movement three or four times. Pause, put your arm down, and rest. Compare your two sides.

   Put your other hand behind your head. Imagine moving your elbow forward and back with the same sense of ease as the other arm. Repeat three or four times. Pause. Put your arms down by your sides and compare sides. Rest. What do you notice now?

   Alternately raise your arms forward and up in the direction of the ceiling. What changes do you notice?

4. **Put your better hand on the opposite shoulder. Gently move its elbow up and down only as far as you can go with ease.** Pause for at least two full breaths and then repeat this movement three or four times. Pause, put your arm down, and rest.

   Put your other hand on the opposite shoulder. Imagine moving this elbow as gently as the other one through as much of its range as your imagination can go. Repeat three or four times. Pause. Put your arms down by your sides and compare sides. Rest. What do you notice now?

   Alternately raise your arms forward and up in the direction of the ceiling. What changes do you notice?

   Stand up, walk around, and notice how your arms move.

REVERSE MIMICRY

A second way to work with bilateral differences that takes advantage of our becoming habituated to limitations is "reverse mimicry." This can be very helpful in recovering from injuries, illness, strokes, and accidents. When we are injured, it is healthy to (1) withdraw our awareness of an area (sensing pain habitually is not helpful) and (2) reorganize our movement to find a way to function without the full use of that area (i.e., we compensate). In the recovery from injury, this is initially healthy. However, often the injury heals but the compensation remains.

The typical response to having one side working better than the other is to endeavor to make the lesser side increase its performance. If the only issue is strength, this usually works well. However, when there is also an internal organizational deficit, this usually fails. Simply put, we do our best on both sides. So, if one side is only 60 percent as functional as the other, that is its current best. Trying to increase this with brute force or strain is not likely to work. After all, if you could use that side as well as the other, you would. However, one can intentionally degrade the better side to perform like the lesser.

As an example of this, we'll use touching the thumb to the pinky (little finger). Touch your right thumb and pinky easily, but let's say you cannot touch your left thumb and pinky. In this example, the following approach would be taken:

First, touch the right thumb and pinky several times to sense how this is done. Rest for a moment to let the brain process this information. Now, without straining, make the best approximation of touching the left thumb and pinky several times. Again, rest. Now imitate with the right hand how you performed this function with the left. Repeat two or three times, looking to copy the "poor" performance as well as possible. Again, rest for a little while. Now go back to making the movement as well as possible on the right. Wait a moment and see how well you do on the left. To the extent the issue is organization and not a physical problem, this typically results in a 20 to 60 percent improvement on the "bad" side. This is dependent on how well you can imitate the problem and how much of the problem is organizational as opposed to a residual physical limitation.

REVIEW: WAYS TO USE KINESTHETIC IMAGINATION

- TRANSFER SENSE OF EASE
- EXTEND PRACTICE
- CHANGE PATTERN OF ERROR
- SPEED RECOVERY FROM INJURY
- FEEL THE SOUND
- SILENT PRACTICE
- SHIFT THE FOCAL POINT
- MIMING THE BETTER SIDE
- REVERSE MIMICRY

NOTES

1. Doidge, Norman. 2007. *The Brain That Changes Itself* (New York: Penguin Group).
2. Doidge, 201–2.
3. Doidge, 204.

CHAPTER 3

Physics of Easy Movement

NEWTONIAN MECHANICS

Our movement, like all movement, is subject to the laws of physics. As a physicist, Dr. Feldenkrais was intimately aware of these laws and incorporated them into his work. Of particular interest, here are Newton's three laws of motion:[1]

Law 1: Every body continues in its state of rest, or of uniform motion in a straight line, unless it is compelled to change that state by a force impressed on it.
Law 2: The change in motion is proportional to the motive force impressed; and is made in the direction of the right line in which that force is impressed.
Law 3: To every action there is always opposed an equal reaction; or the mutual actions of two bodies are always equal, and directed in contrary parts.

The first law is commonly known as the law of inertia, that bodies continue at rest unless an outside force is imposed or, if it is in motion, will continue in a straight line unless outside force is imposed. For our purposes, this implies that we will continue to move as we have done without outside intervention or new information. It also provides a physical reason for the stability of our movement patterns.

The second law describes what happens with an external force, that its impact is the result of the amount of force. Thus the greater the change in motion desired, the greater the force required. The law also states that the direction the force is applied from matters. Billiards illustrates this quite well. The amount of force imparted to the cue ball determines the force it imparts to the target ball when it strikes. Thus, if you want to move the target ball two feet, you hit the cue ball about twice as hard as if you want to move it one foot. The angle at which the cue ball strikes the target ball determines the direction that ball will travel. So controlling where your cue ball and target ball go depends not only on the force imparted to the cue ball, but also the angle at which it strikes the target ball.

It is the third law that is most interesting in the context of Awareness Through Movement (ATM) lessons because we can feel it and utilize it directly. This law is most commonly stated as "for every action, there is an equal and opposite reaction." Any time we make a movement, we also enact force equally in the opposite direction. For example, if we move our right arm forward, our left shoulder and left side of the torso will move backward. Curiously, until this phenomenon is pointed out to us, we seldom notice it. There are two reasons for this: (1) our conceptual conscious attention is a narrow beam,[2] and we focus our attention on our intent, so if our intent is to move the arm forward that is what we attend to, (2) the arm is relatively light compared to the torso, so to offset a large movement by a small mass requires only a small movement by a large mass. Because of our usual lack of awareness of the reaction inherent in our movement, we can often make significant improvements in how we do what we want to do by attending to the reactions of our movement.

ATM: MOVING BACK TO REACH FORWARD

This seated lesson illustrates the third law of motion: that every action has an equal and opposite reaction. In making movements with the arms, we will focus on what is normally the reaction. That is, as an arm goes forward the opposite knee goes backward. This lesson is a reworking of a lesson with only minor changes in the "movement" but with a major change in what we are attending to and how we endeavor to process the information contained in the movement.

1. **Sit forward in your chair. Raise your arms in front of you (forward) to shoulder height.** (Note: Raising your arms means forward to shoulder height in this lesson.) **Alternately reach forward with your left and your right arm. Repeat this three or four times.** Notice how far you go with each arm. How easy is your right arm? How easy is your left? How are you breathing? Stop and rest. Please remember to rest at least half a minute when you rest during this lesson.

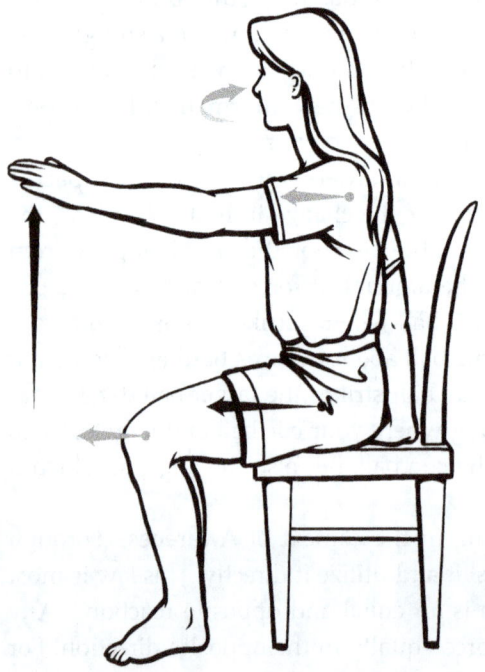

2. **Raise your left arm. Then move your right knee backward, without moving your foot. (Your feet stay fixed in place throughout the lesson.)** The movement comes from the hip. Notice that your right arm and shoulder are moved forward as a result of this movement.

   Lower your arm. Move your right knee backward, being aware of how this carries your left shoulder forward. Repeat this six or more times. Each time see if you can increase your awareness of some aspect of the way the right shoulder is carried by this movement. Pause.

   Now make the same movement with your right knee, but allow your head to turn slightly to the right as you do

so. What does this do for the movement of the shoulder? What does it do for the overall ease of the movement? Repeat four or five times endeavoring to make each repetition easier. Pause and rest.

3. **Raise your right arm. Now move your left knee backward, once, then lower your arm.** Again notice how the arm and shoulder are moved forward by the movement backward on the other side.

   With the arm down, move the left knee backward. Notice how this carries your right shoulder forward as well. Repeat five or more times. Increase your sense of how the back moves the shoulder forward with each repetition. Pause. Notice how you are sitting.

   Again, move the left knee backward, but allow the head to turn slightly to the left as you do so. Repeat four or five times. Pause and rest.

4. **Raise both your arms and alternately move them forward twice. Lower them.** Compare how they move now with how they moved when we began.

   Raise them again and alternately move the knees backward allowing the head to turn slightly in the direction of the retreating knee. Repeat three times, lower your arms, and pause.

   Raise your arms and again alternately move them forward twice. How do they move now? How comfortable? How far? Are you more aware of the reaction movement backward now? If so, where do you most clearly feel this movement back? Pause and rest.

   This is the end of this module. It is a logical place to stop if you cannot do the lesson in one sitting. Resume at step **5**.

5. Notice how you are breathing. Can you feel that as you inhale your chest rises and your sit bones push into the chair? **Take five or six normal breaths noticing how your weight shifts in response to breathing. Now raise your left arm (forward to shoulder height). Inhale and move your right knee backward. Allow the head to turn to the right as you make this movement.** Repeat four or five times. Pause for a moment.

   Now exhale as you move the right knee backward. Repeat three or four times. Is this easier or more difficult than doing the movement on the inhale?

   Try doing this same movement twice while holding your breath. What does this tell you about breathing and movement of the arm? **Breathing while you work, play, or do any other task is vital. When you hold your breath consistently as you perform any task you ensure that you will have problems, particularly with the shoulders, elbows, and wrists. The shoulder blade lies over the upper ribs. Many of the shoulder muscles extend over the ribs. If your breathing is impaired, the movement of your shoulders will be impaired. Likewise, if you have shoulder-related problems this will handicap your breathing. (If this applies to you, try one of the breathing lessons in chapter 7 after you finish this lesson.)** Pause and rest a moment.

6. **Raise your right arm. Move your left knee backward and allow your head to move.** What did you do with your breathing?

    Continue the movement but inhale as you make it. Repeat four times. See if you can integrate the breath into this movement a little bit better each time. Pause with your arm up. **Make the same movement and hold your breath. After you have done this twice, resume exhaling as you move.** Repeat the last movement two times then put your arm down and rest.

    Raise your right arm and move the left knee backward as you exhale. Repeat four times. Does this impede the movement as much as it did on the left?

    Continue the movement and only inhale as you move the arm forward. Repeat four times. Notice how much of a difference there is both in the ease of movement and in the range. Pause, put your arm down, and rest.

7. **Raise both your arms. Alternately move one knee and then the other forward.** (Notice that the other knee moves back at the same time.) **Inhale as you move away from the center and exhale as you move toward the center.** Make five or six movements back and forth like this. Pause and rest with your arms down.

8. **Raise your arms and alternately move one knee and then the other backward.** What are you doing with your breathing? Repeat four times. Pause.

    Lower one arm and move the knee of the lowered arm's side backward. Repeat four times and rest. Notice how this is compared to when you began. What are you doing with your breathing?

    Now lower the arm that is up, raise the other arm, and move the other knee backward several times. Pause and rest. Compare how this moved with the other arm. Which was easier? There is an extremely high likelihood that the arm you chose first was easier. This is the way a healthy organism works. We choose to do what is easiest. This establishes deep-seated habit patterns, which usually serve us well.

    Raise your arms and again alternately move them forward twice. How do they move now? Do you notice any changes from before? Pause and rest.

    This is the end of this module. It is a logical place to stop if you cannot do the lesson in one sitting. Resume at step **9**.

9. **Raise your right arm and move it forward without moving the knee.** Did you move your head? Repeat four times without moving your head. Does your shoulder slide easily over the upper ribs? Where do you feel the reaction movement? Pause with your arm down.

    Again, raise the right arm and repeat the last movement but allow your head to turn to the left as you do so. Repeat four times, then put your arm down and rest.

10. **Raise your left arm and move it forward without moving the knee.** Did you move your head? Allow it to move and repeat five or six times. Each time, see if you can allow the movement to be gentler. Pause and rest.

Resume the movement and alternately inhale as you extend the arm and then the next time inhale as the arm is brought back. Repeat enough times so that it is clear to you which movement facilitates breathing. Pause and rest.

11. **Raise your right arm and move the shoulder back.** Repeat five or six times then put your arm down and rest. Where did you sense the reaction movement?
    Raise your right arm and move the shoulder forward and back. Allow your head to go with this movement. Repeat four or five times. Pause and rest.

12. **Raise your left arm and move the shoulder back.** Repeat four or five times, softening the reaction movement a little more each time, if possible, then put your arm down and rest.

    Raise your left arm and move the shoulder forward and back. Allow your head to go with this movement. Repeat four or five times. Put your arm down and rest.

    Raise both your arms and alternately extend them. Do this a few times. Pay attention so it is clear to you what, if anything, has changed from the movements in this module.

    This is the end of this module. It is a logical place to stop if you cannot do the lesson in one sitting. Resume at step **13**.

13. **Raise your left arm forward to shoulder height. Move it forward leading with the pelvis (the right knee moves backward) then add moving the shoulder. Allow your head to move freely.** Repeat four times. **Then lower your arm.** Pause and rest.

    Raise your left arm again and now move it forward leading with the shoulder. Repeat four times and pause briefly.

    Now move the arm forward, with both shoulder and pelvis involved, aiming to find the most effective way to do so. Repeat four times, pause, and rest. Compare your two sides.

14. **Raise your right arm (forward to shoulder height). Move it forward with the shoulder as the left knee goes backward.** Repeat this combined movement at least eight times. Explore the difference between leading with the pelvis and leading with the shoulder as you do this movement. Pause and rest.

15. **Raise your right arm. Move your right knee forward while you take your right shoulder back.** Repeat three or four times.

    Stop at neutral and reverse this. That is, move the right shoulder forward while the left knee goes *back*. Repeat four or five times then put your arm down and rest.

    Raise your right arm and move forward and back from the shoulder while you move in the opposite direction with the left knee. Repeat four or five times, being careful not to strain. Put your arm down and rest.

16. **Raise your left arm. Move your left knee forward while you take your left shoulder back, twice. Then move the right knee forward while you move the**

left arm forward from the shoulder three times. Put your arm down and pause for a few seconds.

Raise your left arm and move the shoulder in the same direction as the right knee. Repeat four times.

Now move the arm with the shoulder and right knee in opposition. Repeat four or five times, noticing the differences. Pause and rest.

Raise both arms. Alternately move them forward. Repeat several times. Notice the changes since last time. How much of yourself do you feel is involved in this movement? Put your arms down and rest. Stand up and walk around for a moment. Notice how your arms move now.

End of lesson

LEVERS AND LEVERAGE

The lever is a direct application of the third law of motion. By exerting a small force through a large distance, a larger force can be moved a small distance. A child's teeter-totter (seesaw), if it had a movable balance point (fulcrum), illustrates this. If the fulcrum is in the center, equal weights balance, and if one side is heavier, then that side will go down. But move the fulcrum so that it is one-third of the distance from one end, and now the balance point becomes the short side having twice the weight as the long side.

A good example of how this applies to human movement is in lifting the head from the floor. The efficient way to make this movement is to send the sternum (breastbone) in the direction of the floor. Many people will try to lift the head directly from the floor using the relatively weak neck muscles. This puts an enormous load on these muscles, causing or contributing to many a sore neck. However, if you first put the weight down through the sternum, the head lifts much more easily because much of the weight is counterbalanced, just like on a teeter-totter. Moreover, this action distributes the effort among more muscles, thereby reducing the strain on the neck muscles even more than the benefit from counterweighting alone.

Cellist Teresa Kubiak (see interview in chapter 15) offers this insight for playing her instrument with leverage:

> Leverage begins with the quality of one's posture, which comes from a dynamic relationship to gravity—we are always reacting to it. Are we compressing or are we lengthening? The former leads to disease and injury, the latter brings facility and strength.
>
> In the case of cello, leverage creates a technique where weight gets applied, not pressed or squeezed. The elbows are the pivot points. A dynamic posture allows them to be suspended, almost floating, so that weight can pass through in varying degrees as needed.
>
> For the bow arm, one can do an embodiment meditation by observing where the weight needs to be applied (outer two-thirds of the bow) and where

it needs to release (nearer to the frog). Becoming aware of the exact transition point will eventually train the bow arm to relax naturally on a consistent basis, allowing the muscles to breathe and avoiding injury.

On the left side of the body, the elbow is even more important in applying the weight as a lever—the elbow goes up, the fingers go down, like a seesaw. The direction of weight is toward the belly of the cello, or the ground. Though the movement is barely perceptible to an observer, this approach creates a fluid left hand technique that never tires, strains or gets stiff. It also makes shifting much easier and is the best way to bring stability (accuracy) into one's left-hand technique.

POTENTIAL ENERGY AND KINETIC ENERGY

Potential energy is the stored energy in any object or system by virtue of its position or arrangement of parts. Potential energy isn't transferable, and it depends on the height or distance and mass of the object. Thus, if you are lying on the floor, you have less potential energy than if you are seated.

Kinetic energy is the energy of an object or a system's particles in motion. Momentum is related to kinetic energy. The difference is that momentum increases directly with speed whereas kinetic energy increases as the square of velocity.

Let's apply these concepts to an instrumental context:

Harpist, digit poised, unmoving and ready. Harp string, silent and still.
Both = Potential energy
Harpist digit activates to pluck harp string. String vibrates, a musical note sounds.
Kinetic energy!

Some movements can take advantage of potential energy. The following mini-lesson demonstrates how to use potential energy and the third law of motion to easily go from sitting in a chair to standing. Remember to breathe between movements.

ATM: SITTING TO STANDING

1. **Sit near the edge of a flat chair. Put your hands on your legs, slide the hands forward, and allow your back to round so your face is parallel to the floor. Then, return to neutral.** Repeat this movement five to seven times. Pause for at least a breath between movements. Go slowly and gently. Avoid strong or abrupt movements. See if smiling with the movement makes it easier. Stop and rest.

2. **Put your left hand on your left knee. Move your hand down toward the floor along your leg. If you reach the floor and can comfortably extend further, do so. When you have gone to your comfortable limit, pause to take a breath and then**

come up to neutral. Repeat four to six times. Pause and compare your left and right sides.

Now put your right hand on your right knee. Move your hand down toward the floor along your leg. When you reach your limit of comfort, pause to take a breath and then slowly come up to neutral. Repeat four to six times. Pause, notice how erect you feel, and rest a moment.

3. **Put your right hand on your right knee and your left hand on your left knee. Move both hands down toward the floor until you reach your comfortable maximum. Pause, take a breath, and come up to neutral.** Repeat three or four times.

   Come forward on your chair. Again, put your right hand on your right knee and your left hand on your left knee. Move both hands down toward the floor until you reach your comfortable maximum. Now lift your pelvis higher so that it is in the air with your rear end facing the ceiling. Repeat this lifting of the pelvis two or three times, before coming up to neutral. Rest in a seated position.

   The next time you are down, stay there and move your torso left and right. This will move your hands left and right along the floor. Repeat this left and right movement four to six times before returning to sitting. Rest for a moment.

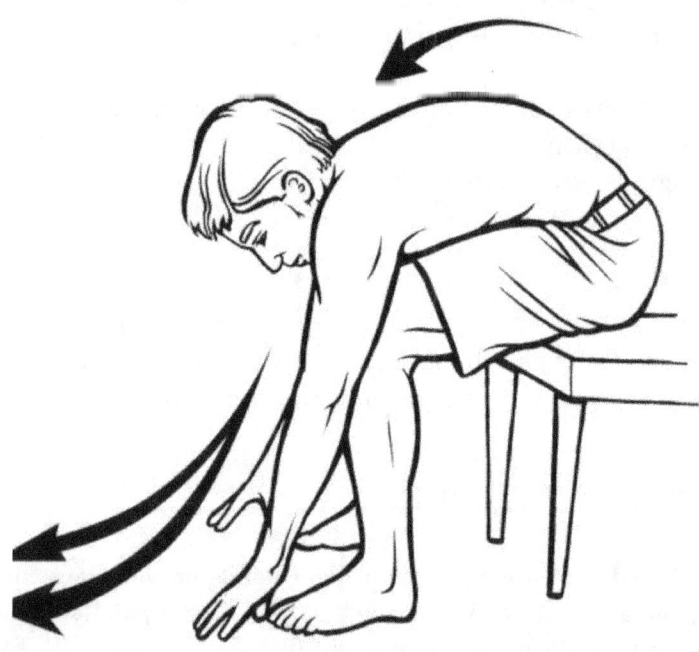

4. **Again, go down with both hands in the middle, pause and lift your pelvis so that your rear end faces the ceiling. From this position, gently come to standing. Then go back to the prior position.** Repeat coming to standing from that position three times. Pause in standing for a short while.

Go back down until your hands are on the floor. Then gently put your rear end back onto your chair. Now go back and forth between going down gently lifting the pelvis standing and then reversing this. Instead of falling into your chair, try and "kiss it" as you resume sitting. Repeat this sitting-standing sequence four or five times until you feel you have some mastery of it.

Now, using this controlled "falling" movement, see if you can use this pattern to come to standing from sitting without putting your hands to the floor. Play with this until it feels easy, comfortable, and natural to come to standing and to sit in this manner.

REVERSIBILITY AND MOMENTUM

Momentum is a dual-edged sword. On one hand, it is needed to keep us moving but on the other, it causes problems when uncontrolled. In the previous lesson (sitting to standing), controlling momentum allows one to both come up to standing with ease and to sit easily. This control provides the ability to reverse direction. A typical example of uncontrolled momentum is falling into a chair. Not only is this bad for chairs, but it is also hard on the pelvis and spine. Efficient walking utilizes both momentum and reversibility. It actually is an act using the momentum of falling forward combined with "catching" oneself and reversing the fall to be able to repeat it. In addition, the arms swing to enhance the movement.

Feldenkrais's martial arts background convinced him of reversibility's importance. Simply put, in martial combat, if you begin a movement and are committed so completely that you cannot do anything but finish it, you make yourself vulnerable to a surprise. At best, you have to partially undo what you've done with concomitant delay, at worst, you lose. For the same reason, stances and sitting should, if possible, be symmetrical. If they are asymmetrical, not only are there alignment concerns, but the ability to move or resist in at least one direction is lost. For example, if you stand with the right foot forward, you cannot move quickly to the right and are unable to resist a forward push from your right rear leftward.

TENSION AND FUNCTION

In physics, tension is a strained state or condition resulting from forces acting in opposition to each other. Translated into physiology, tension becomes the state of having the muscles stretched tight.

And yet, tension is necessary to life. Without any tonus (muscle tension), we cannot stand, sit, or even breathe. Problems arise when tension is excessive, misplaced, or insufficient. If we use more tension than needed to perform any task, that performance will seem strained. We will sense that extra effort is involved. For example, you do not need to clench your jaw while reading this. But do so anyway. Can you feel the sense of strain? Notice your feet while you do this. Do you feel that even they are now slightly tensed? This is what extra (or unnecessary) effort does to us. Over time this extra effort also results in needless wear and tear. Sometimes we do not tense all over but add extra tension in an area that does not further our intent. This has the same result as generalized excessive tension. If you did the jaw-clenching exercise, you have already felt this. If we are persistently tense, after a while we often do not feel this strain. It becomes so habitual that we consider it our normal way of being. But a trained observer will notice it. When we are playing music, the strain will manifest itself in our sound. Unless it is very slight, the impact of tension on our sound will be noticeable. It typically results in a constricted, less pleasing sound.

Insufficient tension also reduces the capacity to produce sound. Without tension, there is no sound, such as with a slack violin or guitar string.

It is rather like the old story about the master guitarist teaching his student with only one string on the guitar. The student asks him, "How can I learn to play with only one string?"

"See how it sounds," says the teacher.

The student strums it and nothing happens. No sound.

"It is too slack," says the student to the teacher. "I can get no sound."

"Okay, then give it to me." The teacher makes an adjustment and hands the instrument back.

The student strums it and it squeaks.

"It is too tight," says the student.

"Okay," says the teacher. "Adjust it until it is just right. Then you will know how to begin to play."

We wish, therefore, to walk the tightrope of ideal tension—just enough to perform and no more. At first, this is difficult. However, as we develop a feel for keeping proper tension, doing so becomes easier, although it still requires us to remain focused. The ideal is to make appropriate tension habitual. When we do so, performing becomes comfortable and has a graceful, easy feel to all involved.

NOTES

1. March, Robert M. 1992. *Physics for Poets*, second edition (New York: McGraw Hill), 35.
2. Tor Nortranders, *The User Illusion: Cutting Consciousness Down to Size*. New York: Viking Press, 1998.

CHAPTER 4

Neuroplasticity

Neuroplasticity is defined as

The brain's ability to reorganize itself by forming new neural connections throughout life. Neuroplasticity allows the neurons (nerve cells) in the brain to compensate for injury and disease and to adjust their activities in response to new situations or to changes in their environment.[1]

Brain reorganization takes place by mechanisms such as "axonal sprouting" in which undamaged axons grow new nerve endings to reconnect neurons whose links were injured or severed. Undamaged axons can also sprout nerve endings and connect with other undamaged nerve cells, forming new neural pathways to accomplish a needed function.

While neuroplasticity is undoubtedly as old as brains, it is only recently that it has been recognized by the mainstream medical profession.

For a very long time doctors and neuroscientists thought that human brain damage was permanent and irreversible.... In the latter part of the twentieth century, the medical world discovered and gradually accepted a revolutionary new idea: our brains can regrow new cells, repair injuries, rewire new connections, and reallocate brain resources to restore lost function. This was neuroplasticity.[2]

Well before the medical profession recognized neuroplasticity, Western techniques were developed to utilize our brains' incredible potential. The earliest of these was developed by a physician, William Horatio Bates. Bates believed that eyestrain and high tonus inhibit vision. He, therefore, developed exercises to relax the eyes. Using his exercises, clients were able to reduce prescriptions, and many could rid themselves of glasses. He also was aware that any approach that modifies muscle tonus and vision always involves the brain. After all, that is where we actually "see." Two of the key techniques espoused by Bates are sunning and palming. In sunning, one exposes their closed eyes up to the sun. In palming, one covers the closed eyes with their palms. The fingers overlap on the forehead. This leads to a greater sense of relaxation throughout the visual system. Bates developed an international following. His students called themselves "natural eyesight educators." Unfortunately, in the era before mainstream medicine accepted neuroplasticity, he was labeled a quack and his work disappeared from medical practice.

Another use of neuroplasticity was in somatic education techniques. These are designed to use a heightened awareness of movement to make changes in how we function. Three prominent methods are the Alexander Technique, the work of Mabel Ellsworth Todd, and the Feldenkrais Method.

F. Matthias Alexander (1869–1955) was an Australian thespian who experienced vocal problems. In the mid-1890s, he developed his technique to resolve these problems. He quickly realized that he could use what he had learned to help others with all sorts of movement-related problems. His work is premised on establishing correct posture of the head, neck, and spine with a strong emphasis on learning and maintaining a correct posture. This work was all hands-on; he never developed any movement lessons.

Mabel Ellsworth Todd (1880–1956) was an American who created what came to be called Ideokinesis. Todd's ideas involved using anatomically based, creative visual imagery and consciously relaxed volition to create refined neuromuscular coordination, presented in her book.[3]

Moshe Feldenkrais, D.Sc. (1904–1984), was both a physicist and electrical engineer. We've provided some of his history in chapter 1. To reiterate, he developed his method during World War II to deal with an old sports injury to his knee. Instead of asking, "How do I fix my knee?" he asked, "If I take one hundred steps and ninety-nine are fine, what do I do differently on the one-hundredth step?" This began his lifelong examination of how we move as a unified organism. This inquiry allowed him to walk without mentionable pain for the remainder of his life.

This led to a major discovery. Feldenkrais realized that many of our aches and pains are not the result of direct trauma, but rather come from poor movement patterns. These could either arise from defects in our early learning, from illness, or from injuries and their related compensations. Learning-improved movement patterns can alleviate these as well as help regain lost functions, as for example, after a stroke, or develop new skills, such as an athlete or musician might require. The Feldenkrais Method is, therefore, an educational approach, not a medical one. His unique contribution was the creation of Awareness Through Movement (ATM) lessons which form the core of this book.

During the course of Feldenkrais's first American training (San Francisco, 1975–1977), he met neuroscientist Dr. Karl Pribram who, with physicist David Bohm, developed the holonomic brain model of cognitive function. After several discussions with Feldenkrais, observing him training and giving Functional Integration lessons, Dr. Pribram stated, "The Feldenkrais Method is not just pushing muscles around, but really changing things in the brain."

THE MEDICAL "DISCOVERY" OF NEUROPLASTICITY

For the latter part of the nineteenth century and almost all of the twentieth century, the idea of brain localization held sway. This began when Paul Broca dissected the brain of a man who had lost the ability to speak and found damaged tissue in the left frontal lobe. Broca found damage in the same location, now known as Broca's area and thought to be key for speech. Soon afterward, physician Carl Wernicke connected damage in another part of the brain to the inability to understand language. Over the next hundred years, new research refined the brain map. These discoveries led to localization going from a series of intriguing correlations to a general theory that every brain function had only one hard-wired location. Localization meant that if a part of the brain was damaged, the brain could never reorganize itself sufficiently to recover a lost function. It was believed that after birth, no neural cells are created. This precluded improvement from programming new cells.

The first break in the wall of localization came not from a medical doctor, but from a psychologist, Donald Hebb. Hebb was an associate of the great neurologist Wilder Penfield. Working with Penfield at the Montreal Neurological Institute, Hebb researched the effect of brain surgery and injury on human brain function. In 1949, he published *The Organization of Behavior*,[4] explaining how the brain processes thoughts, sensation, emotion, and actions. Based on his observations, he proposed that when an action is repeated, brain cells (neurons) fire in a way that is self-reinforcing (or, as is now widely summarized, cells that fire together, wire together).

Twenty years later, physician Paul Bach-y-Rita first demonstrated neuroplasticity in an experiment that was given medical credibility. The trials he conducted in 1969 are now regarded to be the first form of experimental evidence for neuroplasticity and the feasibility of sensory substitution. In 1998, more and more research into neuroplasticity transpired and led to an astounding discovery of neural stem cells in the human brain (neurogenesis). First found active in a region of the brain called the hippocampus (known to be instrumental in the formation of memories), they were later also found to be active in the olfactory bulbs (an area that processes smell) and dormant and inactive in the septum (an area that processes emotion), the striatum (an area that processes movement), and the spinal cord.

Recent research confirms that neurogenesis persists into adulthood.[5]

In addition to new cells, the adult brain has been found to contain millions of "silent synapses."[6] These immature connections remain inactive until they are recruited to help form new memories.

Neuroplasticity was brought to the general public in the writings of Norman Doidge, MD. First in his best-selling book, *The Brain that Changes Itself: Stories of Personal Triumph from the Frontiers of Brain Science*,[7] and, more recently, in *The Brain's Way of Healing; Remarkable Discoveries and Recoveries from the Frontiers of Neuroplasticity*.[8]

HOW DOES NEUROPLASTICITY WORK?

When we examine who we are, it becomes clear that we are constantly reinventing ourselves from moment to moment. Because of our entire history of wiring ourselves to be the person we are, this invention, barring something traumatic, is fairly close to who we were from moment to moment. And yet, over time we change greatly. Can you say at seventy you are the person you were at fifty, or at twenty, the person you were at fifteen? Dr. Michael Merzenich, a leading pioneer in brain plasticity research and co-founder of Posit Science, lists ten core principles involved in the remodeling of your brain:

1. Change is mostly limited to those situations in which the brain is in the mood for it. If you are alert, on the ball, engaged, motivated, ready for action, the brain releases the neurochemicals necessary to enable brain change. When disengaged, inattentive, distracted, or doing something without thinking that requires no real effort, your neuroplastic switches are "off."

2. The more you're motivated, the more alert you are, and the better (or worse) the potential outcome, the bigger the brain change. If you're intensely focused on the task and trying to master something for an important reason, the change experienced will be greater.

3. What changes in the brain is the strength of the connections between neurons that are engaged together, moment by moment, in time. The more something is practiced, the more connections are changed and made to include all elements of the experience (sensory info, movement, cognitive patterns, etc.).

4. Learning-driven changes in connections increase cell-to-cell cooperation which is crucial for increasing reliability. Merzenich explains this by asking you to imagine the sound of a football stadium full of fans all clapping at random versus the same people clapping in unison. He explains, "The more powerfully coordinated your [nerve cell] teams are, the more powerful and more reliable their behavioral productions."

5. The brain also strengthens its connections between teams of neurons representing separate moments of successive things that reliably occur in serial time. This process allows your brain to predict what happens next and have a continuous "associative flow." Without this ability, your stream of consciousness would be reduced to "a series of separate, stagnating puddles."

6. Initial changes are temporary. The brain first records the change, then determines whether it should make the change permanent. It only becomes permanent if the experience is fascinating or novel enough or if the behavioral outcome is important, good, or bad.

7. The brain is changed by internal mental rehearsal in the same ways and involving precisely the same processes that control changes achieved through interactions with the external world (e.g., kinesthetic imagination). According to Merzenich, "You don't have to move an inch to drive positive plastic change in your brain. Your internal representations of things recalled from memory work just fine for progressive brain plasticity-based learning."

8. Memory guides and controls most learning. As you learn a new skill, your brain takes note of and remembers the good attempts, while discarding the not-so-good ones. Then, it recalls the last good pass, makes incremental adjustments, and progressively improves.

9. Every movement of learning provides a moment of opportunity for the brain to stabilize—and reduce the disruptive power of—potentially interfering backgrounds or "noise." Each time your brain strengthens a connection to advance your mastery of a skill, it also weakens other connections of neurons that weren't

used at that precise moment. Thus, positive plastic brain changes work to create a brighter and sharper picture of what is happening, while negative plastic brain changes erase some of the irrelevant or interfering activity in the brain.

10. Brain plasticity is a two-way street. It's just as easy to generate negative changes as positive ones. You have a "use it or lose it" brain. It's almost as easy to drive changes that impair memory and physical and mental abilities as it is to improve these things. Merzenich says that those older people who reinforce negative images of aging are absolute masters at encouraging plastic brain change in the wrong direction.[9]

NEUROPLASTICITY IN ACTION: THE VISUAL SYSTEM

Meir Schneider

Meir Schneider was born in 1954, cross-eyed, with glaucoma, astigmatism, nystagmus (involuntary eye movement), and cataracts. In short, he was blind. After five unsuccessful surgeries on the lenses of his eyes, which left him with massive scar tissue, his doctors pronounced his condition hopeless and he was certified permanently legally blind. He used Braille for reading and schoolwork and was given powerful magnifying lens glasses. With these he could read, but only one letter at a time. At age seventeen, his vision was 20/2,000. A slightly younger teenage boy who had used the Bates method and had found his eyesight to improve taught Meir Schneider the basic exercises of sunning and palming. Although these are normally done for an hour a day, he did them for up to thirteen hours a day. At first he only found the exercises relaxing, but soon noticed that the contrast between light and dark was increasing. After six months, he began to see more clearly. After eighteen months, he was reading without glasses by holding the paper inches from his nose. Using the Bates method as his foundation, he developed many more eye exercises of his own. Originally 20/2,000, his eyesight is now 20/70 despite badly scarred eyes. Meir's right eye is so scarred, less than 1 percent of the lens area admits light; the rest is scar tissue and membrane. Adding self-massage and his own movement work to the eye exercises he found and developed, he created the seven principles of natural vision improvement that he writes about in his book, *Vision for Life*. His exercise system has been found useful for many other physical limitations. He was awarded a PhD in the healing arts for his work with muscular dystrophy.

David Webber

David Webber was born in 1954, the same year as Meir Schneider. He had normal vision until 1996 when he was diagnosed with uveitis. Uveitis is an immune system disorder where the uvea, the middle layer of the eyeball, becomes inflamed. Uveitis can damage vital eye tissue, leading to permanent vision loss. For the next six years, Webber's condition deteriorated. Over that time, he had five operations. These left him in pain and diagnosed with complications, including significant damage to his optic nerves, cataracts, and glaucoma. His right eye was so damaged that it felt dead to him. By 2002, his corrected visual acuity was 20/200 and he was declared legally blind.

Having had extensive training in Buddhist meditation, he sought out Tibetan Buddhist healing practices for his eyes. He was also aware of the Bates method. Unfortunately, he was in too much physical and emotional distress to be able to utilize these practices. He also had heard of Meir Schneider but felt unable to handle traveling to San Francisco to work with him. In 1999, he was living in Toronto and began attending a series of ATM lessons given by a local practitioner, Marion Harris. With eyes very inflamed and out of control, he found awareness directed to gentle movements released chronic tension, making moving around safe and pleasurable. In 2000, he enrolled in the Feldenkrais Method of professional training for self-improvement. During his training he became aware of a lesson Feldenkrais created called "Covering the Eyes." He realized that this was Feldenkrais's exploration and modification of Bates's work and was very similar to the Buddhist exercises. He could feel the changes in his eyes the moment he started doing the lesson. He felt he had the key to relax his eyes and heal his nervous and immune systems. When he finished the lesson, he noticed something totally unexpected: he was able to feel his eyeballs in their orbits. It had brought his eyes back into his self-image. This result was especially surprising for the "dead" right eye. During the course of his blindness, it had disappeared from his body image. This phenomenon, where we withdraw our self-image from a damaged or painful area, is a healthy response to trauma. However, it is also limiting. Recovery from a problem that leads to this withdrawal always involves reintegrating that area. Often, when pain is an issue, it requires some temporary discomfort as we regain our wholeness.

Once he had this key, Webber was able to experience the deep states of calm necessary to relax his entire self and especially the muscles of his eyes, and to utilize Buddhist healing meditations. His vision began to return. He added his own innovations, one being teaching himself to stimulate his eyes by gently squeezing them, using only his external eye muscles. This promoted the draining of dead cells and lowered the pressure in his eyes. By July 2009, he had 20/40 vision in his left eye with glasses, which he needed because his own lenses were surgically removed. His right eye had improved to 20/200 from 20/800. He began developing and adapting Feldenkrais ATMs. One was the Bell Hand, where, with a smaller and smaller gentle opening and closing of the hands, the hands become very relaxed. He then palmed, using these very relaxed hands, and found this allowed the tension in his eyes to dissolve into the emptiness of his hands.

Unfortunately, David passed away in 2018. At the time of his death he was up to 20/20 corrected. He also created two workshops that are available. The earlier one is audio only; the other includes video and is available online from Feldenkrais Access.

Sam Nelson

There are many other aspects of vision besides acuity at a distance. Among them are *convergence*, the ability to make a single image with two eyes, and *accommodation*, the ability to see clearly near mid-range and at a distance. Most people lose the ability to accommodate as they age. As a result, they need reading glasses, computer glasses, progressive glasses, or multifocal lenses. These are less severe visual problems that can often be addressed through movement and training.

When I was a sophomore in college, I went to my optometrist and complained that I was having trouble reading for more than half an hour. The optometrist's response was, "I'm surprised you've been able to read for the last four years. You have an amblyopic condition." Amblyopia is when the two eyes do not work together; this makes it difficult for them to form a single image (converge). Typically, when this happens the weaker eye is suppressed. If the effect of suppression is profound enough, this can lead to functional blindness. Fortunately, my optometrist was considered one of the best visual training optometrists in Michigan. He had simply waited for me to be ready to work on the problem. I spent the next eight weeks making twice weekly visits to do eye exercises in the office. In between visits, I practiced following a hanging string and homolateral crawling. This was followed by an additional eight weeks of work at home, with some different exercises and a slide machine that helped enhance convergence. By the end of this period, my eyes essentially worked together normally and I had no trouble reading. Twenty years later, having moved to upstate New York, I saw another visual training optometrist for the first time. Within two minutes of examining me, he said, "You've had visual training, haven't you."

"Yes," I replied. "How did you know?"

"Nobody organizes their eyes like this without being trained."

As I entered my fifties, I noticed a slight decline in my *accommodation*. This is attributed to the hardening of the lens as we age, leaving the muscles too weak to make the adjustment needed. I began working with the Read Without Glasses Method developed by Ray Gottlieb, OD. Because of this and the earlier work with visual training, I could readily read at full correction to 20/20 and in complete comfort when corrected to 20/30 in each eye. Thus, in my early sixties, when I opted for LASIK to correct nearsightedness, the plan was to undercorrect slightly, so that I would never need reading glasses and only on rare occasion, a weak correction for distance. However, things rarely turn out as planned. It took several months for my system to get used to the new eyesight. During that time I had some trouble reading; using David Webber's "Seeing Clearly" lessons resolved this issue. Less than a year after surgery, my left eye shifted to 20/20, eliminating the need for any distance glasses. Over the next several years, my right eye also became better at distance vision. Currently, at age seventy-six, I see 20/20+ combined. However, in poor light, or with small print, I now need reading glasses.

MOVEMENT

> Sam told me that I'd sleep better, eat less, and start forgetting my cane, and it all happened.—S.B., stroke survivor

At age twenty-six, S.B. suffered a massive stroke. When he began his recovery, he had no use of his left arm, could not make a pincer movement with his left thumb, had poor use of his left leg, and when he stood it took a minute or more of pressure before he knew where his left foot was in space. He was told by one doctor he would never walk again. When he asked his neurologist what the prognosis was for his recovery, he was told "I don't know" because the neurologist had never treated anyone who'd had a stroke of this magnitude before and had lived. Through dint of hard work and determination, S.B. managed to find a way to walk using a cane in his right hand and by twisting his left leg to gain support and some push-off.

About seven years after his stroke, he began Functional Integration lessons with me (Samuel H. Nelson, CFP). At that time, in addition to his movement problems, he needed to eat five meals a day and had trouble sleeping as he couldn't lie on his left side. The five meals were needed to feed the chronic spasticity in his shoulder and to a lesser extent his leg. During the first lesson we were able to reduce the spasticity, free up the arm, and enhance the feeling in the leg. Within a year his gait was more normal, he only ate three meals a day, and he was sleeping on his left side. After a couple of years, he regained the sense of feeling in his left elbow and upper arm. As a result, where before, he could bang his arm against something without feeling it, now it would be painful. When this happened, he'd say "Thanks Sam." For the first couple of years, he came for lessons on a weekly to biweekly basis. Since that time, he comes in for lessons monthly. Now, some twenty-seven years after his stroke, he has a heel strike, no longer uses his cane except when traveling (and then, more as a potential weapon than for support), and has some use of his arm. Furthermore, he continues to make progress every time he has a lesson. Currently, he has regained some feeling in his hand, is improving his shoulder and arm movement, and has increased the ability to pivot with his left leg. The last time he and his wife spent a weekend in New York City, his cane tip never touched the ground.

HEARING

Tomatis

Alfred A. Tomatis was an otolaryngologist whose work with hearing and listening has received some prominence. Alfred Tomatis devised his theory while at the Sorbonne in 1957. Tomatis's approach is based on his idea that the root cause of a variety of ailments is errant hearing. He found that the voices of opera singers had damaged their middle ears. With damaged hearing, they were forcing their voices to produce sounds in registers they could no longer hear, sounds which they were no longer correctly producing. Based on this, he concluded that the voice only contains what the ear can hear. However, like Bates, his work has been mostly ignored by the medical profession. In large part, this is due to his failure to provide a scientific basis for his claims.

He developed the Electronic Ear, a device which utilizes electronic gating, *bone conduction transducers*, and sound filters to enhance the uppermost missing frequencies. The goal is to tonify the muscles of the middle ear to sensitize the listener to the missing frequencies.

Tomatis began treating a number of other problems with the same methods, including reading problems, dyslexia, depression, severe schizophrenia, and even autism. He found evidence that many of these problems result from a failure of communication, which has to do with listening and the ear.

Tomatis theorized that the whole body is involved in the production of speech and language. He stated all reading is an activity of the ear. He recommended reading out loud for thirty minutes a day. He claimed this both stimulates the brain and is the best way to learn.

David Kaetz

David Kaetz recently released *Listening with Your Whole Body: Better Hearing Through the Somatic Experience of Sound*.[10] Central to his book is the idea that if you can make a sound, you can hear it better. He mentions recent experiments that suggest that "the more differentiated is our awareness of the precise work of our tongue and lips, the more differentiated is our ability to attend to different vocal sounds, and by implication to attend to language itself and all that that implies." While cautioning that this approach is unlikely to affect one's hearing as measured by an audiologist, by improving the quality of one's listening, one's effective hearing will be improved. The book contains three appendices which offer practices to improve the quality of listening.

BIMODAL STIMULATION

The most recent innovation for hearing involves bimodal stimulation. This is where two senses are stimulated simultaneously by the same external source. The intent is to teach the brain to distinguish real external sounds from internally generated sounds. When successful, this reduces the ringing in your ears. There are currently two devices available that use bimodal stimulation to ameliorate hearing problems.

Linere markets a device that for tinnitus attaches to the tongue. Sound, in the range of the individual's "buzz," then stimulates the tongue and auditory system. The idea is that the brain will be able to distinguish this from the internal buzz and suppress, to some extent, the tinnitus. They claim about 85 percent of users get notifiable improvement. This device is currently available only in Europe.

Neosensory markets the duo wristband. This wristband has four motors that are each factory tuned to respond to sound. When using the tinnitus program, they claim that sensation on the skin simultaneously with hearing the sound provides noticeable improvement to 87 percent of users. It is available only in the United States. This device has two other programs: "Clarify" and "Sound Awareness."

Clarify helps users with hearing loss in high frequencies distinguish words better. Specifically, the wristband uses machine learning to capture just the high frequency sounds in real time (such as f, ct, s, etc.) and it buzzes in particular ways to tell you whenever one of these sounds has occurred. Thus you can combine signals with the ear taking care of medium and low frequencies and the wristbands clarifying what happens at high frequencies. After practicing for a while with the wristband, the brain fuses these signals, which is why it enables the user to understand speech better.

Sound Awareness is for individuals who are functionally deaf. It allows them to feel sirens, etc. in emergencies, music, voices, and other useful sounds.

Sam Nelson

I have had tinnitus for over forty years and have mild to moderate hearing loss. I tested the duo for tinnitus relief last summer. It did markedly reduce the buzz within five weeks. There was some further improvement over the next month or so. I currently use it to retain this improvement.

I also have been using the Clarify program for several months. So far, I have only noticed a slight improvement when using this program.

NOTES

1. RxList. n.d. "Definition of Neuroplasticity." https://www.rxlist.com/neuroplasticity/definition.htm
2. Pape, Karen. 2016. *The Boy Who Could Run but Not Walk: Understanding Neuroplasticity in the Child's Brain* (Toronto: Barlow Books), 6.
3. Todd, Mabel Ellsworth. [1937] 1968. *The Thinking Body* (Princeton, NJ: Princeton Book Company).
4. Hebb, Donald. 1949. *The Organization of Behavior: A Neuropsychological Theory* (New York: John Wiley & Sons).
5. Abdissa, Daba, Nigusse Hamba, and Asfaw Gerbi. 2020. "Review Article on Adult Neurogenesis in Humans." *Translational Research in Anatomy* 20: 100074.
6. ScienceDaily. November 30, 2022. "Silent Synapses Are Abundant in the Adult Brain." https://www.sciencedaily.com/releases/2022/11/221130114452.htm#:~:text=Neuroscientists%20discovered%20that%20the%20adult,to%20help%20form%20new%20memories
7. Doidge, Norman. 2007. *The Brain That Changes Itself: Stories of Personal Triumph from the Frontiers of Brain Science* (New York: Penguin).
8. Doidge, Norman. 2015. *The Brain's Way of Healing: Remarkable Discoveries and Recoveries from the Frontiers of Neuroplasticity* (New York: Penguin).
9. Merzenich, Michael. 2013. *Soft-Wired: How the New Science of Brain Plasticity Can Change Your Life* (Nashville, TN: Parnassus), 53–59.
10. Katz, David. 2017. *Listening with Your Whole Body: Better Hearing Through the Somatic Experience of Sound* (Hornby Island, BC: River Centre), 36–37.

CHAPTER 5

The Cost of Choice, Intention, and the Power of Habit

OPPORTUNITY COST REVEALED

In economics, there is an important, though oft-neglected, concept called "opportunity cost." In classic microeconomics, this is defined as the value of the best alternative forgone where, given limited resources, a choice needs to be made between several mutually exclusive alternatives.

However, value properly understood includes more than monetary considerations. In particular, time, pleasure, and long-term and total cost need to be taken into account. For example, if a gas station three miles away sells gas for five cents less per gallon and you would save thirty cents, does it justify the extra time to go and come back. And even if it does, what is the added cost of additional driving in terms of wear and tear on tires and other vehicle parts. Finally, there are external costs to many actions, of which environmental degradation is an example. Consideration of all the factors is, indeed, mind-boggling. It is so much easier to just consider the money and run.

This concept applies to all human activity for the simple reason that we have limited time and resources, and lack the ability to actually do more than one thing at one time ourselves. Yes, I can multitask by washing clothes and eating lunch. But only because the clothes washer is actually doing the work without my supervision. Because of these limitations, we can only handle a limited number of options for any particular purchase or task.

The economic decision space is relatively simple. One needs only compare like goods, if any, and cost, both the monetary price and the time and effort it takes to get the goods. Depending on how we value our time and effort, a simple numerical comparison can be made. Then we would purchase what to us is the lowest-cost product.[1]

Now consider a human being at birth. In the words of William James, it is "one great blooming, buzzing confusion" to an infant whose sensory apparatus is "assailed by eyes, ears, nose, skin, and entrails at once."[2] Somehow our brains manage (if not damaged) to make enough sense of this confusion that a normal three-year-old can walk, see, hear and talk, and understand one or more languages. How is this done? Quite simply, our brain develops pathways that function for us and as we grow and develop it reinforces these pathways, as was mentioned in chapter 4.

Because of the many complications involved in making all the choices to do what we want to do, our brain has developed a shortcut: intent.

INTENTION

One of Moshe Feldenkrais's dicta is that if your intention is clear, you will achieve the result you intend. One reason for this is simple. If you don't know what you intend, you are certain not to get it. Another more important reason is that developing intent is the function of our conceptual consciousness, to make clear choices as to what we intend. This is what allows us to accomplish what we set out to do. However, conceptual consciousness can only handle one thing at a time. Think about the color of your shirt and what you had for breakfast simultaneously. Can you do it? Or do they come into your consciousness sequentially? Yet, to function, we must be doing many things: breathing, pumping blood, moving our arms, and moving our legs. And many of these must be done simultaneously. Some we can volitionally control, and some not. But at any given time we predominantly operate on automatic pilot, as it were. Moreover, most of the information we receive is also handled outside our conceptual consciousness. When we are clear on our intent, all this automatic functioning facilitates the enactment of our intent. If we are unclear, other possibilities intrude, and we often fail—thus the importance of clear intention.

Indeed, research shows that most of what we do must necessarily be done without thought. Our brain is divided into seven structures, only one of which, the cerebral cortex, is involved with what we consider thinking and voluntary control of musculature. More important than structures in understanding the relationship of thought to action is information flow. This was investigated in the late 1950s, when it was concluded that maximal information flow of the process of conscious sensory perception is about forty bits per second. Meanwhile, we receive over eleven million bits per second from our external receptors, ten million of which come from the eyes. And yet more information is pouring in from other sensory means, such as the vestibular system, which maintains balance, and proprioception, which is how we know where a body part is without being able to see it. All in all, we are aware of about one-millionth of the information pouring in. The flow of information measured in bits per second is described as the bandwidth, or capacity, of consciousness. The bandwidth of consciousness is so low relative to the information pouring in, it is as if it were a spotlight dramatically illuminating the face of one actor among a vast panoply of characters in an epic. The spotlight can of course move, but it would take a very long time to illuminate all the actors, and in that time they would all have changed position. There is another difficulty with conscious control. Not only is the bandwidth of consciousness narrow, but also there is a time delay of half a second in transmission. That means that you are reacting to past information when you rely on conscious controls. In many cases, such as conversation, this does not matter. However, no one would survive split-second situations if consciousness were always in charge. And in fact it is not. In these situations we are capable of reacting very fast, because a clear intent is (or was) formed and we drop the conscious self and just react. (For more on information flow and the time delay in consciousness, see Norretranders.[3])

Of course, to enact a clear intent, you must know what you are doing. Another of Feldenkrais's dicta is that if you know what you are doing, you can get what you want. It is important, therefore, to learn what you need to do in order to do what you want and to know what this is. Equally important is to know what you don't need to know. It is easy to think that knowing what you are doing means being aware of everything you do. But this is impossible and, therefore, is a trap: the trap of being overly attentive—or, more accurately, being overly attentive to what we do instead of what we intend. The brain's capacity to organize our movement so that we no longer need to think about it is truly amazing. We take the simple act of walking for granted. But how exactly do you do it? What muscles do you move when? You would have to spend a great deal of time studying this simple act to know the answer to this question academically. To do it in real time would probably prove a severe strain on your bladder (unless you camped out a few feet from a bathroom). And this is true of all but the simplest acts. We cannot be aware of all that is going on. Rather, we must focus our intent and rely on our internal sense of proper functioning to perform.

A major obstacle to relying on our inner sense is our desire to be in control. We want to know that we are *doing* something, particularly if we are not confident of our skill or ability. So, if we can feel ourselves doing it, whatever it is, we feel we are performing properly. Even though we know that when we are doing something really well, we are so focused there is no sense of anything but enacting our intent. There is an effortless kind of effort that occurs when we truly perform well. This sensation has many names: flow, oneness, the elusive obvious, being "in the zone." But it is replicating the experience, not naming it, that really matters. To replicate the flow state, we have to allow our natural way of being to occur. Thus, control is anathema to reaching this state.

Consider what happens when we endeavor to actively control some area. For a vocalist, this often seems to occur with the jaw, tongue, breath mechanics, or the soft palate. Operating on a preset notion of how that area should perform, we consciously direct it to perform this way. This actually means *forcing* ourselves to perform a particular way. We would not do this if we felt we were performing properly without this force. After a while this sense of forcing becomes habitual, which often leads us to believe that if the force is not there, we are doing something wrong. Whether habitual or not, a felt sense of force or effort is an indicator of suboptimal performance (i.e., something is wrong). This is true even if we get the sound we and the listener want, because when this occurs, we are using extra effort and/or straining, which ultimately leads to a premature deterioration of ability.

Feldenkrais referred to this extra effort as "parasitic action" (for a brief discussion of this phenomenon, see Feldenkrais[4]). This is action that does not contribute to the desired result. It may be somewhat benign, such as curling the toes when you reach upward. Or it may be injurious, like pulling back with the pelvis as you reach forward with the arm. But even when it is benign, it hinders performance. Because your musculature is linked up to the central nervous system, tension anywhere is in a sense tension everywhere. That is, the interconnectedness of our nervous system, and Newton's third law of motion, results in a minute tightening of our other muscles when we tighten a muscle group. Thus, if something is tightened unnecessarily, it results in slightly more force being needed to perform our intent.

This added effort has three effects: (1) we are more fatigued by performing than we need to be, (2) injuries are more likely, and (3) the sound quality is reduced by the added strain. As fatigue is a function of energy expended versus energy available, obviously, for any given task, the less energy used, the less tired we will be. With extra effort, injuries are more likely both because the extra effort itself leads to added strain and wear and tear and because as we tire, injuries are more likely. As more effort is made, a tense quality envelops the musculature. Since the sound we produce is a product of our entire self, this tense quality colors our sound.

This phenomenon of unnecessary effort is actually widespread. Feldenkrais was well aware of this. Hence he often asserted, "We create our own difficulty." This is an unusual assertion, but it is true. As you become more familiar with this work, you will be able to verify it from your own experience.

It is not clear to what extent this pattern of creating difficulty is innate or social—nor does it matter. Here, quite simply, is how it works: When you endeavor to do something beyond your capacity, the standard approach is to *try harder*. When you try harder, you tense up. This act of tensing up can actually prevent you from achieving your objective; if you do achieve it, it is at a cost, usually of discomfort. For example, open your mouth a little. This is easy. Now open your mouth while pushing up against the jaw with the left hand. Can you feel how the jaw and neck muscles tighten? Even though you are clear that this is not doable (because of the arm's strength), the impetus is to *try* harder and tighten. Did you notice how uncomfortable this was? When something is perceived as difficult, the same pattern occurs: we tighten up to achieve. This tightening results in both excess tension and a feeling of difficulty. Repeat this pattern enough and many things become difficult. This is one reason why "old" people become restricted. They, in effect, practice doing things with difficulty until they do in fact become difficult. (Math anxiety is another manifestation of this.) It is also why, when you have trouble playing a particular piece, after a while it becomes very, very difficult. You've actually practiced doing it wrong (not deliberately, of course) until you've mastered your wrong version. Yet this sense of difficulty is unnecessary. If you can allow yourself to fail with ease, while doing what you intend, you will find that achieving becomes easier. Eventually you will find a way to do what you want to do. And that way will be a way of ease, especially in contrast to earlier efforts.

THE POWER OF HABIT

The strength of habit has been recognized for millennia. Ovid (43 BCE to 17 or 18 CE), wrote *Nil adsuetudine maius*, "nothing is stronger than habit." A musician we know has said her teacher would repeatedly say "habits are stronger than god." In neurological terms, this means that neurons that wire together, fire together.

There is a good reason habits are so powerful: without them we could not function. Without habit you'd have to think about everything you did. Each step would have to be consciously taken. You'd have to think about how to raise your arm, open your mouth, etc.—and we'd all have to use Velcro to tie our shoes. Unfortunately, sometimes we develop habits that become dysfunctional. And these can be just as powerful as habits that are functional at the highest level.

In her book, *The Boy Who Could Walk but Not Run*,[5] Karen Pape, MD, explains that it is neuroplasticity and the power of habit that accounts for the anomaly that is the book's title. The boy in the title was diagnosed with mild cerebral palsy. He walked with a decided limp, moving his left arm somewhat erratically as he walked. As a neonatologist, Dr. Pape worked with him until he was between three and four. Thus, she was surprised when the boy's mother called about three years after he was no longer under her care. She was also surprised and skeptical when the mother said he was playing soccer and running normally. She thought this was another case of a parent exaggerating the accomplishments of a child with difficulty. But when the mother persisted, she agreed to see the boy. He walked into her office with the same inefficient gait she recalled. However, when asked to run he did so normally. This astounded Dr. Pape, who couldn't believe it at first. After some time she came to a simple and profound explanation: cerebral palsy is most often caused by brain damage in utero. From a functional perspective one can think of this as a stroke. Thus, while learning to move, the child does so with a damaged brain. However, the brain can heal, both by creating new cells in some regions and by rewiring everywhere. This potential is highest when we are young. This apparently is what happened in the little boy's case. Running is learned after walking. Typically, it is learned after one is proficient in walking. This little boy was not proficient in walking; however, by the time it came for him to learn to run, his brain had healed. So he learned to run normally. Why then did he not walk normally? Because walking had already been wired and wired in a way that worked, though not well. The bad gait was habitual. And habitual behaviors are difficult to change.

This phenomenon of learning before the system is fully ready may explain how some counterproductive performance habits arise. One possible example of this may be the sitting position of some violinists. Instead of having both feet forward on the floor and more or less squared off, they "kick back" the right leg. This forces them to work hard to maintain their balance. Perhaps when they first started playing, the bow leg had to be moved back to avoid being in the way of the bow.

Even where there is no initial neurological deficit, injuries can reshape our habitual movement patterns in ways that are undesirable. Compensation is the principal culprit here. It is healthy to compensate for an injury to keep going. The problem arises when the injury heals and the compensation remains. Many years ago, we team-taught a class for musicians at Nazareth College in Rochester, New York. On a weekly basis, the class experienced an Awareness Through Movement lesson and then, at some point in the semester, each student got a short five- to ten-minute Functional Integration lesson. The last student to receive this was a young singer who had also been a dancer until a couple of years earlier when she broke her ankle. The ankle was placed in a cast and after a number of weeks the bones fully healed. However, when the cast was removed, she had lost both the capability to point her foot and to fully flex it. When Dr. Nelson started working with her, he began to gently manipulate the foot to see what it could do. He then worked higher up on the leg. After less than ten minutes her ability to point the toes and flex her foot was restored. Astounding as this was, the reason is quite simple. During the time the foot was immobilized, her brain had lost the wiring pattern for moving the foot normally. Instead, the pattern of an immobile foot had become wired in and became habitual.

Fortunately, we are primed for success. Show our nervous system a better way and it adopts it, particularly one that was wired previously. And if there are no physical constraints, it will implement the new program and make it the new and more useful habit. Because of the power of habit, if this way is novel, it takes many repetitions for the entire change to happen. Change proceeds at a pace that the system can handle.

NOTES

1. This will not be the same product for everyone as people have different incomes, time constraints, capabilities, and may value externalities, like carbon consumption, differently.
2. James, William. 1890. *Principles of Psychology* (New York, NY: Henry Holt and Company), 488.
3. Norretranders, Tor. 1998. *The User Illusion: Cutting Consciousness Down to Size* (New York: Viking).
4. Feldenkrais, Moshe, 1985. *The Potent Self*, Michaeleen Kimmy (San Francisco: Harper and Row, 1985), 85–86.
5. Pape, Karen. 2016. *The Boy Who Could Run but Not Walk: Understanding Neuroplasticity in the Child's Brain* (Toronto: Barlow Books).

CHAPTER 6

The Base of Support

The feet and legs form the crucial base of support for performing. This is true of sitting as well as standing. Clearly, you can't play an instrument if you jump and try to keep your feet off the ground. But try it with your feet in the air while seated. It is an enormous strain. No one, therefore, performs or advocates playing in this position. Though your feet and legs are vitally important to performing at your best, not much time or effort is spent on their proper use and care. Learning to use your feet well can be the quickest and easiest way to noticeably improve your playing.

Maximum stability and support are achieved when both feet are firmly on the floor. In this situation, the weight is approximately evenly distributed between the two because no one uses their two sides completely evenly. Indeed, our two sides are usually somewhat different in weight, width, height (at shoulder level), and even depth. In some people the difference is so pronounced that they need different shoe sizes for their two feet. However, when we are in balance, the weight will be distributed between our two legs in accordance with the proportions of our sides. That is, if one side is 2 percent bigger than the other, then that leg will, on average, carry 2 percent more weight.

When the weight is not even, we lean to one side or the other. This compresses the ribs on one side, compromising our breathing. There is also some compression in the neck that impinges on the larynx. Uneven leg length is one common cause of improper weight distribution. This can often be spotted because the person will equalize the weight by having one foot (the long leg) forward of the other. If the discrepancy is small (0.6 centimeter, or a quarter inch, or less), this can be accommodated functionally. That is, how we use ourselves, especially how we curve our spine, allows us to accommodate these relatively small differences without strain. A lift is necessary to properly handle discrepancies of up to about an inch. Greater discrepancies require adaptive shoes. Usually, people who stand with the same leg clearly forward of the other versus parallel or alternating the forward leg have a noticeable leg-length differential. If this does not sound like you, go to the next paragraph. A section at the end of this chapter is devoted to leg-length differentials.

Balance is not a stationary phenomenon. It is a dynamic event. We must remain in balance whenever we shift our weight, and, clearly, we must remain in balance when moving. Otherwise, we would fall instead of being able to walk, run, ski, and so on. But even when standing, we are constantly shifting our weight. No one stands stock-still for long, not even the King of England's guardsmen. The goal is to always be able to shift one's weight easily in any direction. When we can shift easily, we feel secure and in balance. Whenever we are unbalanced, our rib cage is not being properly supported, and we have a feeling of insecurity. And when we feel insecure, we tend to both tighten up and hold our breath. The net result is that we diminish our performance.

It is one of life's paradoxes that we often adopt a strategy that backfires. For example, when we feel unstable, we tense up to prevent ourselves from falling. But that very tensing makes us less stable. Of course, there is some sense in this phenomenon. If we truly are falling, stiffening ourselves to grab on to something often works. But to remain in this holding-on mode when we are not falling is self-defeating. It restricts the ability to flow with changes, putting us out of balance repeatedly. Being out of balance compels us to tighten some muscles to remain upright, move, etc. That we are tightening these muscles more than necessary is both unfortunate and an opportunity. It is unfortunate because it leaves us performing below our potential. It is an opportunity because as we learn to be in better balance so that we more closely approach using minimum necessary force, we will feel and perform better.

How can you tell whether you are really in balance? Clearly, if you feel like you are falling, you have lost your balance. But good balance is much more subtle than not falling. Often, we are a little out of balance and compensate by using extra effort or a suboptimal alignment. Standing with one leg forward to compensate for a leg-length differential is an example of suboptimal alignment. A simple way to see if you are out of balance (or how much) is to see whether you can readily move in all directions. If one leg is forward, you are already committed in that direction. You cannot move further that way without rearranging yourself. At a minimum you have to move your weight onto the back leg to advance your forward leg at all. How much you are out of balance can be gauged by how much, if any, preliminary weight shift you have to make to move in a direction. This will change from moment to moment because we are not static. As long as we are alive, we are in constant movement (however small). Therefore, dynamic balance is crucial. Dynamic balance occurs when our pattern moves us through the position that facilitates movement in all directions most of the time. Think of your central position as homebase. When you are in dynamic balance, homebase is a position that allows easy movement in any direction. When you are going out from, and then returning through, a dynamic homebase, you achieve a sense of balance.

The following lesson is aimed at establishing and retaining a dynamic sense of balance.

ATM: BALANCE IN STANDING

1. Stand with your feet shoulder width apart. If practical, take off your shoes. Have a chair or other support available to place one of your hands on. How does this feel? Do you feel balanced? Supported? **Shift your weight (pelvis) left and right several times.** How evenly did you do this? How easy was this? **Move your weight forward and back several times.** Pause.

2. **Place your right foot directly in front of your left foot, if possible. Place your hand on the chair back if you need to maintain your stability. Put most of your**

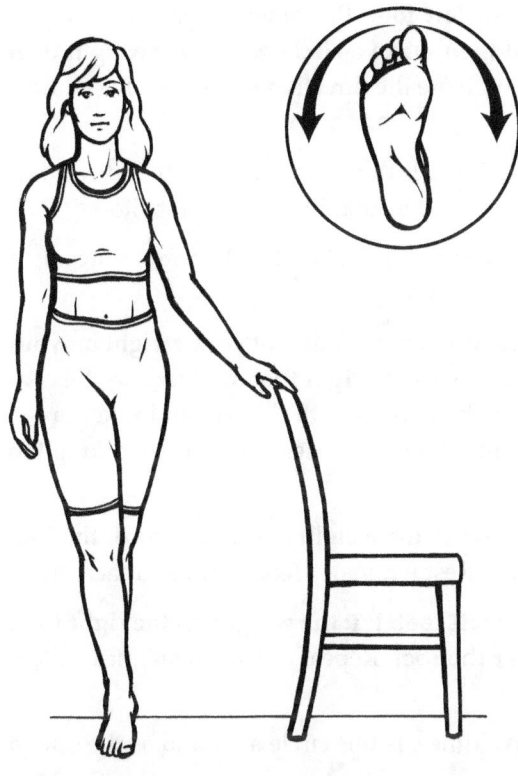

weight on your left foot. Now shift your weight to the front of your left foot and then back to the center. Repeat this shift at least five times. Then pause with your weight still on the center of your left foot.

Shift your weight to the rear of your left foot and then back to the center. Repeat this at least five times. Pause and balance the weight between the two feet for a moment.

3. **Put most of your weight on your left foot. Shift the weight from the front to the rear of your foot.** Repeat this seven to nine times. Where are you shifting weight? Do several of these shifts with the pelvis and a few concentrating on the ankle. What feels best to you? Pause. **Put your right foot parallel with the left and rest a minute.** Which leg seems to support you better?

4. **Place your right foot directly in front of your left foot.** Again, if needed, place your hand on the chair for stability. **Put most of your weight on your right foot. Shift your weight to the back of the right foot and then back to its center.** Repeat this shift at least five times. Pause.

   Shift your weight to the front of your right foot and then back to the center. Repeat this at least five times. Pause and balance the weight between the two feet for a moment.

5. **Put most of your weight on your right foot. Shift the weight from the front to the rear of your foot.** Repeat this seven to nine times. Notice how you do this and try at least one other way. Put your right foot parallel with the left.

   Move forward and back a few times, then shift left and right. How does this feel now? Pause, walk around, and rest for a moment.

   This is the end of this module. It is a logical place to stop if you cannot do the lesson in one sitting. Resume at **step 6**.

6. **Place your right foot directly in front of your left foot. Put your weight on your left foot. Move the weight to the outside of the left foot and back to the center.** Repeat this at least five times and then pause with the weight in the center.

   Now move the weight onto the left foot. Shift it from the center to the inside and back. Repeat this five to seven times. Rest with your feet parallel to each other.

THE BASE OF SUPPORT ■ 55

7. **Place your right foot in front of your left foot. Put your weight on your left foot. Move the weight forward and then make a circle with your weight over the foot.** Repeat this at least five times. Note the direction you chose. Recall how this feels.

   Reverse direction. Circle at least five times. Is this as easy as the other direction? Usually, we choose the easiest route without even thinking about it. Stop.

   Place your feet side by side. Move your pelvis left and right a few times. Is it easier to go in one direction? Rest for a minute.

8. **Place your right foot directly in front of your left foot. Put your weight on your right foot. Move the weight to the inside of the right foot and back to the center.** Repeat this at least five times and then pause with the weight in the center. Remember, if you can't smile while you're doing this lesson, you're working too hard.

   Move the weight onto the right foot. Move the weight to the outside of the foot and back. Repeat this four to six times. Rest with your feet parallel to each other.

9. **Place your right foot in front of your left foot. Put the weight on the right foot. Make a circle with your weight over the foot.** Repeat at least five times. Allow the circle to be more round each time.

   Reverse direction. Repeat at least five times. Is this circle as round as the one in the other direction? Stop.

   Place your feet side by side. Move your pelvis forward and back. Pause. Compare this to when you began. **Move side to side.** Compare this to how it was initially. Pause, walk around, and rest for a moment.

   This is the end of this module. It is a logical place to stop if you cannot do the lesson in one sitting. Resume at **step 10**.

10. **Place your left foot in front of your right foot. Place a hand on a chair if you need support. Put the weight on the right foot. Move the weight from the center to the front of the foot. Now move the weight from the front through the center to the back of the foot and back.** Repeat this ten times. Go slower and slower each time. Pause.

11. **Put your weight onto your right foot. Move the weight to the inside of the right foot then back through the center to the outside. Go back and forth from the inside of the foot to the outside.** Repeat this ten times. Does this weight shift become easier each time? Pause, place your feet parallel to each other, and rest a minute. Notice any differences between your right and left sides. Pay special attention to differences between your two feet.

12. **Place your left foot in front of your right foot. Put the weight onto the left foot. Move the weight from the center to the front of the foot. Next move the weight to the back of the foot and then return to the front.** Repeat this ten times. Notice where you shift your weight and explore shifting from other places. Pause.

13. **Put your weight onto your left foot. Move the weight to the inside of the left foot then back through the center to the outside. Go back and forth from the inside of the foot to the outside.** Repeat this ten times. See how gentle you can be with yourself as you do this. Pause.

    Place your feet side by side. Move forward and back. How is this compared to when you began? Pause. Notice how balanced you feel. Compare this to when you began. Pause, walk around, and rest for a moment.

    This is the end of this module. It is a logical place to stop if you cannot do the lesson in one sitting. Resume at **step 14**.

14. **Place your left foot in front of your right foot. Put the weight onto the left foot. Move the weight from the front to the back of the left foot twice.** Pause.

    Now move the weight between the inside and the outside of the foot twice. Pause.

    Make a circle with the weight on the left foot. Notice the direction of this circle. Go around seven to nine times. See if you can make each movement more circular or easier. Pause.

    Make a circle in the opposite direction to the one you just made. Go around at least six times. Pause and place your feet parallel. Rest a minute.

15. **Place your left foot in front of your right foot. Put the weight onto the right foot. Move the weight from the front to the back of the right foot twice.** Pause.

    Now move the weight from the inside to the outside of the foot twice. Pause.

    Make a circle with the weight on the right foot. Go around seven to nine times. Pause.

    Make a circle in the opposite direction to the one you just made. Go around at least six times. Pause and place your feet parallel. Rest a minute.

16. Imagine that you are trying to balance a plate on your head. **Make a circle with your pelvis without moving either your head or your feet.** Go around five to seven times. Pause.

    Now make a circle in the opposite direction. Go around at least six times. Pause. Notice how balanced you feel now.

    Move your weight forward and back several times. Compare it to when you began. Pause. **Move your weight left and right.** Again, compare with how it was initially. Stop and rest a minute.

    Then walk and observe how you feel. Note your balance from time to time as you resume your normal activities.

End of lesson

USING THE FLOOR

Just as the weight should be distributed evenly between the legs, it also should be distributed evenly over the foot. That is, roughly half the weight is on the front and back, and roughly half is inside (the big toe) and outside. When the weight distribution at homebase is too much in any direction, it distorts and weakens performance while standing. Too much weight on the front of the foot pushes you into overextension. It also gives you the feeling that you might pitch forward. Moreover, it results in a thinner sound by impairing the breathing. If the weight is too far back on the heels, you will feel unsupported as if the chest is behind the pelvis. This makes it more difficult to open your ribs to breathe, and you will have difficulty projecting.

If you tend to collapse to the inside (flat-footedness is the extreme), there is a tightness in the buttocks. This will make it more difficult to open your ribs to the side. You will also have a stretched sensation in the neck. As a result, you will have trouble fully opening up your breathing. Strengthening your arch will reduce the tendency to collapse to the inside. Strengthening the adductors, the muscles that hold your thighs together, can help strengthen your arch. The thigh-strengthening exercise at the end of the chapter will help strengthen the adductors.

If the weight is too far to the outside, the buttocks will be squeezed tight. This will make it harder to open the ribs in the back.

The following lesson is designed to teach you what it feels like to have a more even weight distribution on the feet. It also will help you feel that the best position for the feet in sitting (provided you fit the chair) is with your knees over your ankles.

ATM: THE CONNECTION OF THE FEET THROUGH TO THE HEAD

Take your shoes off.

1. Sit forward comfortably on the edge of the chair. Have your feet in front of you, shoulder width apart. **Keeping the ball of your right foot on the floor, lift your right heel from the floor a couple times.** How easy is it? Pause.

   Now lift the ball of the right foot several times. Is it easier or harder than lifting the heel? Notice the relationship of the knee to the ankle. **Move your leg forward so that the ankle is in front of the knee.** (If you dropped a line from your knee, the ankle would be in front of it.) **Alternate lifting the heel and the ball of the foot several times.** Which movement is easier than before? Which is harder?

   Now move the leg so that the ankle is behind the knee. Alternate lifting the heel and the ball of the foot, once or twice only, very slowly. Has the ball of your foot become quite difficult to lift?

   Now move the leg forward until the ankle is under the knee. Alternate lifting the ball and the heel. Is it easier to go back and forth in this position than in the others?

Move your foot a little forward and back three or four times until you find the best place for alternating between lifting the ball and the heel. Where is it? Compare the relationship of the right knee and ankle to that of the left. Pause and notice how your left and right sides line up.

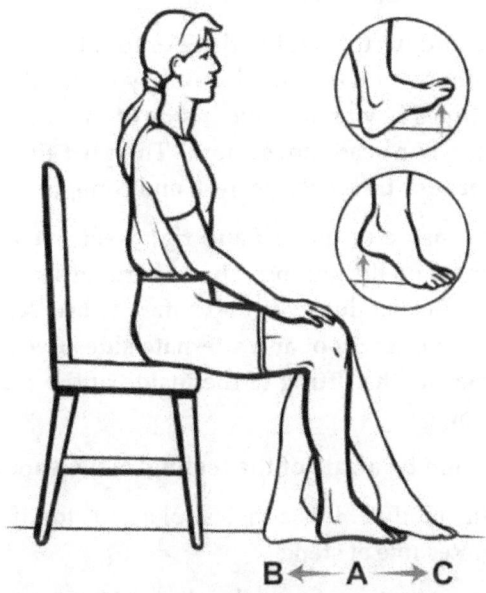

B ← A → C

2. **Now lift your left heel two or three times. Move your foot forward a little and again lift the heel two or three times.** Notice how this position changes the movement. **Then move it back a little from where you started and again lift two or three times.** Notice how this position changed the movement from the previous two positions. Pause a moment. **Then lift the ball of the foot five or six times.** Pause briefly. **Now move the foot forward a little and lift the ball of the foot three or four times.** Pause. **Alternate lifting of the heel and ball of the foot. As you alternate, move the foot forward and back a little into several different positions. Lift two or three times in each position. Find the position where the combined movements seem easiest and lift five or six times.** Compare this placement with that of the right leg.

3. **Alternating between the right and left, lift the heel and the ball of each foot.** Do this four times. Stop and rest a minute. Compare the way your two sides feel. Stand and walk a little.

   This is the end of this module. It is a logical place to stop if you cannot do the lesson in one sitting. Resume at **step 4**.

4. Sit forward on the edge of your chair and remember how your feet were positioned at the end of the previous lesson module. **Alternate lifting the heel and the ball of each foot several times to see if this still feels relatively easy. If not, adjust the position of the leg.**

5. **Now lift the inside of your left foot slowly several times.** Pause. **Slightly raise your right hip.** Gently repeat this movement three or four times. Pause. **Explore lifting the inside of the left foot now.** Is it easier than before? **Add raising the right hip to lifting the inside of the left foot.** Do this three or four times. Pause. **Now just lift the inside of the foot** three or four times. Slowly sit back in your seat and compare the way the two feet fit on the ground.

6. **Move forward again and lift the left hip three or four times.** Pause. **Now lift the inside of the right foot several times.** What does your head do? Pause. **Now lift the left hip several times as you raise the inside of the right foot.** What do you notice about the way your head moves now? **Then lift the inside of the right foot by itself three or four times.** Pause, rest, and compare sides.

7. **Alternate lifting the inside of the left and right feet five or six times.** Pause; notice how your feet are on the ground. **Then alternate slowly raising the right and then the left hip.** Repeat this five or six times. Pause. **Now combine lifting the hip with the inside of the foot and alternate sides five or six times.** Pause. **Return to just alternating the lifting of the inside of the feet five or six times.** How does this feel now?

Stand for a moment and be aware of the feeling. Now walk for a minute.

This is the end of this module. It is a logical place to stop if you cannot do the lesson in one sitting. Resume at **step 8**.

8. Sit comfortably forward on the edge of the chair. **Lift the heel and ball of each foot a few times to check ease of movement and the position of the foot.** Recall the last module. Remember the lifting of the inside of each foot. **Once again alternate raising first the left and then the right hip four or five times.**

9. **Lift the outside of the right foot six to eight times.** What happens in the pelvis when you do this? What do you do with your head? (Note: Some people will move the head to the left a little, others to the right. There is no *correct* way, we just want to draw attention to the relationship.) **Alternate lifting the inside and outside of the right foot six or seven times.** Sit back and rest. While you do so compare your two sides. **Stand and notice how this feels. Walk a little.** What is it like?

10. Come forward in your chair. **Now lift the outside of the left foot six to eight times.** What happens in the pelvis when you do this? Do you feel the same effect with the head as when you lifted the outside of the right foot or is it the opposite? **Now alternate lifting the outside and the inside of the left foot five or six times.** Stop and rest. How do your feet feel against the floor now? How balanced do you feel on the chair?

This is the end of this module. It is a logical place to stop if you cannot do the lesson in one sitting. Resume at **step 11**.

11. Sit comfortably on the edge of the chair. Recall alternately lifting the heel and the toe of each foot. **Do this several times with each foot to find the best position.** Pause. **Now alternate raising the left and right hip two times.** How does that

feel now? **Lift the inside and outside of the right foot four times.** Pause. **Now lift the inside and outside of the left foot three times.** Pause and rest a minute.

12. **Move your right foot forward three to four inches. Lift the front of the right foot into the air a comfortable amount and begin to make circles clockwise.** Slowly continue to circle in this manner for at least four revolutions. Can you allow the movement to become easier? Maybe if you make it smaller, it would be easier.

    Now reverse direction. Again, go around at least four times. What do you notice in your hips as you make this circle? Do you feel any effects of this movement in the position of the head? Stop and move your right foot back. Compare the way the left and right feet feel against the floor. Does either foot feel better connected to the back, to the head? Rest.

13. Come forward in your chair. **Now move your left foot forward three to four inches. Lift the front of the left foot into the air a comfortable amount and begin to make circles clockwise. After each circle pause a moment. Then change either the size, the effort, or the speed at which you make the next circle. What is the relation between size and effort, and speed and effort?** Make at least five circles. How attentive are you if you go faster?

    Now reverse the direction. Go slowly and easily, endeavoring to make this circle seem effortless. As it becomes less effortful, do you feel more or less of yourself involved in the movement? When you sense that all of you is involved in the movement, make one more circle and stop and move your left foot back. How do your feet feel against the floor now? How are you sitting in the chair? Do you feel any shift in your sense of the way the feet support the head?

    Stand up and walk around for a moment. Notice what this feels like now. How easy is walking now compared to when you began? How much can you feel your feet as you walk now?

End of lesson

LEG-LENGTH DIFFERENTIAL

With an acute enough measuring device, we would find that none of us have even leg lengths. In fact, most people have a difference of at least one-sixteenth of an inch. In one study of one hundred asymptomatic soldiers, seventy-one had a leg-length differential of at least one-sixteenth of an inch, whereas thirty-three had a difference of at least three-sixteenths of an inch. In a study of 1,446 school children ages five to seventeen, 80 percent had a discrepancy of at least one-sixteenth of an inch.[1] This lesser leg length imposes a strain on the musculature, because the muscles attempt to correct the resulting distortions in alignment to maintain level head and shoulders. Two other conditions may mimic, compensate for, or add to a leg-length difference. These are a tilting of the sacrum relative to the pelvis and an abrupt lateral angulation in the spine. Because of these factors and the human organism's overall capacity to accommodate, differences of less than one-quarter of an inch are not considered functionally significant for pain creation.

We are capable of accommodating significant differentials without discomfort. A great amount of research has been done on leg-length differential and pain. According to Travell and Simons, a differential of 1.3 centimeters (half an inch) may cause no pain symptoms in a lifetime, provided there is no traumatic event that interferes with the person's ability to compensate for the differential.[2] Because of the strain the leg-length difference puts on the sacroiliac and back, back pain is the common response to this difference. Once a pain problem has been created, discrepancies of three-sixteenths of an inch or more can perpetuate the problem. A study of 443 back patients concluded that a difference of a quarter inch or more should be corrected with a heel lift.

In another experiment, a pain-free, normal individual had a three-quarter-inch elevation added to the heel of the left shoe. On the third day, the subject experienced aching in the buttocks. After three weeks, there was regular night pain in the back and buttocks. When the elevation was removed, the symptoms disappeared in two weeks.

> Gross queried a group of patients with a short leg, regardless of symptoms and found that those with a discrepancy of 9/16 of an inch or less, did not regard their short leg as a problem, did not wear a lift, and did not feel unbalanced. However, those who had discrepancies of 2.0 cm (3/4 inch) and more responded positively to all of these questions. . . .
>
> In our experience, even in the absence of symptoms, correction of a leg length disparity of 1.3 cm or more is of preventive value. . . . When repeated measurements consistently show a discrepancy of 0.5cm (3/16 in) or more in a patient with low back pain, it should be corrected.[3]

Interestingly, leg-length discrepancies of up to three-quarters of an inch are likely to disappear in growing children *if* leg length is equalized temporarily.

What does this mean for performers? Clearly, a leg-length difference that will lead to pain should be corrected with a lift. Pain impedes breathing and interferes with vocal performance (as well as making life miserable). What about lesser differences where there is no pain? One way to accommodate is to place the long leg forward. This is why many people prefer this position and find it stable. Another is to experiment with a slight heel lift to see whether that helps or hinders performance and comfort. No one has really looked into the impact of leg-length differences and performance, so we cannot do more than suggest experimenting until you find what is right for you.

NOTES

1. For a more complete discussion of leg-length differentials, see Travell, Janet M., and David G. Simons. 1983. *Myofascial Pain and Dysfunction: The Trigger Point Manual* (Baltimore: Williams & Wilkins), 104–8.
2. Travell and Simons.
3. Travell and Simons, 106.

CHAPTER 7

The Pelvis

The pelvis (meaning "basin") is the bony ring of the sacrum, ilium, pubic bone, and ischium (or sit bone). It supports and protects the internal organs. However, its most important mechanical function is supporting the head, upper body, and trunk. Powerful muscles connect the pelvis with these areas.

The pelvis or, more correctly, the pelvic girdle (illustrated here), is your power source. It is the location of the most powerful muscles in the human body. It is also the center for movement. The Japanese call this region the *Hara*. They feel it is the key to developing both power in the martial arts and concentration in meditation. A simple experiment will demonstrate this. Lean a little to the left. Did you use your pelvis? That is, did you feel the weight shift from your right to your left sitting bone? Try this movement with just your upper body. Were you able to shift weight as easily? Did you go as far? Or did you have the sense that something central was missing? Another way you can sense the centrality of the pelvis is to stand in a doorway. Now put your buttocks and waist behind you so that you are standing with your rear end in the room behind you. Which room are you really in? If you were to drop straight to the floor, which room would you wind up in? Can you feel that your center is actually in the room behind you? Now that you have felt the central role of the pelvis, it is easy to see its importance. Clearly, then, the more of this power we can use, the better we can project our intent.

The skeleton is the structural framework of the body, just as a building's framework consists of steel beams and girders. Like the building, the framework is made structurally sound by a well-engineered foundation. In the human body, that foundation is the pelvis.

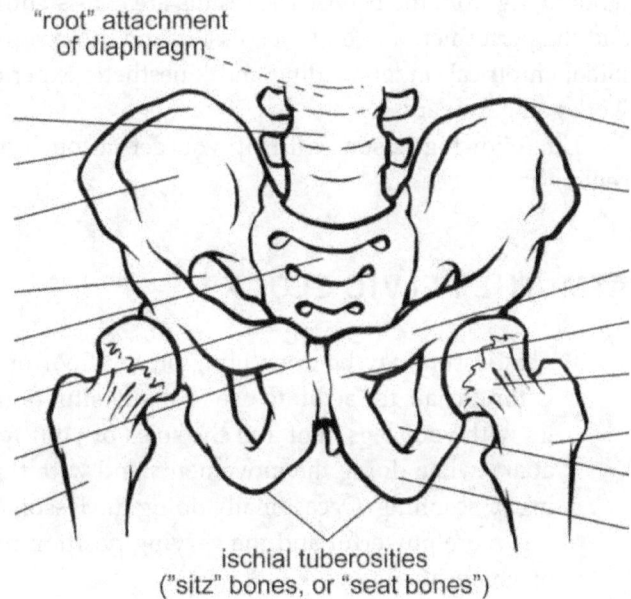

"root" attachment of diaphragm

ischial tuberosities ("sitz" bones, or "seat bones")

63

Mabel Ellsworth Todd, in her excellent book *The Thinking Body*, explains:

> In the human being the pelvis has a threefold function. It must receive from the spinal column the entire weight of the head, shoulders and trunk and transmit it to the legs. It must provide means of motion for the trunk upon the legs, and for the legs upon the trunk. . . . The weight of the head, shoulders and trunk accumulating through the spine and concentrating upon the fifth lumbar, falls upon the sacrum. . . . The two arches [of the pelvis] are the essential weight-bearing portions of the pelvis, and the sacrum is the keystone for both. . . . The pelvic girdle is thus made into a continuous ring, so that the body-load as it travels is distributed around the whole circumference. Why is it so important to acknowledge the importance of the pelvic center for performing? It follows most clearly that the spine has its base in the pelvic girdle and, like a firmly rooted tree, grows up out of the pelvis. The ribs hang off the spine, much like the branches of a tree hang off its trunk. Effective breath function is completely dependent on freedom of the ribs to expand and contract. Therefore, if the pelvis is not appropriately aligned and supported, the domino effect throughout the rest of the system considerably reduces the ability to achieve full potential.[1]

Whenever she teaches a course or workshop on "Body, Mind, and Movement for Musicians," Dr. Blades presents a picture of the human skeleton. She then asks a volunteer to identify the exact lateral midpoint of the body, just by dividing it into halves between head and base of feet. Every time, the volunteers have correctly pointed to the pelvic girdle, even if they do not have the vocabulary to name it (or are too inhibited by social mores to do so!). From that point on, it is very easy to explain the importance and function of the pelvic girdle, its relation to the rest of the skeleton, and, most significantly, its critical participation in efficient breath for singing/playing. She then has the student sing/play again while attending only to the kinesthetic sense of power and center deriving from the pelvis. The results are consistently apparent, both to the listeners and the performer: a freer, fuller, easier, and more responsive sound pours forth. This initial empirical understanding and kinesthetic experience become the basis for their work going forward.

The following lesson will help you get in touch with your pelvis as your power center.

ATM: THE PELVIC CLOCK

0. This lesson may be done lying on the floor or sitting in a chair. This version is for a chair to facilitate use in many situations. To convert to a floor lesson, lie with your legs bent and the soles of your feet on the floor shoulder width apart, when doing the movements and with the legs stretched out when resting or scanning. Occasionally doing the lesson on the floor is recommended as it is more powerful and the varying position reduces the tendency to become mechanical.

1. Sit in a chair that has a firm flat bottom. (With your legs long, note how you fit the floor. Then bend your knees and have your feet on the floor.) **Come forward so that your feet are firmly on the floor. Tilt your pelvis backward so that your back rounds.** Then return to neutral. Repeat this movement *slowly* five or six times. Pause.

   Now rock your pelvis forward as your back arches. Repeat this movement five or six times. Pause.

   Then combine the two movements. Repeat four or five times. *It is very important that you use your pelvis to lead this movement.* It is better to make a small movement where you are certain that you are rocking from the pelvis than a large movement where it is unclear that this is the case.

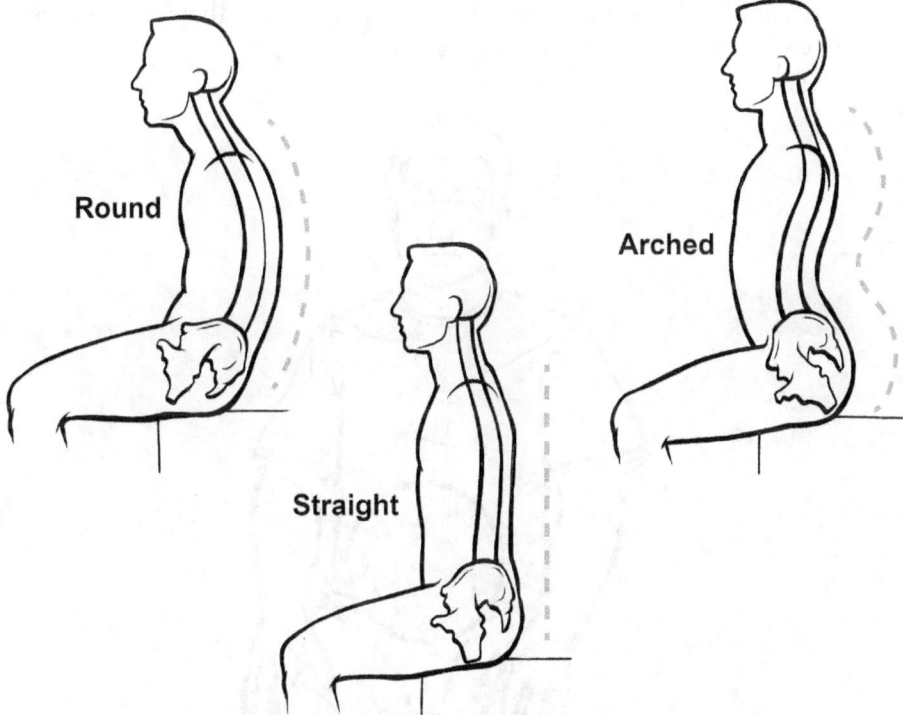

2. **Lift your right hip slightly.** Repeat four or five times and then pause.

   Now repeat the movement only concentrate on putting the weight down through your left hip to raise the right. Pause after another four or five repetitions.

3. **Now lift your left hip. Concentrate on putting the weight down through your right hip as you do this.** Repeat five or six times.

4. **Alternate between lifting the left and right hip.** Do this at least eight times. Have the sense that your pelvis leads this movement. Is it easier to move left or right? Does this movement become more even as you repeat it? Pause.

   Round and arch the back. Repeat three to five times. How has this changed since you did it earlier? Rest.

This is the end of this module. If you stop here, pause a moment before standing. Then stand and walk about a bit.

5. Sit forward in your chair with your ankles directly under your knees. Imagine that there is a clock on your pelvic region. Six o'clock is about an inch above your pubic bone, and you focus there when your back is arched. Twelve o'clock is just above your navel. You focus there when your back is rounded. **Three o'clock is off toward the left hip and nine o'clock off toward the right hip. Put your clock at twelve o'clock. Now, move from twelve o'clock to three o'clock passing through one o'clock and two o'clock on the way. Then return to twelve o'clock through one o'clock and two o'clock .** Clearly sense where one o'clock and two o'clock are as you make this movement. Be very clear that you are making a quarter circle. If it does not feel round, decrease the size until it does. Repeat this movement at least seven times. Go slowly enough so that all the hours are clear to you each time you make the movement. Pause.

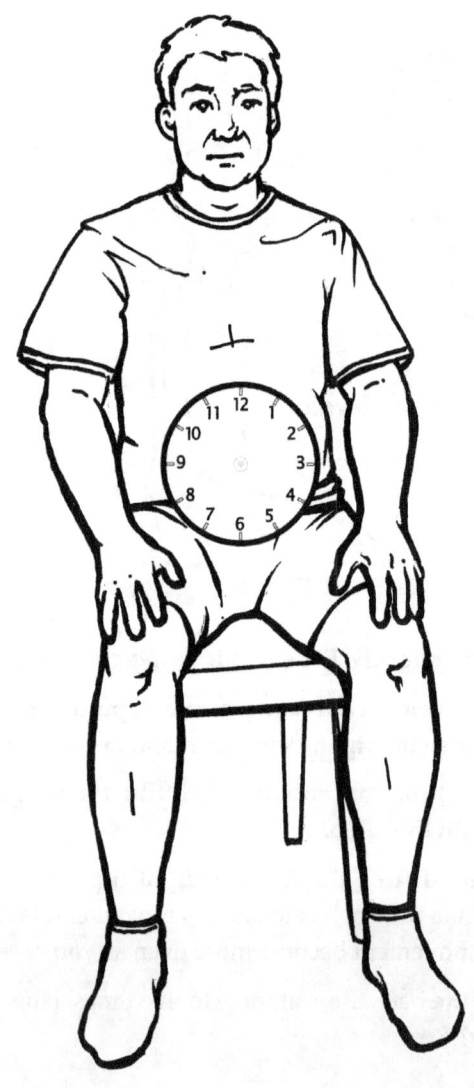

6. **Now go from three o'clock to six o'clock. Pass through four o'clock and five o'clock on the way to six o'clock and then go back to three o'clock.** Repeat this five to seven times, being clear about all the hours. Pause.

    Combine this movement with the last one and go from six o'clock to twelve o'clock via one o'clock, two o'clock, three o'clock, four o'clock, and five o'clock. Do this three or four times and then pause. Rest back in the chair (stretch out legs if on the floor). Compare your left and right sides.

7. **Go from twelve o'clock to eleven o'clock and back.** After you've done this once, extend to ten o'clock. Continue to add an hour after you've gone from twelve o'clock and back to twelve o'clock until you reach six o'clock. Then go back and forth between twelve o'clock and six o'clock via seven o'clock, eight o'clock, nine o'clock, ten o'clock, and eleven o'clock. Do this movement five or six times. Again, be clear that you are moving in a circular fashion. Be aware of each hour as you pass through it. Pause and compare sides.

8. **Beginning at twelve o'clock, make three or four movements around the clock face going clockwise.** Pause and rest. How are you sitting? Stand and sense how tall you feel. How well does your back support you? How is your weight distributed over your feet? (With your legs long, how do you fit the floor?)

    This is the end of this module. If you stop here, pause a moment before standing. Then stand and notice any changes. Finally walk a little and notice if it feels different. Resume at **step 9**.

9. **Again, make clockwise movements starting at twelve o'clock and going around the clock. After you have made three of these, reverse direction and make four counterclockwise.** Which way was easier? How well were you able to feel each hour as you passed through it? Pause.

10. **Move clockwise slowly.** Pay attention at each hour. Where do you feel the movement is sticky or not round? Make a note of these places. Sense which place is stickiest and out of round. Repeat the clockwise movement three times while making these mental notes. Pause.

    Make three counterclockwise movements. Again notice where the movement is not smooth or circular. Pause and rest.

11. Recall the movements you just did. Think where the difficulty was in making a smooth rounded movement the greatest. Place your pelvic clock at that time (i.e., 1:00, 4:20, 9:10, etc.). **Now make a movement of 1.5 hours in either direction from this place.** Thus, if your difficult place was one o'clock, go from 11:30 to 2:30; if it was 8:30, go from seven o'clock to ten o'clock, etc. Repeat this movement four to six times. This is referred to as oiling the clock. Pause and rest for a moment.

12. **Make three movements clockwise and then three more counterclockwise.** Be aware of where your difficult place is now. What happened to the place you just "oiled"?

    Wherever you notice the most difficulty now, oil it as you did in the previous instruction. Pause. Again, make three movements clockwise and counterclockwise. Stop and rest. Notice how you are sitting. Sense your back, your breathing, and how erect you feel. (How do you fit the floor now?)

This is the end of this module. If you stop here, pause a moment before standing. Then stand and notice any changes. Finally walk a little and notice if it feels different. Resume at **step 13**.

13. Sit forward in your chair and be certain that your ankles are lined up below your knees. **Go slowly and as circularly as you can; make a few movements clockwise and a few counter clockwise.** How is this now? Were you clear as to what hour you were at?

14. **Cross your right foot in front of your left foot on the floor. (Bend only your right leg and put your right foot on the floor.) In this position, begin to make clockwise circles.** After you have done three, reverse direction and make three more. Uncross your feet and pause. (Put your right leg long, pause, and then bend the left leg and put the left foot on the floor.) Now cross your left foot in front of your right.

    Once again, make three circles in each direction. Feel whether they are circular. If they are not, adjust your circles so they are. Uncross your feet. Stop and rest a moment.

15. Put the soles of your feet together. **In this position, go clockwise around the clock.** Can you stay aware of the hours as you do this? Were there any sticky places? Repeat three times. Pause.

    Reverse direction and go counterclockwise. Repeat three times. Where did you have the most difficulty doing these movements?

    Go to that time and oil the clock as you did earlier. Then go around the clock in each direction once. What was it like? Were the circles rounder?

    Make several clocks in each direction without concerning yourself about where the hours are. Stop. Separate your feet and put them both on the floor.

16. **Make three clockwise movements. Then reverse direction and make another three movements.** How is this different from before you changed the position of your feet? How erect are you? How easy is it to stay seated like this? Notice your breathing, the feeling in your back, and the feeling in your hips. Stand up and notice how you feel. Walk around for a minute or two and notice how this feels.

End of lesson

There are many possible variants for this lesson. Please do the lesson in the stated form at least four times before exploring the variations. You can change the size of your clock for an easy variation. Another variation is you can put the soles of your feet together and do this lesson as written either seated or if lying propped up on either elbows or with arms extended. These variations act to open up the hip joints. Or you can focus on the movement of the head. Notice that it also describes a clock with the pelvis. Have the head lead the movement. If you are brave, you can try having these clocks going in opposition or starting one at 6 o'clock and the other at 12 o'clock. Yet another possibility is to sit with only one buttock on the chair (one leg up the other down on the floor).

But please, whatever variation you try, stick with the basic idea of the power coming from the pelvis with the torso on top of it. It is easy to dream up variations that seem plausible but which don't work or work too poorly to justify the effort.

THE PELVIS IN SITTING

Because it acts both as a basin and as the support for the trunk, the pelvis is critical to sitting erect. Ideally, the weight should be evenly distributed on your sit bones. When it is, you can press straight down through the shoulders without collapsing the back or causing discomfort. The key to this position is having the pelvis underneath the trunk, not too far forward, as in slouching, or too far back, as when hyperextended. Unfortunately, most people never learn to sit up straight.

Slouching is the almost universal teenage posture, at least for North Americans. While this does not cause significant discomfort when you are young, it always impedes performance. Slouching, or sitting with a rounded back, involves both compressing the sternum and flattening out the ribs. This reduces the capacity to draw in air. Slouching also constricts the muscles around the throat and pulls the jaw downward. Slouch for a moment, and you will be able to feel these effects. Imagine performing while slouching.

However, if slouching is your habitual posture, it will be difficult to remain fully erect for a long time, as the erect position will require unaccustomed effort. The system is not used to balancing properly and will need to use muscular effort to remain balanced. This need not be. When proper erect posture is the norm, it has that effortless quality of rightness. This is because the weight is carried by the spine with just the minimum effort needed to keep it in balance. In this position, the breathing apparatus is fully available and there is reduced excess tension in the shoulders, jaw, and throat.

It is possible to be overly erect, or hyperextended. Female gymnasts use hyperextension as part of their technique. When this is the habitual position, there is a rigidity to the system and a tense feeling overall. The shoulder blades are retracted. As a result, breathing is impeded, and a strained quality is imparted to one's sound. For those who habitually hyperextend, the balanced erect posture will feel like slouching. They will feel as if it is too easy and that something is missing.

Because improper support is deeply ingrained, it seems difficult to change. The admonition to "sit up straight" works only for a few minutes. Most people assume, therefore, that learning to sit properly is a long, arduous task. The following lesson demonstrates that this is not so. If you do the entire lesson, you will feel yourself sitting better, more easily, more completely on your sit bones, and more properly erect. Of course, one lesson will not completely or permanently overcome years of habit. It will take numerous repetitions to make the relaxed upright posture your norm.

ATM: THE ROLE OF THE PELVIS IN SITTING ERECT

1. Sit in a chair with a straight seat, if possible. Do you need to lean against the back of the chair or can you comfortably sit up straight? Now sit toward the edge of the chair. Put your left hand on your left knee and your right hand on the right side of the chair seat behind you. **Move your left knee forward a little and then back to neutral.** (*Because your foot is stationary the movement happens from the hip.* Can you feel this?) Do this *slowly* six to eight times. **Allow the head and eyes to be moved by the movement of the hip and knee.** Pause for as long between movements as it takes to make one movement. Rest in place for about one minute.

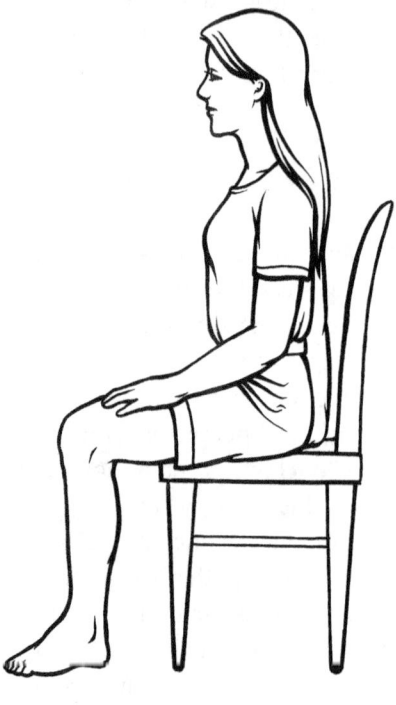

2. **Move your left knee forward, still allowing your head and eyes to turn with the knee. But then stop with the knee forward, turn your eyes and head back to the center and then bring your knee back to neutral.** Repeat four to six times and then move back in your chair. Compare how your left and right sides feel. Pause for a minute. Lean back in your chair if you feel the need.

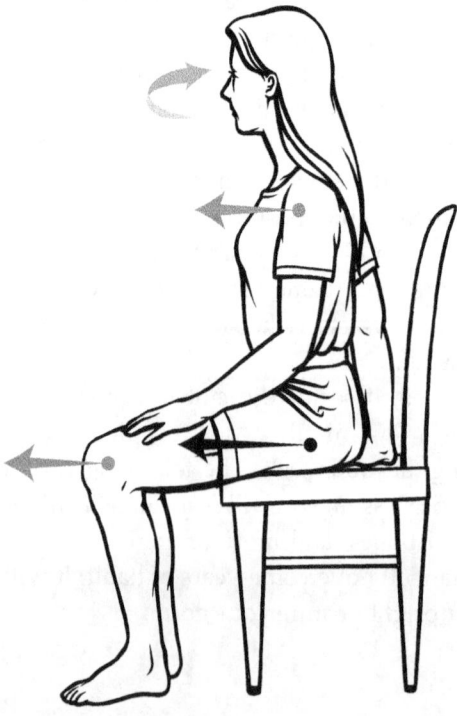

3. Move back to the edge of your chair. Put your right hand on your right knee and your left hand on the side of the chair seat. **Move your right knee forward and back. Allow your head and eyes to move. Notice when you breathe in and when you breathe out as you make this movement.** Repeat six to eight times slowly. Remember to pause between movements. Rest in place.

4. **Move the right knee forward, still allowing your head and eyes to turn with the knee. But then stop with the knee forward, turn your eyes and head back to the center, and then bring your knee back to neutral.** Do this slowly five or six times and then move back in your chair. How do you feel now?

This is the end of this module. It is a logical place to stop if you cannot do the lesson in one sitting. Resume at **step 5**.

5. **Review steps 1 and 3 by doing each a couple of times. Now put your right hand on your right knee and your left hand on your left knee. Slowly move one knee forward and then the other.** What happens to the knee you are not moving forward? Repeat this pattern several times, pausing after each sequence to assimilate the effects of the movement. Stop. How are you sitting now?

6. **Put your right hand on the chair behind you and the left hand on the left knee. Move the left knee forward and leave it there.** The head will be off to the right slightly. Leave it there. **Move your eyes to the center and back several times. Then move everything back to the center.** Do this three or four times. **Now move the left knee forward and back several times.** How does it feel now?

   Then move the left knee forward once and see how far you can see to the right without any strain. Sit back in your chair, rest, and notice any differences in the left and right sides.

7. Come forward on your chair and put both hands on both knees. **Move the right knee forward three times. Then move the right knee forward, stop, and take only the head to the center and back several times.** Pause. **Then move the right knee forward twice and note the changes. Finally alternate moving the left and right knee forward four to six times.** How are you sitting now? Can you feel your sit bones underneath you on the chair? Is sitting straight easier?

   This is the end of this module. It is a logical place to stop if you cannot do the lesson in one sitting. Resume at **step 8**.

8. **Put both the left hand on the left knee and the right hand on the right knee; alternate moving the knees forward three to five times** *slowly*. Notice when you inhale.

   Continue to alternate but fix your eyes on a spot in front of you. Keeping your eyes and head in the center, repeat the movement four to six times. Now let your head and eyes move with the motion of the knees back and forth several times. How does this feel? Rest back in your chair.

9. Come forward in your chair. **Put your left hand on your left knee and your right hand on the chair behind you. When your left knee moves forward, look left with your eyes and head and then bring everything back to the center.** Repeat four or five times.

   Then reverse the hands and look right with your head and eyes when your right knee moves forward. Again, do this four or five times.

   Now place your hands on their respective knees and alternate moving your knees back and forth several times. Notice differences, both between the way you move in one direction and the other, and from before. Rest back in your chair.

10. Come forward in your chair. **Put both hands on your knees and alternate moving the knees forward two times. Continue to alternate moving the knees**

forward but now when the right knee is forward look right and when the left knee is forward look left. Repeat three to five times.

Now go back to letting the head and eyes be moved by the knee movement. Repeat four to six times. How is this now?

Then move your right knee forward and see how far you can see to the left. Try the same thing with the other side. Finally pause and notice how erect you feel. Now stand and notice how this feels. How upright are you standing?

Walk around for a moment or two before going to another activity.

End of lesson

NOTE

1. Todd, Mabel Ellsworth. [1937] 1968. *The Thinking Body* (Princeton, NJ: Princeton Book Company), 113–15.

CHAPTER 8

Breathing

MECHANICS OF BREATHING

Breathing is critical to life. Stop breathing and you die. Breath also plays a crucial role in being in control. When your breath is not free, there is a restriction that impedes performance. This is true no matter what you do. So why do people often hold their breath in a tense situation? Because it once had biological survival value. When faced with danger, one gathers one's resources by taking a big breath, holding it, and then exploding into action. This phenomenon explains the behavior of lions on the hunt. You would think that they would sneak up quietly and then attack their prey without warning. Yet when they get close, they often roar. They do this because the prey's first response is to hold its breath and tense for action. This tensing for action allows a more powerful initial movement and greater speed and endurance over the long haul. However, if the lion reaches its prey before the prey can leap, it has a stationary target and a successful hunt. While holding the breath had survival value when humans were hunter-gatherers, this is seldom true today. Rather, we need to use all our breath, freely. This facilitates our everyday activities.

Proper use of the breath is different in playing a wind instrument than in other activities. In most activities we wish to use as much of our lungs for breathing in and out as possible—that is, to use our entire capacity—because we are using the breath to provide power for the activity. When we run, the amount of air we can take in and expel is one of our limits. When we play a wind instrument, the breath powers the sound. In normal everyday activities, the chest will expand and contract; when we sing, we need to keep the chest open and spacious so as not to collapse inward on the supply of breath or hinder its free flow.

An illustration of the skeleton of the ribs shows that the last two ribs are not attached to the sternum in any way. They are referred to as the floating ribs. Just as thinking of the ribs as a cage can be confining, having a sense of the ribs as mobile is very valuable. Because of both the cartilaginous nature of the connection between the ribs and the sternum and between the ribs and the facets of the thoracic vertebrae and the elastic nature of the intervertebral disks, the ribs are actually quite flexible. They are capable of considerable expansion and deformation. The goal is to expand them properly.

Very simply, the mechanics for breathing involve the following parts: the lungs; the ribs and their intercostal muscles (internal or inner intercostals and external or outer intercostals); and the large, thin, upside-down-bowl diaphragmatic muscle.

When the outer intercostal muscles of the ribs contract, the ribs are expanded; at the same time, the diaphragm contracts downward, flattening slightly. The lungs are attached at the sides to the insides of the ribs and at the bottom to the upper side of the diaphragm. When these partner groups of muscles contract, the action simultaneously expands the lungs both sideways and downward, and a partial vacuum results from the increase in lung volume. Since nature abhors a vacuum and air has weight (14.7 pounds per square inch at sea level), air will rush in to fill the space created. This is inhalation without a sense of effortful "sucking" in the air.

As noted earlier, a look at the ribs reveals several important facts: The ribs increase in size (and weight) from top to bottom; the upper ten ranks of ribs are attached to both the spinal vertebrae and the sternum (breastbone). The lower down the spine, the more flexible and expandable the rib. Finally, the bottom two ribs are free floating because they are only attached at the back. They therefore have the most capability for expansion. It is also significant that the rim of the diaphragm is also attached to the twelfth (bottom-most) rib. Therefore, if a wind player consciously "asks" (and trains) the entire rib cage to "pop" open, a spontaneous spacious expansion can occur. This action must be coupled with a sense of letting go, or release, of any holding in of the abdominal wall and torso, so that the diaphragm, too, has unrestricted freedom to contract and flatten. What results is a low, nearly effortless, and efficient intake of air that occurs almost instantaneously. The performer feels as if they have done very little and yet has a fine supply of air for whatever phrase they need to sing. Conversely, when they "tank up," or try to get a deep breath, the effect is effortful and restricts vocal freedom. (For a much more detailed description of the anatomy and mechanics of respiration, see Bunch 1993, chapter 3.[1])

Just as important as how much air we can take in is how freely we do so. If breathing requires a lot of effort, less is available to power the sound, even if we can get a very full breath. Having a free flow, therefore, is very important. This involves using all of the lungs in a free manner. To do so, you must understand that the lungs are merely empty sacs. They open as we use the muscles to create a vacuum. Because this vacuum is three-dimensional, the lungs open in six directions: forward where the belly and ribs expand; backward where the spine lengthens, the viscera move backward, and the ribs expand; to the left and to the right where both the ribs and belly expand; up, lifting both the scapula and the clavicle; and down into the pelvic girdle, which moves downward into the hips and also expands outward slightly. Should any of these movements be impeded, there will be a corresponding restriction in the flow of air.

Freedom of the shoulders is vital to the free flow of air. Looking at an illustration of the back of the ribs, you will see that the scapula (shoulder blade) sits on top of the upper ribs in the back. If the shoulders are not free, they will directly impede the movement of the ribs backward and up. This will also restrict expansion to the sides, as the upward movement allows more of the torso to expand by lifting the harder portion of the ribs. And the ribs in front also are restricted by the inability to move upward, reducing the capacity of the lungs to open frontally. Therefore, if you are having trouble with your breathing, the quickest and most effective way to address the difficulty is often to free up the shoulders. Clearly, this is the case if you feel the shoulders are tight. However, we often are so used to a habitual holding pattern that we may not recognize tightness when it is present. Chapter 10 is about the use of the shoulders. It contains several useful lessons to provide you with more shoulder ease and freedom.

Keeping a relaxed throat and mouth is also important to the free flow of air. There are many things one can do to maintain openness in this area. Chapter 12 has some lessons to provide more freedom in the mouth.

It is very easy to fall into the trap of thinking that there is one right way to breathe. Actually, there are many options available for breathing. Only a few of these are effective for wind instruments, and for any instrumentalist, there will be a best way to breathe at any time. This may vary depending on health. In general, the optimal way is the one described earlier. However, you need to know other ways so that you can overcome problems and can have options in times of trouble. The following lesson is a useful exploration that will help open your breathing apparatus. It employs the right breathing techniques for learning better breathing, but they are not to be construed as the "right" way to breathe.

ATM: OPENING THE LUNGS

1. This lesson involves directing the flow of air into your lungs separately, so that more of the airflow enters particular areas of the lungs. Before first working with this lesson, it is extremely helpful to read chapter 3 and, if possible, do either, if not both, of the lessons in that chapter. Although this is a seated lesson, part of it can be done lying on the floor. The full lesson is written for the seated version in the expectation that you can lie down flat on the floor with your feet up (down when at rest), and adapt the first two modules.

   Sit forward on your chair with both feet firmly on the ground. Notice how tall you feel and how easy it is to breathe. Take slow full breaths for about a minute or so. Take at least fifteen breaths. Notice where the air flows in easily, and where you sense that you are tight. Also check and see if there are any areas—chest, belly, side, or back—that you do not feel participating in your breathing. Pause, and sit comfortably for a minute; let your breathing come and go normally without paying any particular attention to it.

2. **Again take slow full breaths, only now concentrate on drawing air into the right lung.** Take at least twenty breaths with this intent. As you continue to concentrate on the right lung, let your awareness move around. First, sense the general movement of the right lung. Then see where it feels easiest to breathe. Now notice where you sense you have difficulty. Go back to where it is easy and concentrate on those areas, letting them expand gently with each breath. **After at least twenty breaths, when you lose interest in following the breath, let go of this concentration and breathe normally.** Pause like this for a minute and notice the sensation in your two feet.

3. **Once more take slow full breaths, this time concentrating on drawing air into the left lung.** Again, take at least twenty breaths as you examine how your left lung is working. Can you tell that your left lung is smaller than your right lung? For all but the rare individual who has a reversed heart and lung (only about 0.1 percent of humans), the right lung has three lobes while the left has two in order to make room for the heart. And while the upper and lower left lobes are somewhat bigger than those of the right, the middle lobe makes the right lung noticeably larger. **After at least twenty breaths when you lose interest in following the breath, let go of this concentration and breathe normally.** Pause like this for a minute.

4. **Again take slow full breaths. Only this time, alternate between concentrating on the left and right lung every two breaths.** Take at least twenty breaths, five full sequences, as you sense the differences between your two lungs. Notice the difference in the way your two lungs fill. Does this difference (if you notice one) change as you continue alternating? What do you notice in your shoulders as you continue to breathe in this fashion? Pause.

   Breathe normally. Notice how tall you feel now. How easy is it to breathe now?

   This is the end of this module. It is a logical place to stop if you cannot do the lesson in one sitting. Resume at **step 5**.

5. **Taking slow full breaths, concentrate on filling the lower lobe of your left lung.** Take at least twenty breaths. First, concentrate on filling this area as completely as possible. When you sense you have completed the filling process, begin to notice where the lung expands well and where you feel "blocked." Leave the areas where you feel blocked alone and concentrate on increasing the quality of ease where you sense you breathe well. You may notice that the area of ease expands when you do this, but just allow this to happen, do not force anything. Remember, if you can't *smile* while you're doing this, you're working too hard. Pause for a moment and compare the sense of weight in your feet.

6. **Now as you take slow full breaths concentrate on filling the upper lobe of your left lung.** Take at least twenty breaths. At first, get a general sense of how this area fills. Then take at least four breaths to notice the interaction of the shoulder with the movement of the breath. How well does your shoulder blade slide over your ribs? Next notice the movement of the collarbone and sternum (breastbone) while you take several more breaths. Then focus on the way your lung moves out to the side. Now notice how the back beneath your shoulder blade moves with the breath. And then return to your general sense of the upper lobe of your left lung. Maybe this has changed, maybe not—just notice. Pause for a moment. Compare the way your two sides feel. How much weight is on your left sitz bone versus the right? Does one side feel as though it is shorter than the other?

7. **Again take slow full breaths, only now concentrate on filling the lower lobes of your right lung with slow full breaths.** Take at least twenty breaths. Can you tell that this lung area is larger than the lower lobe of the left? Spend a while making this a gentle, soft movement, noting what moves without force. Then

compare the ease with which the front and back open without trying to change anything. Pause for a moment and see if your weight sits differently.

8. **Return to taking slow full breaths, this time concentrating on the upper right lung.** Take at least twenty breaths. At first, get a general sense of the movement, then concentrate on the relationship between the right ear and the right shoulder. After a few breaths like this, notice how well your chest expands as you concentrate on the shoulder and ear. Then switch your concentration to the expansion of the chest. After several breaths concentrating on your chest, see how your right shoulder moves. Pause and rest. Did the shift in focus change what happened where you focused? Did it change the other area? Ponder the implications of this phenomenon.

    Breathe normally. How tall do you feel now? How easy is it to breathe now?

    This is the end of this module. It is a logical place to stop if you cannot do the lesson in one sitting. Resume at **step 9**.

9. **Sitting forward in the chair, take slow full breaths and sense how the air goes into your back.** Take at least twenty breaths like this. **At first sit up straight. Then round your back ("slouch" a little). Finally return to sitting straight.** Slouching closes down the ribs in front and opens them up in the back. You likely found it easier to sense the air flow in the back when you were in the rounded position. Because we face forward and focus our attention there and because of the back's structure, most of the lung expansion is forward. Therefore, it is easy to forget about the expansion behind us. This is why we often find it difficult to concentrate on the backward airflow. Pause and rest a moment.

10. **Again take slow breaths. Only this time, alternate between concentrating on the back of the left and right lung every two breaths. You may play with rounding and straightening the back as you do this.** Take at least twenty breaths. Can you sense the relationship of the shoulders to the ribs behind? Pause and rest a moment. What does your breathing feel like now?

11. **Interlace your fingers and place your hands on top of your head. In this position take slow full breaths.** Take at least ten breaths. Note where this feels freer in your breath and where it is more restricted. Pause and rest briefly in this position.

    Again take slow full breaths. Now alternate your awareness from your left to your right lung every second breath. Take at least twelve breaths. How much movement do you feel in front? How much behind? Are your fingers tense? If so, what happens when you relax them? Pause, put your hands down, and rest.

12. **Put your hands on the chair behind you. In this position take slow full breaths.** Take at least ten breaths. How well are you able to breathe like this? Pause and rest briefly in this position.

    Again take slow full breaths. Now alternate your awareness from your left to your right lung every second breath. Take at least twelve breaths. Pause and rest. What does this position do to the movement in front and back? What have you noticed about the interplay between breathing and shoulder tension?

Put your hands back into the position they were initially. Now take several slow full breaths. Compare what this feels like now to when you began.

Stand and walk around for a minute. Notice what walking feels like now.

End of lesson

RECOVERY FROM ILLNESS

Everyone falls ill at times. Usually, it is only a minor cold. However, any respiratory problem can dramatically reduce your ability to perform. Most annoying is the way the difficulties hang on. We seem to have fluid in our sinuses and lungs long after the infection appears to be gone. It would seem that this "crud" is responsible for our difficulty. Yet even when we have cleared our system, the breathing difficulties remain. This is partially because we may not have fully regained our strength. However, another reason that difficulties hang on is the structure of our breathing apparatus.

Our lungs are surrounded by a membrane called the pleura. The pleura adjoins the lungs, then doubles on itself and adjoins the ribs. The space inside the pleura is filled with a highly viscous fluid. This double membrane, plus fluid, means that there is very little friction when the lungs and ribs slide against each other. When there is an infection, areas of the pleura may be inflamed. (A generalized pleural infection is called pleurisy.) Pleural inflammation profoundly retards breathing because it dramatically raises the friction in that area of the lung. This higher friction causes us to need more effort to breathe and also creates some to a great deal of discomfort in that area. The lack of movement in any area causes a pulled feeling.

The following lesson concentrates on freeing the lungs via the ribs, thereby freeing up the pleura. As you do the lesson, you will be letting go of places where the lungs and pleura feel stuck. A useful lesson in general, this is extremely helpful for overcoming the pulled or compressed feeling that usually accompanies respiratory difficulties.

ATM: FREEING THE RIBS

1. Lie on your back with both legs stretched out straight. You will need about two feet of clearance in either direction. Notice how your back fits the floor. Take a breath. Notice how you are breathing.

    Bend your right knee and put your right foot on the floor. Put your right hand into your left armpit. Then put your left hand over your right arm and shoulder above the area of the armpit. Do not put your hand up by your neck. Extend your left hand and arm to the right. Your hand comes off your right shoulder as you do this. The right hand can gently pull on the left shoulder blade to facilitate this movement. The head turns to the right as part of the movement. If you can, reach out along the floor with your left arm. Do not strain. Only go a comfortable distance. Repeat this movement, slowly, six to eight times. Always pause for as long as it takes to make the whole movement sequence before beginning the next.

    Pause and remain in this position for a moment.

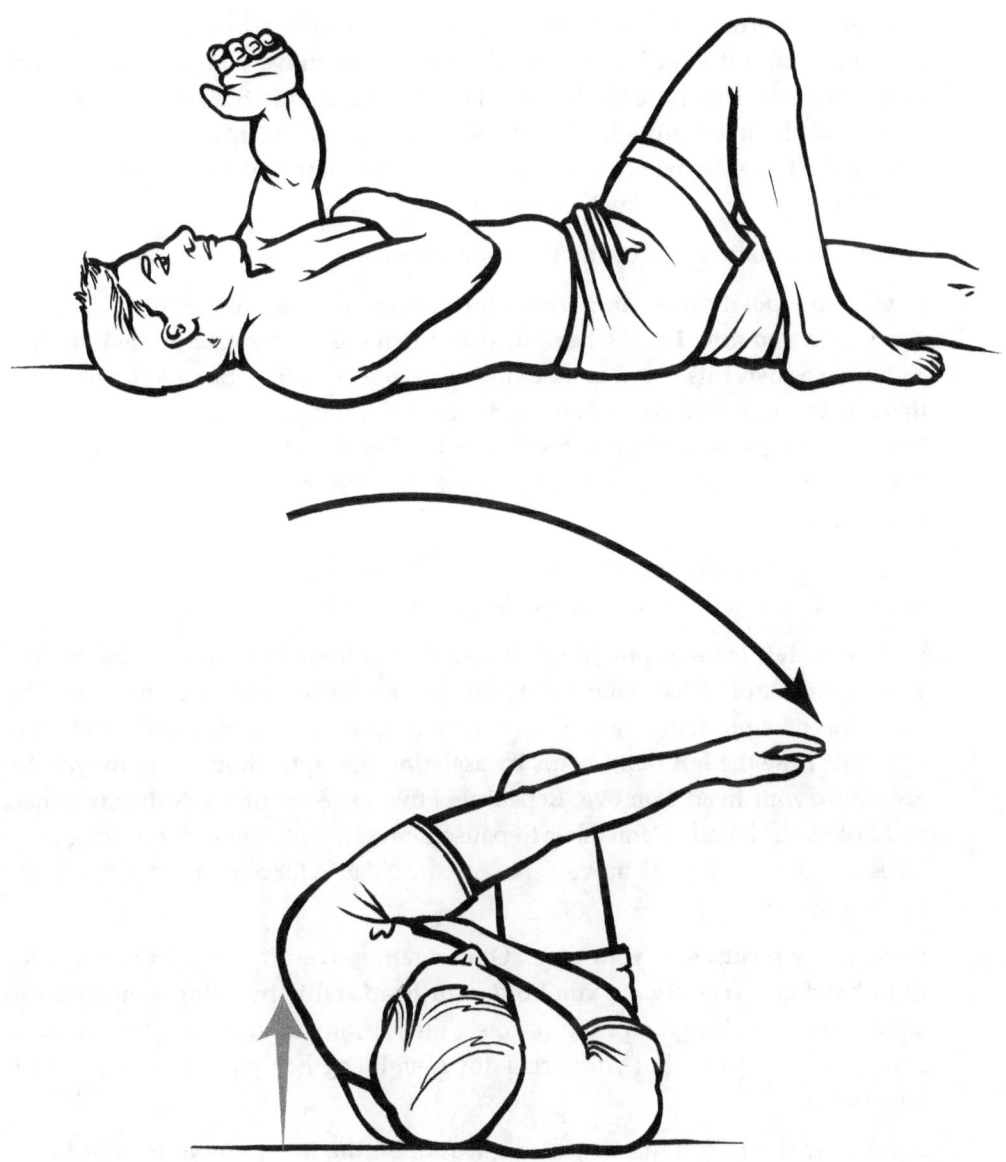

2. **Reverse the position of your arms (i.e., put right arm over left). Now once again move off to the right with your left hand and arm. Let it come out of your armpit and slide toward the floor. Again the right arm assists by gently pulling on the left shoulder blade, the head turns to the right, and there is a rotation of the upper torso.** Of course, the arm position prevents the left arm from extending as far. So don't aim for distance; aim for the same sense of ease you felt in the prior movement pattern. Repeat five to seven times. Pause.

Put your arms down and lengthen your right leg. Compare your two sides. Then rest a moment.

3. **Put your left arm into your right armpit and your right arm over it. Bend your left knee and put your left foot on the floor. Now move your right hand and arm to the left. This time the left hand helps by assisting the right shoulder to move and the head turns to the left.** Repeat this movement six to eight times. Remember to pause in between movements. See if you can make the movement smoother or easier each time you repeat it.

   Pause and remain in this position for a moment.

4. **Reverse the position of your arms. Once again move off to the left with your right hand and arm. Let the head turn and feel the torso rotate to the left. The right arm assists this movement.** Repeat five to seven times. See if you can make this movement easier than when the right arm is on top. Pause.
   Put your arms down and lengthen your left leg. Compare your two sides. Do they feel more even? How does your back fit the floor now? What is your breathing like? Rest.

   This is the end of this module. If you stop here, pause a moment before standing. Then walk and notice any changes. Resume at **step 5**.

5. **Bend your left leg and put your left foot on the floor. Put your left hand into your right armpit. Place your right hand over your left arm and shoulder. Fix your eyes on a point on the ceiling. Now move your right hand and arm to the left. This time the left hand helps by assisting the right shoulder to move. Do not allow your head to move.** Repeat this five to seven times. Notice whether you hold your breath. Remember to pause between movements for as long as it takes to make a complete movement sequence. Pause for a moment and remain in this position.

6. **Reverse the position of your arms. Once again move off to the left with your right hand and arm. Again, you hold your head stable by fixing your eyes on a point on the ceiling.** Repeat four to six times. Can you make each movement easier, lighter? Pause. Put your arms down and lengthen your left leg, and rest for a moment.

7. **Bend your right leg and put your right foot on the floor. Put your right hand into your left armpit. Place your left hand over your right arm and shoulder. Fix your eyes on a point on the ceiling. Now move your left hand and arm to the right. This time the right hand helps by assisting the left shoulder to move. Your head stays still.** Repeat six to eight times. Is this easier or more difficult than going to the left? How does the movement change as you repeat it? Pause for a moment and remain in this position.

8. **Reverse the position of your arms. Keeping your head stable by fixing your eyes on a point on the ceiling, move your left hand and arm to the right.** Repeat five to seven times. Can you smile as you make this movement? Pause.

   Put your arms down, lengthen your left leg, and rest for a moment. Compare your two sides. How does your back fit the floor now? What is your breathing like? Rest.

This is the end of this module. If you stop here, pause a moment before standing. Then walk and notice any changes. Resume at **step 9**.

9. **Bend your right leg and put your right foot on the floor. Put your right hand into your left armpit. Place your left hand over your right arm and shoulder. Now move your left hand and arm to the right. This time the right hand helps by assisting the left shoulder to move. At the same time, your head turns to the left**. Repeat this six to eight times. Go slowly so that the movement of head and arm is simultaneous. Smile occasionally to ensure you are not using too much effort. Pause for a moment and remain in this position.

10. **Reverse the position of your arms. Again, move your head to the left as you move your torso and left arm to the right.** Repeat this five to seven times. See if you can make each movement a little clearer. Pause, put your arms down, lengthen your right leg, and rest for a moment.

11. **Bend your left leg and put your left foot on the floor. Put your left hand into your right armpit. Place your right hand over your left arm and shoulder. Move your right hand and arm to the left. At the same time move your head to the right.** Repeat this five to seven times. How does your head turn in this direction compared to going left? Are you trying to go as far with your arm as earlier? Or are you content to go only as far as you can easily? Pause for a moment in this position.

12. **Reverse the position of your arms. Now move your torso and right arm to the left as you move your head to the right.** Repeat this four to six times. How do you breathe as you do this movement? Are you inhaling and exhaling in a pattern? Just be aware of what you are doing. Pause.

    Put your arms down, lengthen your left leg, and rest for a moment. Compare your two sides. How does your back fit the floor now? What is your breathing like? Rest.

    This is the end of this module. If you stop here, pause a moment before standing. Then walk and notice any changes. Resume at **step 13**.

13. **Bend both your knees and put both your feet on the floor. Cross your arms with the one going into the armpit and the other on top, in the way that you prefer. Now move your right hand and arm to the left. The left hand helps by assisting the right shoulder to move and the head turns to the left. When you return to the center, continue over to the right. The right hand now assists the left arm and the head turns to the right.** Repeat this sequence of going left and right five to seven times. Pause between every other sequence for as long as one back and forth takes. Allow the movement to be pleasurable and light. Pause for a moment in this position.

14. **Reverse your arms. Start the movement in the direction you prefer and then go the other direction.** Repeat this sequence four to six times. Pause in this position.

15. **Again start the movement of your arms in the direction you prefer. Only have your head go in the opposite direction. This means it moves toward the rising shoulder.** Repeat this sequence four to six times. Can you keep the movement light? Did you remember to pause after every other movement? Pause.

    Reverse the position of your arms and resume the movement. Repeat this sequence four to six times. Do you find your feet and buttocks moving relative to each other? If so, this may be reversed by having the head move in the same direction as the leading arm. Pause and remain in this position.

16. **Bend your right knee and put your right foot on the floor. Put your right hand into your left armpit. Then put your left hand over your right arm and shoulder above the area of the armpit. Do not put your hand up by your neck. Extend your left hand and arm to the right.** Repeat three or four times. Put your arms and legs down and rest.

    Bend your left knee and put your left foot on the floor. Put your left arm into your right armpit and your right arm over it. Now move your right hand and arm to the left. Repeat three or four times. Put your arms and legs down and rest.

    Compare your two sides. How does your back fit the floor now? What is your breathing like? How free do your ribs feel? How long does your back feel? Rest a moment.

    Slowly sit up. Stay seated for a moment and then come to standing. Stand for a moment and notice what this feels like. Then walk around and notice how this feels.

End of lesson

NOTE

1. Bunch, Meribeth. 1993. *Dynamics of the Singing Voice* (Vienna: Springer-Verlag).

CHAPTER 9

Upper Trunk Flexibility

THE UPPER TRUNK

The upper trunk consists, roughly, of the ribs and thoracic spine. This region is intimately involved in breathing. As noted in chapter 8, the ribs must move freely for the lungs to open freely and easily. When the ribs cannot properly contract, the vacuum created in the lungs is reduced. This causes a reduction in the ability to bring in air. The ribs most capable of moving are the floating ribs.

The following lessons explore spinal rotation, which is important for both proper positioning to play any instrument and easy movement (walking, running, etc.).

MINI-ATM: SPINAL ROTATION

1. **Sit forward in a flat chair.** Scan yourself. How do your feet fit the floor? How tall do you feel? What is your breathing like? **Now cross your right leg over the left. Gently tilt the legs to the right and then back to the center again.** Repeat this ten to fifteen times. Do not go your full range at first. Instead let the legs tilt a little at a time, moving only so far as you can go easily and effortlessly. Notice, as you make this movement, where you sense lengthening, and how far up the spine you feel rotation. (Note: View drawings from overhead in a chair. They depict the lesson done on the floor.)

   Stop. Uncross your legs. Rest for a minute. What changes, if any, do you notice?

83

2. **Put your palms together. Extend your arms forward until the elbows are straight. Take your arms to the left without bending the elbows and then return them to center. Allow your head and eyes to move with your arms.** Repeat this movement six to eight times. Do each movement slowly and lightly. Pause for as long as it takes to go left and then back to the center before starting left again. How far down your back can you feel this movement? Stop, put your arms down and rest for a minute.

   Now once again cross your right leg over the left. Gently tilt the legs to the right and then back to the center again. Do this three or four times. Compare the ease and range of this movement now to what it was before you did the arm movements. **Stop. Uncross your legs.** Rest for a minute. Let go of comparing; just notice whatever it is you notice.

3. **Cross your left leg over your right. Gently tilt the legs to the left and then back to the center again. As you start out make small movements and gradually increase the range.** Repeat ten to sixteen times. Always stay well within your range to avoid strain and maximize your learning. Avoid the trap of always seeing how far or how well you can do. Remember, if you stay within your range, it will increase and you will find greater ease. But, if you keep testing your limit, it will not improve, and you risk going too far and injuring yourself.

   Stop and uncross your legs. Rest for a minute. Enjoy whatever sense of quiet you find.

4. **Put your palms together. Extend your arms forward until the elbows are straight. Take your arms to the right without bending the elbows and then return them to center. Again, allow your head and eyes to move with your arms.** Repeat this movement six to eight times. Slowly begin by moving about 50 percent as far as you think you can. Then allow the range to increase gradually. Stop, put your arms down, and **rest** for a minute.

   Now, once again, cross your left leg over the right. Gently tilt the legs to the left and back to the center. Do this three or four times. Compare this movement now to what it was before you did the arm movements. **Stop and uncross your legs.** Rest for a minute. How do you feel now?

This is the end of this module. It is a logical place to stop if you cannot do the lesson in one sitting. **Stand and walk around for at least a minute.** Resume at **step 5**.

5. **Put your palms together and extend your arms. Take your arms to the right but do not follow this movement with your head and eyes.** Repeat this slowly six to eight times. Put your arms down and rest for a minute.

6. **Put your palms together and extend your arms. Pick a point on the wall and keep your eyes focused on it. Now take your arms to the right and follow with your head while keeping your eyes focused on that point.** Repeat seven to nine times. If this bothers your eyes, close them as you keep them fixed on that point. Put your arms down. Stay like this briefly.

   Put your palms together, extend your arms, and take them to the right with your head and eyes. Repeat three to four times. What differences do you notice in your back from turning the head and eyes? Do you notice any changes from when you did this movement before? Put your arms down. Rest briefly.

   Cross your left leg over the right. Gently tilt the legs to the left and then back to the center again. Do this three or four times. Compare this movement now to what it was like earlier. Stop, uncross your legs, and rest for a minute.

7. **Put your palms together and extend your arms. Take your arms to the left, but do not follow this movement with your head and eyes.** Repeat 7 to 9 times. How smoothly do you make this movement? Put your arms down and rest for a minute.

8. **Put your palms together and extend your arms. Pick a point on the wall and keep your eyes focused on it. Now take your arms to the left and follow with your head while keeping your eyes focused on that point.** Repeat 6 to 8 times. Can you find a way to allow this movement to be smoother? Put your arms down and rest briefly.

   Extend your arms and take them to the left with your head and eyes. Repeat 3 to 4 times. Do you notice changes from the last time you did this movement? Put your arms down and rest.

   Now cross your right leg over the left. Gently tilt the legs to the right and then back to the center again. Do this 3 or 4 times. Compare this movement now to what it was like earlier. Stop, uncross your legs, and rest.

   This is the end of this module. It is a logical place to stop if you cannot do the lesson in one sitting. **Stand and walk around for at least a minute.** Resume at step 9.

9. **Put your palms together and extend your arms until the elbows are straight. Take your arms to the right and follow with your eyes without moving your head.** Repeat 6 to 8 times. You may find this easier with your eyes closed. Can you feel the impetus to move your head when your eyes move? Put your arms down and rest like this for a minute.

10. **Put your palms together and extend your arms. Take your arms to the right with your head and eyes, pausing when you are as far to the right as you can**

comfortably go. Now bring your arms back to the center. **As you tilt your arms back to the right, move your head and eyes to the center.** Repeat this alternating pattern 6 to 8 times. Go slowly as it may be disorienting. Put your arms down and rest.

Extend your arms and take them to the right with your head and eyes. Repeat 3 to 4 times. Do you notice changes from the last time you made this movement? Lower your arms down and rest.

Now, cross your left leg over the right. Gently tilt the legs to the left and then back to the center again. Do this 3 or 4 times. Compare this movement now to what it was like earlier. Stop and rest.

11. **Put your palms together. Extend your arms until the elbows are straight. Take your arms to the left and follow with your eyes without moving your head.** Repeat 5 to 7 times. Is this easier than on the other side? Do you close your eyes? Can you feel the impetus to move your head when your eyes move? Put your arms down and rest for a minute.

12. **Put your palms together. Extend your arms . Take your arms to the left with your head and eyes, pausing when you are as far to the left as you can comfortably go. Now bring your arms back to the center. As you take your arms back to the left move your head and eyes to the center.** Slowly repeat this alternating pattern 6 to 8 times. Do you concentrate more on the hands or the head and eye moving? Put your arms down and rest.

Extend your arms and take them to the left with your head and eyes. Repeat 3 to 4 times. What changes do you notice from the last time you did this movement? Put your arms down and rest.

Cross your right leg over the left. Gently tilt the legs to the right and then back to the center again. Do this 3 or 4 times. Compare this movement now to what it was like earlier. Stop and rest. How straight are you sitting now?

This is the end of this module. It is a logical place to stop if you cannot do the lesson in one sitting. **Stand and walk around for at least a minute.** Resume at step **13.**

13. **Cross your right leg over the left. Gently tilt the legs to the right and then back to the center again as your head turns in the same direction as your legs.** Repeat 6 to 8 times. Do you lead with your legs or your head? Can you find a way to make the movement simultaneous? Can you reverse your normal lead? Pause in the middle.

14. **Gently tilt the legs to the right and then back to the center again as your head turns in the opposite direction.** Do this 7 to 10 times. Go slowly and enjoy the sense of stretch. Stop and rest

Cross your right leg over the left. Gently tilt the legs to the right and then back to the center again. Do this 3 or 4 times. Compare this movement now to what it was like earlier. Stop, uncross your legs, and rest briefly.

Extend your arms and take them to the left with your head and eyes. Repeat 3 to 4 times. What changes do you notice from the last time you did this movement? Put your arms down and rest.

15. **Cross your left leg over the right. Gently tilt the legs to the left and then back to the center again as your head turns in the same direction as your legs.** Repeat 6 to 8 times. Play a little between leading with your head or your legs. Try this both while tilting left and returning to center. Pause.

16. **Gently tilt the legs to the left and then back to the center again as your head turns in the opposite direction.** Do this 7 to 10 times. See if you can make both movements happen at the same time. Sense how long you feel when your legs are tilted one way and your head the other. Stop and take a short rest.

Extend your arms and take them to the right with your head and eyes. Repeat 3 to 4 times. What changes do you notice from the last time you did this movement? Put your arms down and rest.

Cross your left leg over the right. Gently tilt the legs to the left and then back to the center again. Do this 3 or 4 times. Compare this movement now to what it was like earlier. Stop, uncross your legs, and rest for a minute. How are you sitting now?

Stand up. What does standing feel like? How tall do you feel? How straight? **Walk around for a minute or so.**

End of lesson

THE MID-SPINE

Each of the ribs is attached to the spine. There are facets on both sides of the vertebrae where the ribs (actually cartilaginous connecting tissue) attach. Because of this close connection, any difficulty in moving the spine will impede movement of the ribs and hence breathing.

The spine moves in three planes. It can move up and down, left and right, and forward and back. By combining these, the spine is also capable of rotation. Thus you can twist to your right to look behind yourself. Various areas of the spine can move more or less. However, the key to good movement is for the entire spine, from the neck to the pelvis, to move in unison. A stuck place anywhere leads first to difficulty and ultimately to discomfort and pain, although usually the pain is not where we are stuck. Instead, the pain is usually where there is extra movement or effort to compensate. Of course, we can only hope to approximate even and appropriate movement. And it is easy to be deceived by how well one moves when young, because we can move one area of the spine excessively to substitute for a tightness elsewhere. Although the spine can be said to move in three planes—back and forth, left and right, and up and down—in actual movement, it moves some in at least two and usually all three directions at once. Thus, movement forward or back inevitably involves some up-and-down movement, and so on.

The first lesson in this chapter involves rotation of the spine. The following lesson is about moving the spine left and right. As you become familiar with it, you may look at how your movement deviates from this plane and includes some forward-and-back, or up-and-down, or rotational movement as well. If you find that the movement left is significantly different from that to the right, you may have scoliosis, or curvature of the spine.

ATM: LATERAL FLEXION

1. Sit forward in your chair. **Turn your head left and right/notice what this is like.** Pause. **Without bending forward, move your right arm toward the floor by bending sideways three or four times.** Pause. Notice how far you went and how easy this felt. Compare your two sides.

    Now do the same movement to the left three or four times. Which hand was closer to the floor? Was it easy or more difficult to do the movement in this direction? Stop and rest.

2. **Tilt your head to the right. Do this without turning the head. That is, the nose faces forward and your right ear moves toward your shoulder.** Repeat this four to seven times. See how gently you can do this movement. Let your breath out as you move your head downward to the right. Does this help the movement? Stop and rest.

3. **Tilt your head to the left. Again the nose faces forward.** Repeat this four to seven times. How is the movement on this side different from that on the right? What are you doing with your pelvis when you do this movement? Pause.

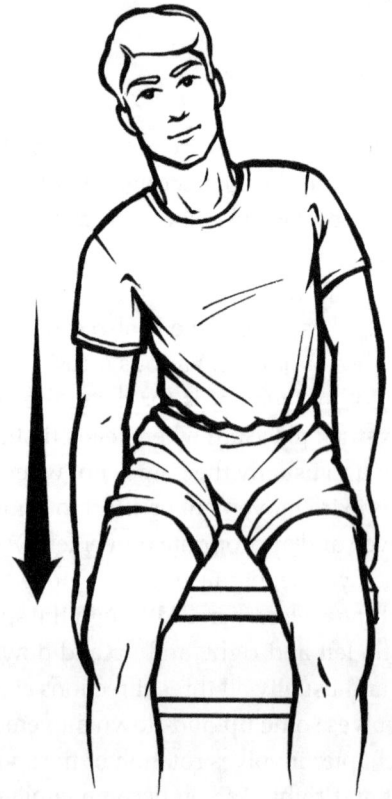

4. **Tilt your head once to the left and then once to the right,** *slowly*. Repeat this six to eight times, taking a full breath between each iteration. Notice differences between the two sides. Do you remember to exhale as the head goes to the side? What other movement do you notice in conjunction with the movement of the head? Rest a minute.

   Make the first movement, that is, alternately move the right arm and then the left arm toward the floor. Notice if anything has changed. If you notice changes, repeat the motion two or three times and see if you can notice any other changes. Pause.

   Turn your head left and right. Stop.

   This is the end of this module. It is a logical place to stop if you cannot do the lesson in one sitting. Resume at **step 5**. If you stop, stand and walk for a minute noticing changes, if any.

5. **Gently move the right hip toward the right shoulder, slightly. Keep this a very small movement. The buttock need not lift from the chair.** Repeat this movement four or five times. As you do so, see what happens if you put weight down through the left buttock to help raise the right hip. Does it make this movement easier?

   Continue this movement and at the same time tilt the right ear toward the right shoulder. Repeat four to seven times. Rest. Did you put the weight down to the left buttock as you did the last movement? Compare your two sides. Is there a difference in your breathing?

6. **Gently move the left hip toward the left shoulder. Remember to keep this movement small.** Repeat this movement four to six times. Did you put weight down through the right buttock to help make this movement?

Continue this movement, at the same time tilting the left ear to the left shoulder. Repeat four to seven times. Pause. Compare your two sides. Rest a moment. Sit back in your chair if you need to.

7. **Move forward in your chair. Alternately move the left hip toward the left shoulder and right hip toward the right shoulder. Keep the movements small and aim for equal *effort* on each side, not equal distance.** Repeat five to eight times, *slowly*. Pause.

8. **Now alternate between moving the left ear toward the left shoulder while you move the left hip toward that shoulder and moving the right ear toward the right shoulder while you move the right hip toward the right shoulder.** Repeat this five to eight times. Again, equality of effort is what counts. If you can stay in your comfort zone and do each side well, they will both improve. Usually the improvement will be greater on the side that moves less well. Thus, if you do not strive for evenness of result you will get it. This is a paradox of performance that occurs repeatedly. Pause.

   Put your arms down by your sides. Move your right arm toward the floor as in step 1. Then do the same thing to the left. Compare this with how you did at the end of the last module. Breath in and notice how you are breathing.

   This is the end of this module. It is a logical place to stop if you cannot do the lesson in one sitting. Resume at **step 9**. If you stop, stand and walk for a minute noticing changes, if any.

9. **Put your hands on your legs. Move your left shoulder toward your left hip.** Repeat four to six times. Do not strain while you make this movement. Pause.

   Move your left shoulder toward your hip as you raise your left hip, slightly. Repeat four to six times. Pause.

   Now add turning your head gently to the right while moving your left shoulder toward your hip as you raise your left hip. Repeat four to six times. Do you breathe in or out as your head turns? Stop, compare sides, and rest.

10. **Move your right shoulder toward your right hip.** Repeat four to six times. Do not strain while you make this movement. Pause.

    Move your right shoulder toward your hip as you raise your right hip, slightly. Repeat four to six times. Pause.

    Now add turning your head gently to the left while moving your right shoulder toward your hip as you raise your right hip. Repeat four to six times. How far down your back can you feel movement as you turn your head? Stop and rest.

11. **Alternate moving your right and left shoulders down.** Repeat three or four times, taking a couple breaths in between each movement. Pause.

    Add in the movement of the head and hip as you alternate moving your shoulders down. Repeat three or four times. Again, take a couple breaths between movements. Stop and rest. Notice how you are breathing.

12. **Put your arms down by your sides. Move your right arm toward the floor as in step 1. Then do the same thing to the left.** Compare this with how you did at the end of the last module. Breath in and notice how you are breathing.

    Turn your head left and right. What is this like now? Rest.

    When ready, slowly stand and walk for a minute.

End of lesson

SCOLIOSIS

Scoliosis is a deviation left or right in the curvature of the spine. Virtually everyone has some scoliosis, but for the vast majority it is so slight as to be unmeasurable. The cause for this slight scoliosis is hand dominance. All humans have a dominant hand, even those who are ambidextrous. This is because perfect ambidexterity, where there is no preferred hand, is dysfunctional. If you have no automatic preference, you have to think about which hand to start with whenever you initiate an action. In today's cultures, this would make you somewhat uncoordinated. In less civilized times, the delay in moving could be fatal. The lion or opposing swordsman would slay you before you moved. Thus, even people who are considered ambidextrous have hand preferences. These preferences simply differ from one task to another. This hand dominance means that there will be differential mechanical stress placed on the spine from the two arms. This accounts for the "normal" scoliosis of most people.

Some people have measurable scoliosis. It is not entirely clear why. What is important is that it may affect their ability to function. Typically, scoliosis increases with age. This increase is due both to the strain from hand dominance and to the dynamics of fighting gravity when one is off-center. For some people, the scoliosis can become so large that it threatens mobility and even health. A surgically inserted rod is used to stabilize the spine in these cases. But for most people with notable scoliosis, pain is the problem.

Functionally, scoliosis impinges on the lung on one side and also acts like a short leg. (See the discussion of leg-length differential in chapter 3.) There are lessons to help cope with problems caused by scoliosis. These lessons will allow individuals with slight scoliosis to function, at least for a time, as if there were no scoliosis. Lessons that in large part involve spinal rotation are helpful. The first lesson in this chapter is in that category. The second type of lesson involves feeling the differences in pelvic movement. The following mini-lesson belongs to this category. It can also be helpful for people with minor leg-length differentials.

MINI-ATM: EVENING THE SIDES

Stand and notice how even your two sides feel. Take off your shoes and lie on your back. Extend both your legs. Notice how your back fits the floor. How even do your two sides feel? Which side feels longer? Is that the side that feels freer? **Extend the heel**

on the side that feels freer away from your head. **This is not a movement of the ankle but of the hip. So be clear that the whole leg is involved in this movement.** Can you feel the pelvis titling in this direction? If not, you are not involving the hip. Repeat this movement five to seven times. Go slowly and gently as you do this.

Pause for a moment. Compare how your two sides feel now.

Now extend your other heel. Again, move from the hip so that the pelvis shifts in this direction. Repeat six to eight times. Pause between repetitions for as long as it takes to slowly make this movement. Aim to do the movement as easily as on the other side. If this means a smaller movement, so be it. If this movement is difficult, you can assist by pulling up the other hip.

Pause for a moment. Compare how your two sides feel now.

Alternate extending your heels. Can you feel how one hip goes up as the other extends? Can you use this to even out the effort on the two sides? Repeat this movement six to eight times.

Pause for a moment. Then alternate extending your heels a couple more times. Did the feeling change while you paused?

Stop. Compare how your two sides feel now. Notice how you are breathing on each side. Slowly sit up. Sit for a moment and notice any changes in sitting. Slowly stand and compare how your two sides feel in standing now. Then walk for a minute and notice what this feels like.

End of lesson

The final lesson in this chapter involves the relationship of the hips, pelvis, and legs to the spine, especially the mid-spine. Instead of a long explanation of its benefits, etc., try it and find out if it's useful for you.

ATM: CIRCLING THE LEGS

0. Bend your knees and put your feet on the floor, which is best performed by bending your knees out to the side and rotating your legs around. To straighten, reverse this process. This is the safest way to take your legs from laying flat to having the feet on the floor. This circular movement uses the most muscles and puts the least strain on any individual muscle groups well, as reducing the maximum strain on the back compared to a straight-line movement.

1. Please lie on your back. **Roll your head left and right several times.** Notice how far it rolls, how easily, and how much of yourself you feel is involved in this movement.

   Bend your knees and put your feet on the floor. Gently slide your right foot downward about a foot or so and then bring it back. Only go as far downward as you can while all the toes of your right foot touch the floor. Repeat this ten to twelve times. Intend to make this movement easier as though you were painting the floor with your foot. Pause.

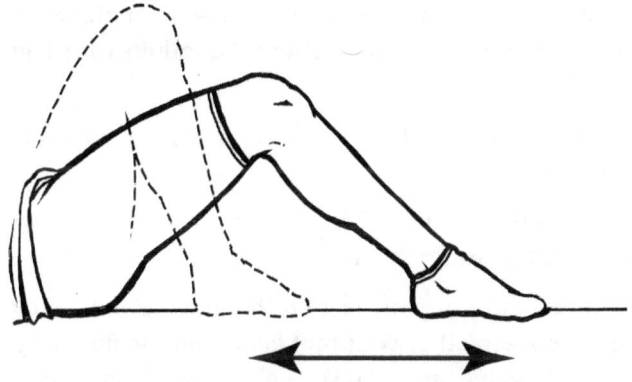

Extend your left leg and resume sliding the right leg downward with the entire foot touching the floor. Repeat this four to six times, noting how this changes from having the left leg bent. Pause.

Bend your left leg again and resume painting the floor with your right foot. Repeat this six to eight times. Sense how your foot is fitting the floor. Aim to have it feel easy. Avoid a sense of strain, if possible. Pause. **Lengthen your legs.** Compare your two sides and rest for a minute.

2. **Bend your knees and put your feet on the floor. Gently slide your left foot downward about a foot or so and then bring it back. Again, only go as far downward as you can while all the toes of your foot touch the floor.** Repeat this ten to twelve times. Is painting the floor easier on this side? Pause.

   Extend your right leg and resume painting the floor with the left foot. Repeat this four to six times, noting how this is different from when the leg is bent. Pause.

   Bend your right leg again and resume painting the floor with your left foot. Repeat this six to eight times. Pause. **Lengthen your legs.** Compare your two sides and rest for a minute.

3. **Bend your knees and put your feet on the floor. Gently move your left foot left and right about three to four inches.** Repeat this nine or ten times. Go no further than you can feel all your toes against the floor? Pause.

   Extend your right leg and resume moving your left leg gently left and right. Repeat this four to six times.

   Bend your right leg again and resume moving your left leg gently left and right. Repeat this four to six times. Pause. **Lengthen your legs.** Compare your two sides and rest for a minute.

4. **Bend your knees and put your feet on the floor. Gently move your right foot left and right about three to four inches.** Repeat this seven or eight times. Can you make the movement softer each time? Pause.

   Extend your left leg and resume moving your right leg gently left and right. Repeat this four to six times.

Bend your left leg again and resume moving your right leg gently left and right. Repeat this four to six times. Pause. **Lengthen your legs.** Compare your two sides.

Roll your head left and right several times. Notice how far it rolls and how easily it rolls now.

This is the end of this module. It is a logical place to stop if you cannot do the lesson in one sitting. Resume at **step 5**.

5. **Bend your knees and put your feet on the floor. Paint a circle with your left foot on the floor. Keep all of your foot gently on the floor as you paint.** Repeat this circle at least twelve times. Make two or three circles and pause for a breath. See how well you can keep the circle round or make it rounder each time. Pause.

   Now reverse the direction of your circle. Repeat at least ten times. Again, make two or three circles and pause for a breath. Is it as easy to go in this direction? Probably not. We have a strong tendency to start movements going in our best direction. Which, if you think about it, is the sign of a healthy organization. Pause. **Lengthen your legs.** Compare your two sides and rest for a minute.

6. **Bend your knees and put your feet on the floor. Paint a circle with your right foot on the floor.** Repeat this circle at least twelve times. Make two or three circles and pause for a breath. Is it easier to make a circle on this side? Can you paint more softly and also with more control as you continue around? Stop.

   Now reverse the direction of your circle. Repeat at least ten times. Again, make two or three circles and pause for a breath. Once more aim to make each circle at least as round, easy, and smooth as the one before. Pause. **Lengthen your legs.** Compare your two sides and rest for a minute.

7. **Roll over onto your stomach. With your head in a symmetrical comfortable position, alternately bend your knees.** Repeat this several times. Which knee bends better?

   Straighten the knee that bends less well. Is this the leg that made easier circles on the floor? **Now make a circle with the bent leg.** Have the sense that this foot has an extension and is painting the ceiling. Repeat this six or seven times. Pause.

   Reverse the direction of your circle. Repeat five or six times. See if you can go as easily in this direction. Pause. **Unbend your knee.** Rest like this for a minute.

8. **Bend the knee that was straight and make a circle with this leg.** Repeat this at least ten times. Is it easier or more difficult to circle this leg? Pause.

   Reverse the direction of your circle. Repeat five or six times. See if you can go as easily in this direction. Pause. **Unbend your knee. Roll over onto your back.** Rest for a minute.

   Bend your knees and put your feet on the floor. Make a few circles with your right foot. Has this changed from what it was like before you rolled onto your stomach? Pause.

Now make a few circles with your left foot. Lengthen your legs. Stop and rest a moment.

Roll your head left and right several times. Notice how far it rolls and how easily it rolls now.

This is the end of this module. It is a logical place to stop if you cannot do the lesson in one sitting. Resume at **step 9**.

9. **Bend your knees and put your feet on the floor. Begin to make slow circles, in opposition, with each foot.** Do the feet meet in the center when they return, or does one foot lead the other? Try to keep the two circles even. Repeat this twelve to fifteen times, doing no more than three circles in a row before pausing for a couple of breaths. Pause.

    Resume the circles in the same direction, only go faster and without noting how evenly the feet move. What is your back doing? How much movement do you feel in the vertebrae opposite the shoulders? Repeat about twelve times, again no more than three in a row before pausing for a couple of breaths. **Now do a few slow even circles.** Stop, lengthen your legs, and rest a moment.

10. **Bend your knees and put your feet on the floor. Begin to make slow circles, in opposition, in the other direction than you did before with each foot.** Is it easier or harder for the feet to meet in the center going in these directions when they return than in the directions you first chose in step 9? Repeat this about fifteen times, following the same process as in step 9, concentrating on keeping the feet both moving in circles. Do you find that one side tends to become an oval first? Pause.

    Resume the circles in the same direction, only go faster and without noting how evenly the feet move. Does your back move as before, or has the movement changed amplitude or area? Repeat ten to twelve times, again no more than three in a row before taking a few breaths. Stop, lengthen your legs, and rest a moment.

11. **Bend your knees and put your feet together on the floor. Make circles with both feet going in the same direction.** *Because you are holding the feet together, they will move at the same speed and amplitude.* Repeat about twenty times going slowly at first and building up speed. Where do you feel this movement in your back? Pause with your feet still together.

    Now reverse the direction of your circles. Repeat about fifteen times aiming for a soft movement with lots of control. Stop, lengthen your legs, and rest a moment.

12. **Bend your knees and put your feet on the floor. Make equal circles with both feet going in the same direction.** Because they are not together, it will require attention to keep the circles even and the feet opposite each other. Repeat about twelve times. Pause.

    Now reverse the direction of your circles. Repeat about ten times, noting where you feel this movement in your back. Pause.

    Now make a few circles with the feet in opposition where you concentrate on the sense of painting control. Pause.

Reverse direction and make a few more circles. Pause. Lengthen your legs.

Roll your head left and right several times. Notice how far it rolls and how much of your back you can feel participating in this movement. What are your feet doing on the floor? Pause and rest a minute.

Sit up and then stand up. Notice how tall you feel, how your shoulders feel and how your arms hang. **Walk around for a minute or two.** How are your arms moving?

End of lesson

CHAPTER 10

Shoulder Girdle and Arms

SHOULDERS AND BREATH

The shoulders play an important role in breathing. Referring to an illustration, you can see that the shoulder blade (scapula) sits directly over the ribs. Free movement of the shoulder blade is vital to free breathing. Any tightness in the muscles holding the shoulder blade will impede rib movement and thus breathing.

Much of the musculature of the shoulder also overlies the ribs. In particular, the trapezius and rhomboids, the serratus anterior and latissimus dorsi in back, and the pectoralis muscles in front connect the scapula to the ribs. Clearly, tightness or dysfunction in these areas will impede breathing. This musculature was heavily involved in the lesson in chapter 8, "ATM: Freeing the Ribs."

Because shoulder muscles attach to vertebrae for virtually the entire length of the spine, they are susceptible to being pulled by problems with the back. Think about this interrelatedness for a moment. Can you see why releasing tightness anywhere could have a positive impact everywhere and, conversely, why working one area without addressing other related areas might cause problems? This is the infamous law of unintended consequences. Or, "It's hard to remember the goal was to drain the swamp when you are up to your ears in alligators." It is also another example of Newton's third law of motion in our lives.

The muscles that attach the shoulder to the neck and arm can cause problems in the muscles that attach the shoulder to the back. Anything that causes strain in these areas disorders the movement or the stability of the shoulder. This disorder is transmitted to all muscles involved in the shoulder, and all shoulder-connected musculature must work to counteract the strain. Accordingly, any lesson involving the shoulder will have a wide-ranging impact. The following lesson, "Reach and Drop," involves the relationship of the shoulder to the torso. It therefore can markedly affect breathing and the back, in addition to the shoulders.

ATM: REACH AND DROP

An audio lesson is available at https://on.soundcloud.com/NouE4.

This lesson is somewhat more effective on the floor where you have the help of gravity when dropping and then the support of the floor throughout much of the lesson. If you can only do the lesson on a chair, the following modifications are suggested. Raise your arm(s) until they are parallel to the floor. Unless moving the arm forward, move the shoulder back about half an inch. This is the neutral position for the rest of the lesson. It mimics keeping the shoulder on the floor.

1. **Lie on your back.** Notice how you are breathing. How do your shoulders and back fit the floor? **Bend your right knee out to the side and then rotate the leg so that your foot stands on the floor with the knee in the air. Now repeat that with your left leg. For the rest of the lesson, we will refer to this as, "Rotate your legs to standing." Raise both your arms forward (toward the ceiling). Extend your right arm toward the ceiling.** How much of your shoulder blade leaves the floor as you do this. Did you exhale? **Repeat this movement exhaling as you do so. Then leaving your right arm forward, extend your left arm toward the ceiling.** How does this shoulder move compared to the right? Did you exhale as the arm went forward? **Repeat this movement exhaling as you do so.** Pause, leaving your arms in this position.

   Alternate extending your left and right arms. Extend each arm four to six times. As you extend, compare how easily and completely you move on each side. Pause, put your arms and legs down, and rest a minute. When putting your legs down, reverse the rotation that you used to raise them. Based on comfort and range of movement, decide which arm extends better. We'll label that the preferred arm and the other arm is the other arm.

2. **Rotate your legs to standing. Raise your preferred arm forward. Gently drop the shoulder blade into the floor, keep it there and move the arm to the inside two to three inches and back to neutral. (We will call this position, "keep your shoulder blade against the floor.")** Allow enough freedom of movement for the shoulder blade to move while maintaining contact with the floor. You will feel the back of the shoulder blade move in the opposite direction (right) against the floor as you make this movement. Repeat this movement seven to ten times. Each time, see if you can allow more movement in the shoulder or chest. Pause in place for a short while.

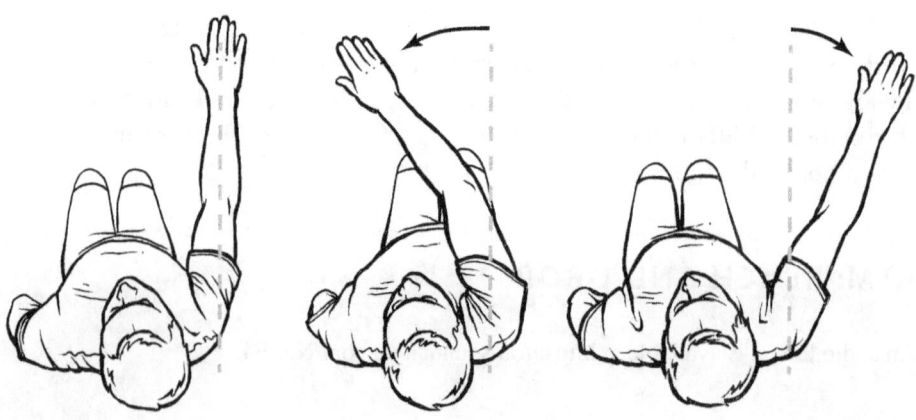

Now move your arm to the outside one to two inches while maintaining floor contact with the shoulder blade. Repeat this movement five to eight times. How soft can you make this movement while still sensing the contact and movement of your shoulder blade relative to the floor? Pause, put your arm down, and rest a minute.

Raise your preferred arm forward. While keeping your shoulder blade against the floor, alternately move your arm left and right. Stay in the range established above. Repeat six to eight times shifting your awareness between the movement of the arm, shoulder blade, and chest. When do you breathe in? Pause, put your arm and legs down, and rest a minute.

3. **Rotate your legs to standing. Raise your other arm forward. Keeping the shoulder blade into the floor, move the arm to the inside an inch or two as you exhale, and then return to neutral.** Repeat seven to ten times. How easy is this movement? Is the contact with the shoulder blade clearer on this side? Pause in place and rest a while.

    Now move your arm to the outside one to two inches. while maintaining floor contact with the shoulder blade. Repeat this movement five to eight times. How freely are you able to breathe as you make this movement? How well is the shoulder blade moving? Pause, put your arm down, and rest a minute.

    Raise your other arm forward. While keeping your shoulder blade against the floor, alternately move your arm left and right. Repeat six to eight times, shifting your awareness between the movement of the arm, shoulder blade, and chest. Pause, put your arm and legs down, and rest a minute.

4. **Rotate your legs to standing. Raise both your arms forward. Extend your right arm forward several times.** How does this movement compare to earlier? Pause briefly.

    Extend your left arm forward several times. How easy is this compared to earlier? How do you feel this arm moves relative to the right? How much of yourself do you feel moving as the left arm extends? Pause, and put your arms down for a short while.

    Raise both your arms forward. Alternate extending your left and right arms. Extend each arm four to six times. How does this compare to earlier? Are the movements of the left and right more or less similar than they were before? Pause, put your arm and legs down, and rest a minute.

    This is the end of this module. It is a logical place to stop if you cannot do the lesson in one sitting. Resume at **step 5.**

5. **Rotate your legs to standing. Raise your preferred arm forward. Keeping the shoulder blade into the floor, move the arm upward in the direction of the floor above your head about one to two inches, and then return to neutral. Repeat this four to six times. Breathe in as the arm moves upward. Let this be a gentle movement. Put your arm down and rest.**

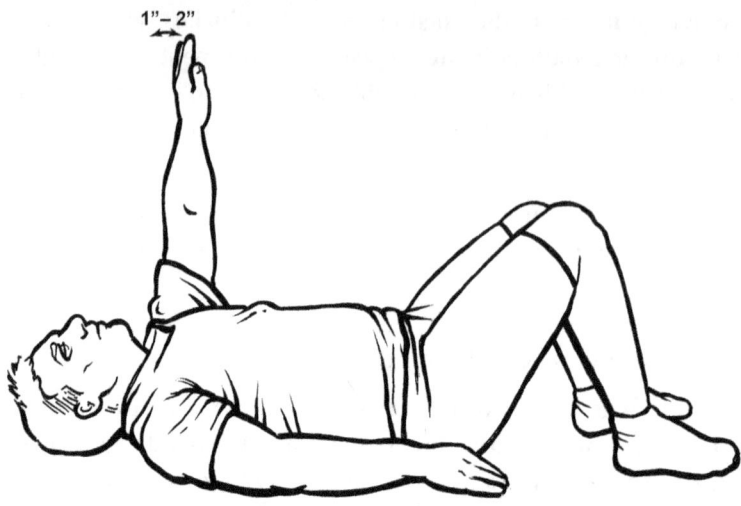

6. **Raise the same arm. Keeping the shoulder blade into the floor, move the arm downward in the direction of the floor about an inch and then return to neutral.** Repeat this four to six times. Exhale as the arm moves downward. Move slowly and smoothly. Put your arm down and pause briefly.

   Once more, raise the preferred arm forward. Keeping the shoulder blade into the floor, move your arm up and down about an inch in either direction. Repeat five to seven times. Sense the movement of the shoulder blade against the floor as well as the movement of the arm in the air. Can you track both movements at the same time? Put your arm and your legs down and rest.

7. **Rotate your legs to standing. Raise your other arm forward. Keeping the shoulder blade into the floor, move the arm upward in the direction of the floor above your head about one to two inches and then return to neutral.** Repeat this four to six times. Let the movement coming back to neutral be a soft letting go. Pause briefly.

   Keeping the shoulder blade into the floor, move the arm downward in the direction of the floor about an inch and then return to neutral. Repeat this four to six times. What moves downward as the arm lifts to neutral: the pelvis? The legs? Somewhere else? Put your arm and your legs down and rest.

8. **Rotate your legs to standing. Raise your other arm forward. Keeping the shoulder blade into the floor, move your arm up and down about an inch in either direction.** Repeat five to seven times. Sense the movement of the shoulder blade against the floor as well as the movement of the arm in the air. What is your breathing like? Put your arm down and rest.

   Raise both your arms forward. Alternate extending your left and right arms. Extend each arm four to six times. How does this compare to earlier? Are the movements more or less similar than they were before? Pause, put your arms and legs down, and rest a minute.

   This is the end of this module. It is a logical place to stop if you cannot do the lesson in one sitting. Resume at **step** 9.

9. **Rotate your legs to standing.** Notice what your breathing is like. **Raise your preferred arm forward. Keeping the shoulder blade into the floor, move your arm in a circle with a radius of about an inch.** Repeat eight to ten times. Alternately notice the quality of the movement of the arm in the air and that of the shoulder blade against the floor. Pause, put your arm down, and rest a minute.

10. **Raise your preferred arm forward. Keeping the shoulder blade into the floor, move your arm in a circle with a radius of about an inch in the opposite direction than you made last time.** Repeat seven to nine times. Can you allow this movement to become smoother and more circular? Pause, put everything down, and rest a minute. How are you breathing now?

11. **Rotate your legs to standing. Raise your other arm forward. Keeping the shoulder blade into the floor, move your arm in a circle with a radius of about an inch.** Repeat eight to ten times. See what happens to the quality of this movement if you make the circle a little bigger or a little smaller each time. Pause, put your arm down, and rest a minute.

12. **Raise your other arm forward. Keeping the shoulder blade into the floor, move your arm in a circle with a radius of about an inch in the opposite direction than last time.** Repeat seven to nine times. Pause, put your arm down, and rest a minute.

    Rotate your legs to standing. Raise both your arms forward. Alternate extending your left and right arms. Extend each arm four to six times. How does this compare to earlier? Are the movements of the left and right more or less similar than they were before? Pause, put your arms and legs down, and rest. What is your breathing like now?

End of lesson

The following lesson is designed to clarify the relationship between the shoulders, head, and neck.

ATM: WINGING IT

1. Sit in a chair with a flat bottom. **Turn your head left and right as far as you can easily.** Repeat this three or four times and then pause. Notice how far your head turns in each direction.

    Put your right hand behind your head with your right elbow pointing to the right. Gently move your right arm forward and back. Repeat six to eight times. Is it easier or more difficult to keep your head and eyes looking forward when this arm is up? Does your breathing coordinate in any way with this movement? Pause, put your arm down, and rest a moment.

2. **Make a fist with your right hand. Gently raise your right shoulder straight up until the movement becomes sticky or discontinuous.** Straight up means that the top of the shoulder moves toward the ceiling and the arm stays parallel to the

torso. **Gently lower your arm opening your fist as you do so.** Repeat this six to eight times. Pause.

3. **Put your left hand behind your head. Gently move your left arm forward and back.** Repeat six to eight times. Can you keep your head and eyes looking forward the entire time? Do you feel your shoulder blade moving over your upper ribs as you make this movement? Pause, put your arm down, and rest a moment.

4. **Make a fist with your left hand. Slowly raise this arm (same way as the right in step 2) and then gently lower it, releasing your fist as you do so.** Repeat four to six times. Pause.

    Put your left hand behind your head. Gently move your left arm forward and back. Repeat two or three times. How does this movement feel now?

    Put your right hand behind your head. Gently move your right arm forward and back. Repeat two or three times. Pause.

    Turn your head left and right as far as you can easily. What is this like now? Compare this to the movement you made initially. Stop and rest.

    This is the end of this module. It is a logical place to stop if you cannot do the lesson in one sitting. Resume at **step 5**.

5. **Put your left hand behind your head. Gently move your head and arm together as a unit with the head going right as the arm moves forward and left as the arm moves back.** Repeat seven to ten times. Can you make this movement easier and smoother as you repeat it? Pause, put your arm down, and rest a moment.

6. **Put your left hand behind your head. Gently move your head to the left as your arm goes right and vice versa.** Repeat seven to ten times. Can you make this differentiated movement without strain? Check your breathing, your mouth, and your toes as you perform this movement for signs of unnecessary tension. (Feldenkrais referred to this useless tension as parasitic.) Pause, put your arm down, and rest a moment.

    Turn your head left and right as far as you can easily. Is there a difference between the ease of moving left and that of moving right? Pause.

    Put your left hand behind your head. Gently move your left arm forward and back. Repeat two or three times. What is this movement like now? Put your arm down and rest.

7. **Put your right hand behind your head. Gently move your head and this arm together as a unit.** Repeat six to nine times. What is it like coordinating the movements of your head with this arm? Are you able to make the movement gentler as you repeat it? What happens if you look slightly upward as you turn? Pause, put your arm down, and rest a moment.

8. **Put your right hand behind your head. Gently move your head in opposition to your arm.** Repeat six to eight times. Notice if there is any "parasitic" tension. Allow yourself to relax, each time making the movement a little easier. Pause, put your arm down, and rest a moment.

Put your right hand behind your head. Gently move your right arm forward and back. Repeat two or three times and notice how easy this movement is now. Pause, put your arm down, and rest a moment.

Turn your head left and right as far as you can easily. Is there a difference from before? How far down your back do you feel movement? Pause and rest.

This is the end of this module. It is a logical place to stop if you cannot do the lesson in one sitting. Resume at **step 9**.

9. **Put your left hand behind your head. Move your head left and right, leaving your arm stationary.** Repeat seven to nine times. See if you can use the same level of effort as you earlier used to turn your head left and right. Can you allow the movement to be equally easy in either direction? Pause.

   Now gently move your left arm forward and back. Repeat two or three times. What is this movement like now?

10. **Put your left hand behind your head. Move your head up and down.** Don't strain to see how much of the ceiling or floor you can see. Instead, make this a simple, flowing, comfortable movement. Repeat this eight to ten times. Pause, put your arm down, and rest a moment.

    Turn your head left and right as far as you can easily. Is there a difference between the ease of moving to the left and that of moving right? Pause and rest.

11. **Put your right hand behind your head. Now move your head left and right leaving your arm stationary.** Repeat six to eight times. Can you find a way to make this movement softer each time you make it? Pause, put your arm down, and rest a moment.

12. **Put your right hand behind your head. Move your head up and down.** Repeat this eight to ten times. What do you sense in your shoulders as you make this movement? How is it different between the right and the left? Pause; slowly lower your arm and rest.

    Put your right hand behind your head. Gently move your right arm forward and back. Repeat three times, noticing what this feels like.

    Turn your head left and right as far as you can easily. Compare how your head turns to either side now. How has it changed from before? Pause and rest.

This is the end of this module. It is a logical place to stop if you cannot do the lesson in one sitting. Resume at **step 13**.

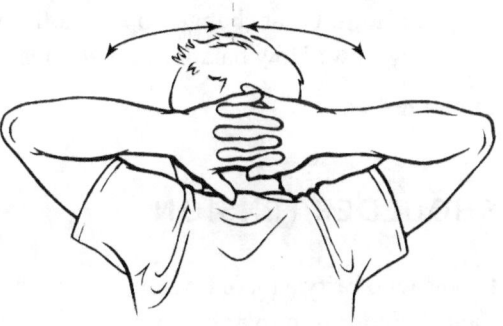

13. **Interlace your fingers and put your hands behind your head. Move your head left and right while leaving your hands in place.** Repeat this movement

nine to eleven times. How, if at all, does the hand position limit this movement? What do you notice about your breathing? Put your arms down, pause, and rest a moment.

14. **Interlace your fingers and put your hands behind your head. Open and close your arms, without moving your head.** Repeat this gentle movement seven or eight times. See if you can equalize the effort between the arms, as opposed to equalizing the range of movement. Pause.

    Now move both arms to the right and then to the left. Your elbows go in the same direction as you make this movement. Repeat this movement nine to twelve times. Pause, put your arms down, and rest.

15. **Interlace your fingers the non-habitual way and put your hands behind your head.** Non-habitual means that you switch the order of the fingers so that if the left index finger is on top you switch it with the right index finger and continue through the other fingers and vice versa. **Move your head right and left as you move both arms to the right and then to the left.** Repeat this movement nine to eleven times. Pause after the first four or five times to assimilate this movement and then continue. Then put your arms down and rest.

16. **Interlace your hands and put them behind your head. Move your head right and left as you move your arms in the opposite direction.** Repeat this eight to ten times. Pause.

    Now go back to moving the arms and head in the same direction. Repeat three or four times. Do you notice any changes? Pause, put your arms down, and rest.

    Put your left hand behind your head. Gently move your left arm forward and back. Repeat two or three times. How does this movement feel now? Put your arm down and rest briefly.

    Put your right hand behind your head. Gently move your right arm forward and back. Repeat two or three times. How free is this movement now? How much effort does it take compared to earlier? Put your arm down and rest briefly.

    Turn your head left and right as far as you can easily. What changes do you notice? How easy is this now? What do you notice in your seat as you make this movement? Stop and rest.

    When you are ready, stand up. What changes if any do you notice? **Now walk around.** What change do you notice in your walking? How are your arms moving now? How balanced do you feel?

End of lesson

SHOULDER TENSION

People who carry a lot of tension in their shoulders often complain that it feels as though their shoulder is in their ear. Actually, their shoulders are elevated. It may be a habitual response to tension in a person's life to raise the shoulders and locate the tension there. Or it may be a function of the type of work the person does. People who work at their desk writing a lot tend to keep their shoulders elevated. This elevation may persist even when they are no longer working at their desk. Elevated shoulders may also be a response to poor posture. It is as if some people try to hold themselves erect with their shoulders.

Whatever the cause, a high shoulder impedes a performer. Like any other shoulder dysfunction, this will interfere with breathing. It also will constrict the throat and may cause jaw problems. (One of the lessons in chapter 11 explores these relationships in depth.) This particular shoulder difficulty results in tightening of the muscles that connect to the neck and occiput (the back of the skull). This makes it more difficult to keep the throat open, and it may pull on the jaw indirectly. The following lesson is designed to "lower" the shoulder.

ATM: DROP YOUR ELBOW

After each movement, return to neutral unless directed otherwise. For example, if the direction says drop your elbow, one movement consists of dropping your elbow and then returning to neutral.

1. Sit comfortably in a chair. Let your arms hang or place them on the armrests. **Turn your head left and right several times and see how far and how easily it moves.** Pause and rest.

    Place your hands on your legs near or on your knees. Allow yourself to make this placement comfortable. Now drop your right elbow down and back towards the floor. Repeat this movement seven to nine times. Leave at least as much time between movements as it takes to make the movement. Be very gentle with yourself. This is an unusual movement and straining is likely to cause discomfort later. Notice how your shoulder slides over the upper ribs as you make this small movement. Pause in place and rest for a minute.

2. **Now drop your left elbow down and back towards the floor.** Repeat this movement seven to nine times. Allow the movement to have a slow luxurious quality. Remember to allow at least as much time between movements as it takes to make the movement. Notice how you breathe as you make this movement. Can you allow the movement to feel easier each time? Pause in place and rest a minute.

3. **Alternate dropping your right elbow and your left elbow.** Compare the two. Let them drop with the same sense of relative ease that the easier of the two has. If the other elbow drops less far or less fast, fine. We are seeing if we can equalize effort and let go of the result (for now). Repeat this alternating movement eight to ten times. Pause, sit comfortably, and rest a minute.

4. **Place your hands on your legs near or on your knees. Again, alternate dropping your right elbow and your left elbow. Each time you drop an elbow, breathe in. After dropping both elbows twice, pause for a complete breath cycle.** Repeat this cycle five to seven times. Pause and rest for several breaths.

Let your arms hang or place them on the armrests. **Turn your head left and right several times and see how far and how easily it moves.** Compare this to how it moved earlier. How are you breathing now?

This is the end of this module. It is a logical place to stop if you cannot do the lesson in one sitting. Resume at **step 5**.

5. **Place your hands on your legs near or on your knees. Now very gently raise your left elbow up toward your ear a little.** Repeat this movement seven to nine times. Allow the movement up to be as slow and gentle as the movement back to neutral. **Take a breath between each movement. Each time see if the movement can be slower and softer.** Pause, sit comfortably, and rest a minute.

6. **Place your hands on your legs near or on your knees. Now slowly raise your right elbow up toward your ear a little and then just as slowly return it to its initial position. Take a breath between each movement.** Repeat this movement six to eight times. Pause and rest a minute.

7. **Place your hands on your legs near or on your knees. Round your back while exhaling. As you inhale, return to your original position.** Repeat this movement seven to nine times without straining or forcing the breath. Let the breathing out and the rounding be a harmonious unit.

Pause with your hands in this position and rest a minute.

8. **Alternately raise your right and left elbow. Take a breath between each movement.** Repeat this movement cycle six to eight times. Pause and rest for a minute.

Let your arms hang or place them on your knees. **Turn your head left and right several times and see how far and how easily it moves.** Compare this to how it moved earlier. How are you breathing now?

This is the end of this module. It is a logical place to stop if you cannot do the lesson in one sitting. Resume at **step 9**.

9. **Place your hands on your legs near or on your knees. Raise both your elbows at the same time. Take a breath and repeat four or five times. This is a shrugging movement. Can you smile as you make this motion?** Pause briefly.

Now lower both your elbows at the same time. Take a breath and repeat three or four times. Pause and rest a moment.

10. **Place your hands on your legs near or on your knees. Move your right elbow a little to the right once.** Continue to make this movement but only go half as far. Repeat this movement seven or eight times. Pause and rest. Compare how your two sides feel.

11. **Place your hands on your legs near or on your knees. Now move your left elbow to the left with the same ease you felt with the right when you went about half as far as you could go.** Repeat this movement seven or eight times. Concentrate on making the movement easier each time. Pause and rest in place.

12. **Alternately move your elbows out to the side. Aim for the same sense of ease each time. Really try and keep the sense of ease the same and not the size of the movement.** Repeat six or seven times. Pause and rest a minute.

    Turn your head left and right several times and see how far and how easily it moves. Compare this to how it moved earlier. How are you breathing now?

    This is the end of this module. It is a logical place to stop if you cannot do the lesson in one sitting. Resume at **step 13**.

13. **Bring your right elbow against your side. Hold it there as you breathe slowly and easily. Keep your arm there for about ten full breaths. Release your arm, sit there for a minute, and compare your sides.**

14. **Bring your left elbow against your side. Hold it there as you breathe slowly and easily. Keep your arm there for about ten full breaths. Release your arm and sit there for a minute.**

15. **Place your hands on your legs near or on your knees. Make a circle with your left elbow going down, right, up, and left.** Repeat this five or six times.

    Now reverse the direction. Again repeat five or six times. Pause and rest. Compare your breathing on the left side to what it was like before and what it is like on the right side.

16. **Place your hands on your legs near or on your knees. Make a circle with your right elbow going down, left, up, and right.** Repeat this five or six times. Notice what happens in your shoulder while letting this be a soft movement with the emphasis on your elbow circle. **Now reverse the direction.** Again repeat five or six times. Pause and rest.

    Turn your head left and right several times and see how far and how easily it moves. Compare this to how it moved earlier. How are you breathing now?

    Stand up and walk around for at least a minute. Notice how your arms are moving.

End of lesson

CHAPTER 11

Head and Neck

POSITIONING THE HEAD

The head contains the mouth, tongue, sinuses, brain, eyes, ears, and nose. It balances on the seven vertebrae of the neck (cervical spine). The neck, which is the top portion of the spine, curves in the same direction as the lumbar spine and the opposite direction of the thoracic spine. At the base of the spine is the pelvis, which, like the head, is relatively heavy. Because of their mass and relative positions, the head and pelvis tend to move in opposition. Move the head forward, and the pelvis goes backward, and vice versa.

The neck is relatively delicate compared to the head. The head must balance on the neck. The head should turn freely up and down and left and right upon the neck. When these movements are restricted in more than a minor way, your sound will be impaired. The lessons in this chapter are designed to provide free and easy movement of the head and neck.

People commonly make poor and injurious use of the head and neck by using the neck muscles to directly lift the head when sitting up from lying. The neck muscles are relatively weak and have little mechanical advantage for lifting the head. As a result, people who habitually lift their head this way eventually wind up with either discomfort or stiffness in the neck. There are better ways both to sit up and to directly lift the head. The preferable way to sit up is to bend your knees, roll to the side, and, without stopping, come up to sitting by moving your head in a semicircular trajectory. This makes use of the momentum of the legs going down to help lift the head. And moving the head and back in a circular manner to sit up both involves more muscles and reduces the peak muscular load compared to the linear movement of coming straight up to sitting.

To safely lift the head directly up from lying, first push down on the sternum (breastbone). This greatly increases leverage over using only the neck muscles to lift the head. It also involves more musculature, thereby reducing the load on the neck muscles. If you want to try this, lie down with your feet on the floor. Then take your hand and push down the lower part of your sternum a couple of times. Can you feel this freeing the neck? After you feel this connection, lift your head at the same time as you press down. When this becomes easy, press the sternum down without the help of the hand as you lift the head. Can you feel how much easier your head lifts this way? If not, try lifting with just the neck muscles and repeat lifting while pressing down on the sternum for contrast.

Head positioning is a key element in maintaining balance. The head is relatively heavy and is our highest point. Therefore, even relatively small deviance from optimal will impair balance. To find out for yourself, stand up. Then move your head back about one inch, the distance from the tip of your index finger to the first knuckle. You will find yourself tensing up your back and feeling as if you are going to fall over backward. People whose balance is poor often do something very curious with their head. In response to the threat of falling, they look down toward their feet. This better view of the ground gives them a better sense of security, yet at the same time it makes them more likely to fall by tipping the head and torso forward. It is important, therefore, to learn to balance your head properly and also to realize when you are poorly positioned.

The following lesson will clarify the relationship of the head and pelvis. It will also help you position your head more optimally. When you internalize this optimal position, you will know when you are out of position and will have the tools to get back toward optimal.

ATM: RELATING HEAD AND PELVIS

1. Sit in a chair that has a firm flat bottom. **Gently tilt your head back (arch your neck) and then lower it so your chin goes toward your sternum (breastbone).** Go only as far as you can comfortably. *Do not force your head back or push to touch your chin to your sternum.* Just allow yourself to feel what your comfortable range is. Repeat this movement two times. Pause a moment.

   Now begin rocking your pelvis forward and backward so that your back rounds and arches. Do this three times. *Be certain that you lead this movement with your pelvis.* Pause and rest for a moment.

2. **Slowly turn your head left and right several times.** How far does it go in each direction? How easy is it to turn your head?

   Raise your right hip slightly. Did you do this by lifting up on the right or putting the weight down through your left buttock? **Raise your right hip two more times, focusing on putting the weight down through the left buttock.** Pause and rest.

   Now raise the left hip slightly three times, focusing on putting the weight down through the right buttock. Stop and rest. Notice how you are sitting now. How is your weight distributed? How heavy does your head feel?

3. **Slowly rock your pelvis forward, arching the back as you tilt your head upward.** Repeat this four times, pausing after each movement for as long as it takes to make the movement. Did you lead this movement with your pelvis or your head?

   Repeat this movement and switch the lead. How did this feel? Can you tell now why it is preferable to lead with the powerful pelvic muscles when there is a choice? **Arch your back and look down with your head (round your neck).** Repeat this three times. Pause for a moment.

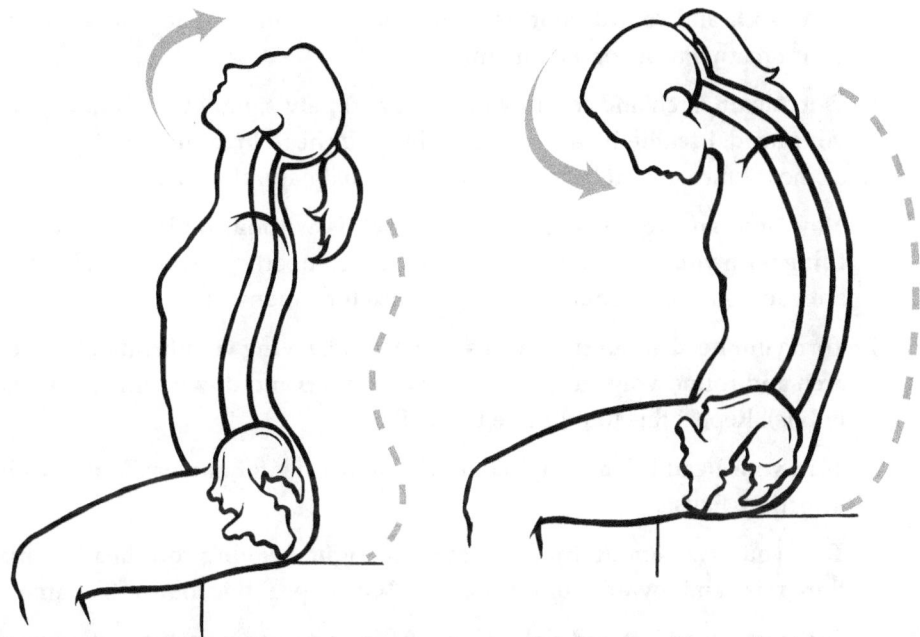

Now combine the two movements so that you rock forward and back with your pelvis as you look up and down. Go slowly and see if you can allow this to be a unified movement where both the head and pelvis move through their range at the same time. Repeat four times. Sense how you are sitting now. What are your thought patterns like now?

4. **Turn your head to the left as you raise your right hip.** Repeat this four times, having the sense that the weight goes down through the left hip to lift the right.

   Now turn your head to the right as your left hip rises. What does your chest do as you make this movement? Repeat the movement four more times. Pause for a moment.

   Combine these movements so your head goes left and right as the opposite hip rises. Repeat three to five times until you have a sense that this is smooth and easy. Rest.

   With your head in the center, raise and lower your head and pelvis twice. How does this feel now?

   This is the end of this module. It is a logical place to stop if you cannot do all of this lesson in one sitting. Resume at **step 5**.

5. Sit forward and be aware of your breathing. **Arch and round your neck and pelvis, leading with the pelvis.** Notice that you tend to breathe in as the head goes up and breathe out as the head goes down. **Deliberately breathe in as the head goes up and out as it goes down.** Repeat this combination three or four more times. Pause.

HEAD AND NECK ▪ 111

Now arch and round your neck and pelvis. Notice what you are doing with your breath. Pause for a moment.

6. **Once again, arch and round your neck and pelvis, only this time as you lower your head, breathe in, and as you raise your head breathe out.** Repeat this four or more times until it begins to feel somewhat natural. Pause.

   Now arch and round your neck and pelvis without deliberately doing anything with your breath. How does this feel compared to when you began? What are you doing with your breathing? Pause for a moment.

7. **Turn your head about two inches to the left. Leaving your head in this position, arch and round your neck and pelvis (look up and down with your head and pelvis).** Repeat this four or five times. Pause.

   Turn your head left and right, and compare how far and easily it goes in each direction. Pause.

8. **Turn your head about three inches to the right. Leaving your head in this position, raise and lower your head and pelvis.** Repeat this four or five times.

   Turn your head left and right. Compare how it goes in each direction now.

   With your head in the center, arch and round your neck and pelvis twice. How does this feel now?

   This is the end of this module. It is a logical place to stop if you cannot do all of this lesson in one sitting. Resume at **step 9**.

9. Sit forward in your chair. **Simultaneously turn your head about two inches to the left and arch your neck and pelvis.** Repeat this four times. Each time, see if you can do this in a smoother, more continuous manner. Be as aware and smooth as you return to neutral as when you go upward.

   Now make a similar movement going downward. Repeat this three or four times, smoothly. Pause.

10. **Turn your head left and right.** How is it? **Simultaneously turn your head about two inches to the right, and arch your neck and pelvis.** Repeat this four times. Again, see if you can find a way to make it smoother each time. Pause.

    Now make a similar movement going downward. Repeat this three or four times, smoothly. Pause.

11. **Look up while turning your head to the right two inches then back through neutral and then look down while again turning your head to the right two inches.** Repeat this four or five times then rest for a moment.

    Now turn your head left and right and compare to earlier.

12. **Look up while turning your head to the left two inches then back through neutral and then look down while again turning your head to the left two inches.** Is this as smooth as the arc to the right? Repeat three or four times, pausing between every other arc to avoid a mechanical feeling.

Again, turn your head left and right. Has anything changed since last time?

Look up and down with the head and pelvis and see what this is like. Pause.

This is the end of this module. It is a logical place to stop if you cannot do all of this lesson in one sitting. Resume at **step 13**.

13. **Look up and down with your head and pelvis.** Did you stay in the range that was easy? How far was this? How much effort did you use?

    Now, look up with your head as you round your back. If this is difficult, think of gazing at the stars. Repeat four or more times until this feels easy. Pause.

    Look down with your head (round your neck) as you arch your back. Repeat four times and pause for a moment.

14. **Look up and down with your head as your pelvis moves in opposition. That is, combine the previous two movements.** Repeat this three to four times. Does it feel more normal?

    Now go back to the simultaneous looking up and down of the head and pelvis a few more times. What is this like now? Pause.

15. **Look to the right as you lift your right hip (by putting the weight down through the left).** Repeat this four to six times until it feels very comfortable. Pause.

    Now look to the left as your left hip lifts. Repeat three or four times and pause a moment.

    Combine these movements so your head goes left as the left hip rises and then to the right as the right hip rises. Repeat four times. **Now turn your head left and right and see how far and easily it turns.** Pause and rest a moment.

16. **Round and arch your back.** Compare this with how it was when you began. In particular, how clear is the movement's origin in the pelvis? How well does the movement travel through your spine? Pause a moment.

    One last time, arch and round your neck and pelvis. What is this like now? Think of three ways in which this movement feels different. How aware are you of the role of the pelvis in this movement? When sitting erect? How straight are you sitting now? How free do your head and neck feel? Stand up and pay attention to how tall you are standing and how free your neck feels. Vocalize a little and notice what this is like. Then walk and feel what this is like in walking.

End of lesson

NECK AS EXTENSION OF THE SPINE

A stiff or sore neck not only impedes one's sound, it can also take much of the joy out of playing, as one has to work hard to overcome this impediment.

There are three spinal sections which in ascending order are lumbar, thoracic, and cervical. The cervical spine is the structural component of the neck. Just as the lower spine can be accessed by moving the head and neck, the neck can be freed up by moving the lower spine.

The following lesson allows one to free up the neck without having to directly move it. Typically, we move the head and neck relative to the torso. But we can reverse this and move the torso while stabilizing the neck. The following lesson is an exploration of our ability to free the neck without directly moving it.

ATM: NECK TURNED PASSIVELY

1. **Please lie on your back and roll your head left and right as far as it can easily go several times.** How far does your head turn easily? How much effort did this movement take? Does your head turn more readily in one direction, and if so, which one? Pause. Remember to take your time making these movements. Pausing occasionally for as long as it takes to make a movement is very helpful.

    Rotate your right leg so the knee points right and then bring the leg to stand so that your right foot is on the floor (this movement will be referred to as "place your leg[s] to standing"). **Push through your right heel to move your right knee forward (toward the ceiling) thus lifting the right hip and buttock from the floor. Allow your head to be gently rolled by this movement.** Repeat this movement nine to eleven times. Do your eyes go in the same direction as your head? Let the knee/hip movement be gentle. Allow the movement back to the floor to have the sense of returning to homebase or almost without effort. Then see if you can make the movement forward with the same sense of effortlessness. Pause, put your right leg down, and rest a minute. Compare the way your two sides feel.

2. **Place your left leg to standing (remember, this involves rotating the leg to the outside, knee points left). Move your left knee forward, by pushing through the left heel, so as to lift the left hip and buttock from the floor. Allow your head to be gently rolled by this movement. Let your eyes move in the same direction as your head.** Repeat four or five times. Again, see if you can make this movement softer as you repeat it. Then try it with your eyes closed (open if they were closed) four or five more times. Is this movement easier than the previous one where it was the right leg that was standing? How does this difference, if noticeable, relate to the difference felt earlier in turning your head. Pause, put your left leg down, and rest a minute. Compare the way your two sides feel now.

    Place both your legs to standing, shoulder width apart. Alternately move your left and right knee forward to lift the hip and buttock at the same time, allowing your head and eyes to be gently rolled by this movement. Repeat seven or eight times. Try and equalize the sense of ease in either direction, not the result. If you can allow the movement to be equally pleasurable in each direction, you may be surprised by what happens. Pause, put your legs down, and rest a minute.

3. **Place your right leg to standing. Move your right knee forward so as to lift the right hip and buttock while allowing your head and eyes to gently roll. Repeat**

six to eight times. What, if anything, do you notice in your shoulders as you make this movement? Pause, put your arms and right leg down, and rest a minute.

Place your left leg to standing. Place your arms across your chest so that your elbows are not on the floor. Move your left knee forward so as to lift the left hip and buttock from the floor. Allow your head and eyes to be gently rolled by this movement. Repeat six to eight times. How is this different from having your arms on the floor? Pause, put your left leg down, and rest a minute. Compare the way your two sides feel. Is this different from before?

4. **Again place your arms on your chest and put both legs to standing. Alternately move your knees forward to lift the hip and buttock at the same time, allowing your head and eyes to be gently rolled by this movement.** Repeat seven or eight times. Does this movement seem more even than the last time you went in both directions? Can you keep the movement easy? Pause, put your arms and legs down, and rest a minute.

Roll your head left and right as far as it can easily go several times. How far does your head turn easily now? If your head turns more readily in one direction, is it the same as before? Has the difference in ease changed? Pause and rest.

This is the end of this module. It is a logical place to stop if you cannot do the lesson in one sitting. Resume at **step 5**.

5. **Place both your legs to standing. Raise your left arm and bend it so that the forearm is over your torso. Grab your left elbow with your right hand. Gently pull your left arm to the right three or four inches. Allow your head to be moved to the right slightly from this movement.** Repeat nine to eleven times. How well does your head move with this shoulder? Can you let your left shoulder soften a little more each time you do this movement? Can you also let your neck soften as you do this movement? Pause, put your arms back down by your side and put your legs down, and rest a minute.

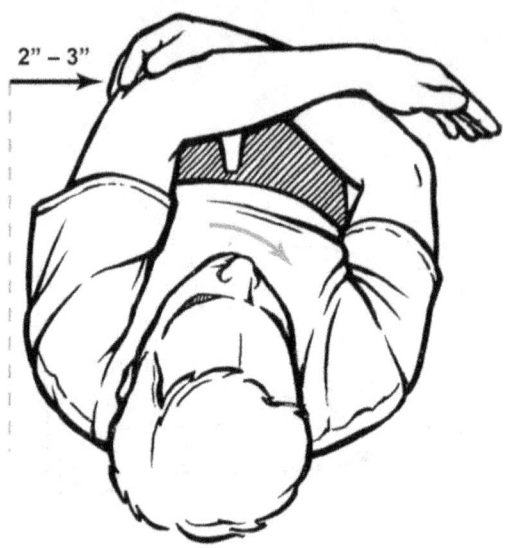

6. **Place both your legs to standing. Raise your right arm and bend it so that the forearm is over your torso. Grab your right elbow with your left hand. Gently pull your right arm to the left about the same distance you pulled the left arm to the right in the previous movement (step 5). See if you can make the sense of effort equal to that in the previous movement, rather than trying to equal the movement. Allow your head to be moved to the left slightly from this movement.** Repeat eight to ten times. Are you able to soften your neck as readily in this direction as you did the other way? Go slowly enough so that you can clearly feel the connection between the movement of the shoulder and that of the neck. Pause, put your arms back down by your side and put your legs down, and rest a minute.

   Place both your legs to standing. Raise both your arms forward and bend them across your torso. Grab your left elbow with your right hand and your right elbow with your left hand. Gently pull your arms left and right. Aim for an equal sense of ease in each direction. Allow your head to be moved by this movement. Repeat six to eight times. How far into your back do you sense this movement? See if you can let this be like a dance going left and right with a feeling of grace and ease. Allow this gentle back and forth movement to sharpen your focus and lull your mind so that those many thoughts: "How long have I been doing this? Can I get everything I need to do, done today? Can the cow really jump over the moon?" recede into the background and your mind becomes quieter. Pause, put your arms back down by your side and put your legs down, and rest a minute.

7. **Place your right leg to standing. Raise your right arm and bend it so that the forearm is over your torso. Grab your right elbow with your left hand. Gently pull your right arm to the left about three to four inches. Again, allow your head to move.** Repeat six to eight times. Does the left leg being long make the movement of the head easier than before? Where do you feel softer moving now? Are you able to allow the movement to the left and the return to the center to feel

equal in effort? Pause, put your leg down and put your arms back down by your side, and rest.

Place your left leg to standing. Raise your left arm and bend it so that the forearm is over your torso. Grab your left elbow with your right hand. Gently pull your left arm to the right about three to four inches. Allow your head to move. Repeat six to eight times. How stable does your left leg feel as you move your arms? Pause, put your leg down and put your arms back down by your side, and rest.

8. **Place both your legs to standing. Raise both your arms and bend them. Grab your left elbow with your right hand and your right elbow with your left hand. Gently pull your arms left and right. Aim for an equal sense of ease in each direction. Allow your head to be moved by this movement.** Repeat four or five times. How easy is this movement now? Pause, put your arms back down by your side and put your legs down, and rest a minute.

    Roll your head left and right as far as it easily goes several times. How far does your head turn easily now? If your head turns more readily in one direction, is it the same as before? Has the difference in ease changed? Pause and rest.

    This is the end of this module. It is a logical place to stop if you cannot do the lesson in one sitting. Resume at **step 9**.

9. **Slowly extend your left leg as far as is comfortable pushing the heel downward as you make this movement. Allow your head to turn as part of this movement.** Repeat nine to eleven times. Let this be a slow luxurious lengthening. Stop and rest a minute. Notice any changes.

    Now slowly extend your right leg as far as is comfortable, pushing the heel downward as you make this movement. Allow your head to turn as part of this movement. Repeat eight to ten times. Are you able to lengthen this side more easily as you continue the movement? Is this side easier than the left? How well can you feel the connection between lengthening and the movement of your head? Stop and rest a minute.

10. **Alternate between extending your left leg and your right leg. See if you can equalize the sense of effort between the two sides. Allow your head to gently turn in response to this movement.** Repeat seven to nine times. Pause and rest a minute.

11. **Place both your legs to standing. Raise your left arm and bend it so that the forearm is over your torso. Grab your left elbow with your right hand. Gently pull your left arm to the right three or four inches. At the same time, move your left knee forward so as to lift the left hip and buttock from the floor. Allow your head to be gently rolled by this movement.** Repeat seven to nine times. How well do you feel you combine these two movements? Does it provide more impetus for your head to move? Pause, put your arms and legs down, and rest a minute.

12. **Place both your legs to standing. Raise your right arm and bend it so that the forearm is over your torso. Grab your right elbow with your left hand. Gently pull your right arm to the left three or four inches. At the same time, move your right knee forward so as to lift the right hip and buttocks from the floor. Allow your head to be gently rolled by this movement.** Repeat six to eight times. Do you lead this movement with your arm or your hip? Pause, put your arms and legs down, and rest a minute.

   Roll your head left and right as far as it can easily go several times. How far does your head turn easily now? If your head turns more readily in one direction, is it the same as before? Has the difference in ease changed? Pause and rest.

   This is the end of this module. It is a logical place to stop if you cannot do the lesson in one sitting. Resume at **step 13**.

13. **Place your right leg to standing. Place your left palm on your forehead. Move your right knee forward while rolling your head to the right with your hand. Go slowly and gently as you make this movement.** Repeat eight to ten times. Let your neck be soft so that, as much as possible, the moving of the neck is performed by the left hand and arm. How long do you feel you are as you make this movement? Pause, put your hand and leg down, and rest at least a minute.

14. **Place your left knee to standing. Place your right palm on your forehead. Move your left knee forward while rolling your head to the left with your hand. Go slowly and gently as you make this movement.** Repeat four or five times. Pause. **Now make the same movement, only pause with your head to the left and take in a full breath before returning to neutral.** Repeat three or four times. What do you notice when you breathe in like this? Pause, put your hand and leg down, and rest a minute.

15. **Place your left knee to standing. Place your left palm on your forehead. Move your left knee forward while rolling your head to the right with your hand.** Repeat six to eight times. Notice whether you lead with your leg or hand in making this movement. Can you reverse the lead? Pause for a short while. **Resume the movement, trying to make the hand and leg move simultaneously.** Hint: Pay attention to your breath. Repeat two or three times. Pause, put your hand and leg down, and rest a minute.

16. **Place your right leg to standing. Place your right palm on your forehead. Move your right knee forward while rolling your head to the left with your hand.** Repeat eight to ten times. Once you know what your usual tendency is in leading this movement try the other options from **step 15**. Is the movement smoother on this side? Pause, put your hand and leg down, and rest a minute.

    Place both your legs to standing. Alternately move your right and left knee forward to lift the hip and buttock at the same time, allowing your head and eyes to be gently rolled by this movement. Repeat three or four times. What does the movement feel like now? Pause, put your legs down, and rest.

Roll your head left and right as far as it can easily go several times. How far does your head turn easily now? If your head turns more readily in one direction, is it the same as before? Has the difference in ease changed? How does your back feel against the floor? Pause and rest.

Stand up, walk around for a minute, and notice any changes.

End of lesson

HEADACHES

The predominant type of headache is a tension headache. It is caused when tension tightens the neck muscles, restricting the flow of blood to the brain. There are numerous other causes for headaches, the most common of which are sinus problems and eyestrain. If pressing on the sinus areas below the eyes is very painful or if the headache worsens significantly if you look down with your head, it is likely that you have a sinus headache. The most pernicious common headache is the migraine. Migraines can debilitate sufferers for up to several days. Fortunately, most people do not suffer from migraines. Some causes of headaches—stroke, brain aneurysm, tumor—can be life-threatening. Therefore, severe headaches that come on suddenly and do not let up or repeated headaches that occur for no clear reason are a medical problem, and you should consult a doctor immediately.

The following mini-lesson is superb at relieving tension headaches. It may also help a migraine if you can do the lesson before the migraine has progressed to nausea. If you have a sinus headache, the mini-lesson may actually make it feel worse. The lesson works by showing the nervous system that there is excess tension in the muscles of the back of the neck and occiput. This tension is then released, lengthening the muscles. The release of tension ends the constriction of blood to the brain that is causing the headache. Experience indicates that if you can touch your chin to your sternum, you cannot have a tension headache. And if you do have a tension headache and free the neck enough to touch your chin to your sternum, the headache will disappear. Some people cannot touch their chin to their sternum. Fortunately, that is not a prerequisite for not having a tension headache. Rather, a significant lengthening will result in considerable reduction, if not termination, of the pain. This lesson can sometimes stop headaches as they begin.

MINI-ATM: RELEASING THE NECK

1. Sit on a flat chair. **Look up and down.** Notice how far you can go. **Then look up. Stay in this position and open your mouth.** You will feel your head go back a little further. **Close your mouth while keeping your head in this new position, if you can without strain.** Repeat this sequence slowly three more times. If your head does not shift position on the repetitions, that is alright. *Do not force any movement!* **Bring your head back to neutral and pause for a minute.**

2. **Look down. Stay in this position, open your mouth, and then close it.** You will likely feel your head drop slightly when your mouth closes. **Stay in this new position as you open your mouth again.** Repeat this sequence slowly two more times. **Then return your head to neutral and pause a minute.**

3. **Look up. Stay in this position and look down only with your eyes.** Do this lightly so that you do not strain your eyes. **Then look up again with your eyes.** Does your head go back a little further? **Stay in this new position as you look down with your eyes again.** Repeat this sequence slowly two more times. **Then return your head to neutral and pause a minute.**

4. **Look down. Stay in this position and look up only with your eyes. Then look down again with your eyes.** Does your head go down more? **Stay in this new position as you look up with your eyes again.** Repeat this sequence slowly two more times. **Then return your head to neutral and pause a minute. Look up and down, moving your head.** How much more range do you have now? If you had a headache, what is it like now? Slowly stand and walk around for a minute. Notice how your head moves as you walk.

End of lesson

You may find that **steps 1** and **2** are sufficient. If so, then there is no need to continue. Also if the second two, involving the eyes work, better for you, start with them.

CHAPTER 12

Hands and Mouth

The muscles of the hand connect, indirectly but closely, to the shoulder muscles. Tightness in one will inevitably result in tightness in the other. The most common hand pain problem, carpal tunnel syndrome, is an example of this interrelation. The presenting problem is that the nerve passing through the carpal tunnel is inflamed. Medical doctors will try to reduce the inflammation with drugs or, failing that, use surgery to enlarge the tunnel. The procedure does work, though usually with some reduced mobility in the wrist and a period of considerable discomfort and rehabilitation. However, in the preponderance of cases, *the problem is not actually in the carpal tunnel but in the shoulder or even the lower back!* If the shoulder problem is resolved, the carpal tunnel syndrome usually goes away. The wrist troubles occur because it is possible to overuse the wrist to compensate for weakness or dysfunction in the shoulder. If you pick up a small hammer and make pounding movements, you will realize this. You can make the entire movement with your wrist (note how much this strains the wrist). Or you can make the movement entirely from the shoulder and observe how much wrist strain there is. Or you can try a combination of wrist and shoulder movements.

This is an example of an important movement rule: you want power to come from the largest and best leveraged muscles available, then smaller, more local musculature is available to provide precision.

Sam created a lesson for a lovely woman in his class named Melanie. She had been dealing with rheumatoid arthritis for over thirty years and was facing surgery on her thumb. The lesson was taught with the class lying on the floor. The effect was profound: her curled-up hand opened and lay flat on the floor. As a result of this change, she no longer needed surgery.

Here is that lesson, designed to provide freedom in the hand and wrist.

ATM: MOBILE WRISTS, AKA "MEL'S LESSON"

0. If you do this lesson on the floor, bend your knees when not resting. **Raise your arms and alternate reaching forward with each arm.** Pause. How easy is this? How far did the arms go?

1. **Place your left hand on your belly. Grab your left elbow with your right hand. If you can't reach the elbow, move your left hand further to the right. Gently move your elbow forward and back.** Repeat this movement five or six times. Put your arms down and pause.

2. **Place your right hand on your belly. Grab your right elbow with your left hand. If you can't reach the elbow, move your right hand further to the left. Gently move your elbow forward and back.** Repeat this movement six or seven times. Put your arms down and rest.

   Round and arch your back. Repeat six or seven times, noticing how you breathe as you make this movement. Pause for a moment.

   Put your hands on your knees and resume rounding and arching your back. Repeat six to seven times. Pay attention to the interaction between your torso and your shoulders as you make this movement. Stop and rest.

3. **Interlace your fingers and put them on your belly. In this position, slowly and gently move your right elbow forward and back.** Repeat this movement seven or eight times. Take your fingers apart, put your arms down, and rest. Compare your two arms. Do they feel the same length?

   Interlace your fingers and put them on your belly. In this position, slowly and gently move your left elbow forward and back. Repeat this movement six or seven times. Take your fingers apart, put your arms down, and rest. How do your two arms feel now?

4. **Interlace your fingers and put them on your belly. In this position, slowly and gently move both your elbows forward and back.** Repeat this movement seven or more times. Let your awareness move from your hands, your shoulders, and elbows, breathing as you make this movement. Stop, put your arms down, and rest.

   Raise your arms and alternate reaching forward with each arm. What is this like now? Put your arms down and rest.

   This is the end of this module. It is a logical place to stop if you cannot do all of this lesson in one sitting. Resume at **step 5**.

5. **Interlace your fingers the non-habitual way and put them on your belly.** (Switch pinkys from the habitual and then continue to switch positions of your other fingers.) **In this position, slowly and gently move your left elbow forward and back.** Repeat this movement six or seven times. How was this different from when you had the habitual interlacing? Pause in position for a moment.

   Now slowly and gently move your right elbow forward and back. Repeat this movement five or six times. Pause in position for a moment.

   Now slowly and gently move both your elbows forward and back. Repeat this movement seven or more times. Let your awareness move from your hands, shoulders, and elbows, breathing as you make this movement. What do you notice that is different with this interlacing? Stop, put your arms down, and rest.

6. **Interlace your fingers and put them on your belly. In this position, slowly and gently move both your elbows forward and back.** Repeat three or four times, noticing what, if anything, has changed since the last time you did this. Stop, put your arms down, and rest.

7. **Bend your left forearm so that it faces forward and is parallel to the floor. Drop your shoulder blade (scapula) to lift the forearm at a slight angle and then raise the shoulder blade.** Repeat this movement five or six times very slowly and carefully. This is a small, very unusual, and silly movement. (It might feel like a Praying Mantis.) If you can't smile while doing this movement, you are working too hard. Pause, put your arm down, and rest briefly.

    Bend your right forearm so that it faces forward and is parallel to the floor. Drop your shoulder blade to lift the forearm at a slight angle and then raise the shoulder blade. Repeat this movement five or six times gently. How does this compare to the movement on the left? Pause, put your arm down, and rest a moment.

    Raise both your forearms parallel to the floor. Alternate raising one shoulder blade then the other. Repeat five or six times. Put your arms down and rest. How are you breathing?

8. **Interlace your fingers and put them on your belly. In this position, slowly and gently move your right elbow forward and back. Breathe in as your elbow moves forward and out as it moves back.** Repeat this movement seven or eight times. Take your fingers apart, put your arms down, and rest.

    Interlace your fingers and put them on your belly. In this position, slowly and gently move your left elbow forward and back. Breathe in as your elbow moves forward and out as it moves back. Repeat this movement six or seven times. Take your fingers apart, put your arms down, and rest. How do your two arms feel now?

    Interlace your fingers and put them on your belly. In this position, slowly and gently move both your elbows forward and back. Repeat this movement seven or more times. Let your awareness move where it is drawn as you make this movement. Stop, put your arms down, and rest. How did the movement feel this time?

    Raise your arms and alternate reaching forward with each arm. What is this like now? Put your arms down and rest.

    This is the end of this module. It is a logical place to stop if you cannot do all of this lesson in one sitting. Resume at **step 9**.

9. **Raise your right arm and bend your elbow so that it is in front of your torso. Grab your right elbow with your left arm. With your left arm, guide your right arm to the left three to four inches.** Repeat seven or eight times. What do you do with your breathing as you make this movement? Look to find ways to make the movement more enjoyable as you repeat it. Put your arms down and rest.

Raise your left arm and bend your elbow so that it is in front of your torso. Grab your left elbow with your right arm. With your right arm, guide your left arm to the right three to four inches. Repeat six or seven times. What do you notice happening in your shoulder blades as you make this movement? Put your arms down and rest.

10. **Put your hands on your knees and round and arch your back.** Repeat six to seven times. Pay attention to the interaction between your torso and your shoulders as you make this movement. Is it clearer than before? Do you notice anything different about the movement? Stop and rest.

11. **Interlace your fingers and put them on your belly. In this position, slowly and gently move your right elbow forward and back. Breathe in as your shoulder moves forward and out as it moves back.** Repeat this movement seven or eight times. Take your fingers apart, put your arms down and rest.

    Interlace your fingers and put them on your belly. In this position, slowly and gently move your left elbow forward and back. Breathe in as your shoulder moves forward and out as it moves back. Repeat this movement six or seven times. Take your fingers apart, put your arms down, and rest. How do your two arms feel now?

12. **Interlace your fingers and put them on your belly. In this position, slowly and gently move both your elbows forward and back.** Repeat this movement seven or more times. Be aware of how your wrists are feeling. What changes do you notice? Stop, put your arms down, and rest. How did the movement feel this time?

    Raise your arms and alternate reaching forward with each arm. What is this like now? Put your arms down and rest.

    This is the end of this module. It is a logical place to stop if you cannot do all of this lesson in one sitting. Resume at **step 13**.

13. **Raise your right arm and bend your elbow so that it is in front of your torso. Grab your right elbow with your left arm. With your left arm, guide your right arm to the left three to four inches. At the same time, look to the left.** Repeat three or four times. **Make a fist with your right hand.** Continue the movement two more times. **Let go of the fist.** Make another two movements. What happens to your breathing as you make this movement? Look to find ways to make the movement more enjoyable as you repeat it. Put your arms down and rest.

    Raise your left arm and bend your elbow so that it is in front of your torso. Grab your left elbow with your right arm. With your right arm, guide your left arm to the right three to four inches. At the same time, look to the right. Repeat three or four times. Find ways to make this movement fluid and easy. **Make a soft fist with your right hand.** Continue the movement two more times. **Let go of the fist.** Make another two movements. What do you do with your eyes as you move your head? Pause, put your arms down, and rest.

14. **Interlace your fingers and put them behind your head. Move your left elbow forward and back.** Repeat six or seven times. Let the movement be easy. How

does this position change the movement in the wrist? What do you notice in your shoulders? Put your arms down and rest.

Interlace your fingers and put them behind your head. Move your right elbow forward and back. Repeat six or seven times. Aim for the same sense of ease you felt on the left. Notice your breathing. Put your arms down and rest.

Interlace your fingers and put them behind your head. Move both elbows forward and back. Try this with both alternating elbows and with both together. Repeat at least six times. What happens in your spine when you move both elbows together? What did you notice about alternating elbows that was different from moving them together? Put your arms down and rest.

15. **Raise your right arm and bend your elbow so that it is in front of your torso. Grab your right elbow with your left arm. With your left arm, guide your right arm to the left. At the same time, look to the right. Continue with your head moving opposite your arms.** Repeat seven or eight times. What happens to your breathing as you make this movement? Look to find ways to make the movement more enjoyable as you repeat it. Put your arms down and rest.

    Raise your left arm and bend your elbow so that it is in front of your torso. Grab your left elbow with your right arm. With your right arm, guide your left arm to the right. At the same time, look to the left. Continue with your head moving opposite your arms. Repeat six or seven times. Find ways to make this movement fluid and easy. What happens to your sense of height as you move your head to the left? Pause, put your arms down, and rest.

16. **Interlace your fingers and put them on your belly. In this position, slowly and gently move your right elbow forward and back.** Repeat this movement seven or eight times. How are your fingers moving? What do you notice in your wrists? Take your fingers apart, put your arms down, and rest.

    Interlace your fingers and put them on your belly. In this position, slowly and gently move your left elbow forward and back. Repeat this movement six or seven times. What are your fingers doing with this movement? Take your fingers apart, put your arms down, and rest. How do your two arms feel now?

    Interlace your fingers and put them on your belly. In this position, slowly and gently move both your elbows forward and back. Repeat this movement seven or more times. Be aware of how your wrists are feeling. What changes do you notice? What were you doing with your breathing? Stop, put your arms down, and rest. How did the movement feel this time?

    Raise your arms and alternate reaching forward with each arm. What is this like now? Put your arms down and rest. How long do your arms feel?

    Stand up and walk around for a minute. Notice how your hips move now. What are your arms doing?

End of lesson

There is an intimate connection between the hands and shoulders. The following short mini-lesson, which is an excellent warm-up, involves this relationship in freeing up the fingers. Every instrumentalist relies on finger mobility and accuracy to perform. The fingers themselves are connected muscularly all the way up to the shoulder.

On a recent vacation, I (Sam) became friendly with a fellow who was an amateur guitarist. When I found out he played, I asked what his biggest physical problem was when playing. He said tightness in his fingers. I thought about it and the next morning put together this short lesson. When I taught it to him that day, he was quite pleased.

MINI-ATM: FAST FINGER RELEASE

An audio lesson is available at https://on.soundcloud.com/NouE4.

1. **Hold your right arm with your left hand just above the elbow. Gently raise your right arm and shoulder straight up with your left, until the movement feels sticky or discontinuous in the shoulder (from the rest of this lesson when you lift your arm, this is the point to stop lifting and begin letting down).** The shoulder goes up parallel to the neck and the arm remains parallel to the torso. This is a small movement, no more than three to four inches. Repeat this three times. Pause and **let go of the right arm.** Compare the left and right sides.

   Now make a soft fist and lift the right arm in the same manner as before, using only the muscles of the right arm. Let the arm down in a slow relaxed fashion, simultaneously opening the fist, a controlled letting go. Repeat three times and pause. Pause. Compare your two sides.

2. Reprise step 1, only lifting and releasing the left arm.

3. **With your arms hanging downward, slowly extend the fingers of your left hand.** This is a soft gentle movement. You may do all the fingers at once or each one sequentially,

whatever appeals to you now. Repeat this three or four times, slowly, taking a couple of breaths between repetitions.[1] Pause and compare your two sides.

4. Reprise step 3, only extending the fingers of the right hand.

End of lesson

RELATIONSHIP OF THE HANDS AND TONGUE

One of the more surprising close neurological relationships is the one between the tongue and the hands. Dr. Nelson first became aware of this during the third year of his Feldenkrais training. One of his trainers was giving a lesson to another member of the class. She had sat up when all of a sudden, her hands locked up. She could not move them; they were extremely tense and uncomfortable.

The trainer said that there was an important connection between the hands and tongue and requested a piece of paper towel. The trainer grabbed the student's tongue using the paper towel. Then he manipulated her tongue very gently. You could see her hands relax. After three or four minutes, her hands had returned to normal. The trainer explained that there were two reasons for this close connection: first, as the fetus develops, the hands and tongue are joined and then bud off from each other. Second, both are highly represented in the sensory system, and these representations are very near each other.

Recent research indicates that this phenomena may be reflected in the cortex. Neurobiologists at Duke University have identified a previously uncharted area of the cortex, which they are calling the "oromanual region" in mice, that coordinates movement between the two. They suspect this region is also found in humans. It could help explain why so many people gesture as they talk, and why children learning to write often twist their tongues as their fingers shape letters.[2]

While relaxation anywhere in the system relaxes it everywhere, as we noted before, the relationship between tongue and hands is a much closer and tighter connection. Very early in our collaboration, Dr. Nelson took advantage of this during a voice lesson with Dr. Blades. She noted that there was a great deal of tension and "thickness" in his tongue. Then she watched, with considerable surprise, as Dr. Nelson spent several minutes doing hand manipulations. When he had finished and resumed vocalizing, the tongue tension was gone.

The following mini-lesson will help clarify the hands.

MINI-ATM: CLARIFYING THE HANDS

1. Sit with your hands on your knees. Take a few easy breaths. Put your dominant hand palm down on the thigh of the same side leg.

    Take your other hand, hold the fingers lightly together, and place the end of the little finger just below the wrist on the outside of the hand. This will be just below the large prominence. Using the tip of your little finger, slide your hand along the outside of the little finger bones of your dominant hand. As you proceed along

the hand, allow the other fingers to slide along as well. **Then reverse direction.** Go up and down slowly six or more times, taking at least one breath between each iteration. Pause for at least three breaths.

Move the sliding fingers to where the ring finger bones originate at the wrist. Again, slide the little finger along the bones of the finger to the end and back. Let the other fingers of the sliding hand participate where it happens easily and naturally. Go up and down slowly six or more times. Pause again for at least two breaths.

Continue to slide your finger along the bones of the remaining three fingers in the same fashion. Each time, go up and down slowly six or more times. **Then pause briefly before moving to the next finger.** Rest, after sliding your fingertip(s) along the thumb. Notice any differences in the way your two sides feel.

2. **Take your other hand and place the palm just above the wrist of the dominant hand. Now slide the palm along this hand past the end, bring the sliding hand back to the wrist.** It's as if you were washing your hands. Repeat at least four times. Rest. Let both your arms hang down. What differences, if any, do you notice?

3. Put your other hand palm down on the other leg.

   Take your dominant hand, hold the fingers lightly together and place the end of the little finger just below the wrist on the outside of the hand. Using the tip of your little finger, slide your hand along the outside of the little finger bones of your dominant hand as you did with the other hand. Then reverse direction. Go up and down slowly six or more times. Pause for two or three breaths.

   Continue to slide your finger along the bones of the remaining three fingers and the thumb in the same fashion. Each time, go up and down slowly six or more times. Pause for two or three breaths before moving to the next finger. Rest after sliding your fingertip(s) along the thumb.

4. **Take your other hand and place the palm just above the wrist of the dominant hand. Now slide the palm along this hand past the end, bring the sliding hand back to the wrist,** what we call "washing." Repeat at least four times. Rest. Let both your arms hang down. What differences, if any, do you notice from before? What is your breathing like now?

   This is the end of this module. It is a logical place to stop if you cannot do the lesson in one sitting. Resume at **step 5.**

5. Put your dominant hand palm up on the same side leg.

   Place the little finger of your other hand on the outside of your palm where it meets the wrist. Slide this finger along the line to the tip of your little finger. Allow any other finger that feels right to you to slide along as well. After your index finger (or last finger you use) reaches the tip, reverse direction and go back to where the palm meets the wrist. Go up and down slowly six or more times. Pause.

   Move the sliding fingers to where the ring finger bones originate at the wrist. Again, slide the little finger along the bones of the finger to the end and back.

Let the other fingers of the sliding hand participate where it happens easily and naturally. Go up and down slowly six or more times. Pause.

Continue to slide your finger along the bones of the remaining three fingers in the same fashion. Each time, go up and down slowly six or more times. **Then pause briefly before moving to the next finger.** Rest after sliding your fingertip(s) along the thumb.

6. **Take your other hand and place the outer edge of the palm along the palm of the dominant hand at the wrist. Slide this hand past all the fingers and return to where you began your slide.** Repeat this "washing" motion at least four times. Rest.

7. Place your other hand palm up on its leg.

    Place the little finger of your dominant hand on the outside of your palm where it meets the wrist. Slide this finger along the line to the tip of your little finger. Allow any other finger that feels right to you to slide along as well. After your index finger (or last finger you use) reaches the tip, reverse direction and go back to where the palm meets the wrist. Go up and down slowly six or more times. Pause.

    Continue to slide your finger along the bones of the remaining three fingers and the thumb in the same fashion. Each time, go up and down slowly six or more times. **Pause briefly before moving to the next finger.** Rest after sliding your fingertip(s) along the thumb.

8. **Take your dominant hand and place the outer edge of the palm along the palm of the dominant hand at the wrist. Slide this hand past all the fingers and return to where you began your slide.** Repeat this "washing" motion at least four times. Rest.

End of lesson

Because they are so highly represented in our nervous system, our hands can have a profound impact on our emotional state. The following lesson is both calming and helpful when you have trouble sleeping.

It is most impactful lying on the back, as written. However, it is quite potent when done in a chair. Just be sure the seat is flat and your feet are on the floor.

MINI-ATM: SOFTENING THE HANDS FOR CALM

An audio lesson is available at https://on.soundcloud.com/NouE4.

1. **Lie on your back.** Scan. How do you fit the floor? Where do you feel the least discomfort? Where are you most comfortable?

2. **Bend your knees and put your hands on your lower ribs with the elbows resting on the floor. Slowly lift your right thumb, index finger, middle finger, and ring finger into the air.** Thus, your pinky will act like a hinge, so that the palm is opened toward your face. **Then just as slowly put those fingers back down. Exhale as you raise your fingers and inhale as you put them down.** Repeat this movement eight

to ten times and take one or two breaths in between each iteration. Go slowly, notice the tendency of your hand to curl a little, and see if you can soften your hand as you make this motion.

Pause.

Resume the motion of lifting, starting with your thumb. With closed eyes, look down toward your hand as the thumb and other fingers rise and return eyes to neutral as you put your hand down. Repeat this four or five times, again breathing between iterations so that there is a freshness to each movement. Stop, put your arms and legs down, and rest.

3. **Bend your knees and put your hands on your lower ribs with the elbows resting on the floor. Now begin with your right pinky to lift your hand.** Slowly and gently repeat this eight to ten times, pausing between each iteration to take a full breath or two. Pause.

   Return to the movement of lifting, starting with your right pinky. What are your eyes doing? **Either continue to let the eyes look up if they are already or look up with the eyes as the back of the hand rises.** Repeat six to eight times, again with breath in between each movement. Allow the movements to be slow and soft. Pause.

   Now alternate lifting your right hand once from the pinky and then from the thumb. Gently go back and forth around ten times. Put your arms down by your sides and lengthen your legs. Compare the way your two sides feel. Rest.

4. **Bend your knees and put your hands on your lower ribs with the elbows resting on the floor. Slowly lift your left thumb, index finger, middle finger, and ring finger into the air.** Thus, your pinky will act like a hinge, so that the palm is opened toward your face. **Then just as slowly put those fingers back down. Exhale as you raise your fingers and inhale as you put them down.** Repeat this movement eight to ten times and take one or two breaths in between each iteration. Go slowly and see if you can soften your hand as you make this motion.

   Pause.

   Resume the motion of lifting, starting with your thumb. With closed eyes look down toward your hand as the thumb and fingers rise and return eyes to neutral as you put your hand down. Repeat this four or five times, again breathing between iterations so that there is a freshness to each movement. Stop, put your arms and legs down, and rest.

5. **Bend your knees and put your hands on your lower ribs with the elbows resting on the floor. Now begin with your left pinky to lift your hand.** Slowly and gently repeat this eight to ten times, pausing between each iteration to take a full breath or two. Pause.

   Return to the movement of lifting, starting with your left pinky. What are your eyes doing? **Either continue to let the eyes look up if they are already or look up with the eyes as the back of the hand rises.** Repeat six to eight times, again with breath in between each movement. Allow the movements to be slow and soft. Pause.

Now alternate lifting your left hand once from the pinky and then from the thumb. Gently go back and forth around ten times. Put your arms by your sides and lengthen your legs. Compare the way your two sides feel. Rest.

6. **Bend your knees and put your hands on your lower ribs with the elbows resting on the floor. Now move both hands simultaneously to open the palm toward the eyes and your feet. Follow the movement with your eyes.** Repeat seven to nine times. Again, remember to go slowly, gently, attentively. Pause to take a breath after every two or three movements. Pause.

   Resume moving the hands together, only now have the eyes reverse their movement so that you look at the back of the hands, then up as the palms face upwards. Repeat four or five times. Notice what this does to the ease of movement, to the tension in your eyes, and to your overall sensation. **Then return to moving the eyes to look at the palm facing upwards. Bend your knees and put your hands on your lower ribs with the elbows resting on the floor.** Repeat three or four times. What changed when you reverted back to the "preferred" way of using your eyes? Rest.

   While resting, put your hands over your eyes with the palms over the sockets and the fingers of one hand atop the other (palming).

7. **Bend your knees and put your hands on your lower ribs with the elbows resting on the floor. Now move your hands in opposition so that as the palm faces up on the right it faces down on the left and vice versa.** Go back and forth about twelve times. Notice where your eyes look. Do they shift from side to side? And if so, when? Most likely, you look at the palm facing the eyes.

   Now look the other way. Repeat four or five times. **Then revert to looking your preferred way.** Repeat three or four times and rest.

   Bend your knees and put your hands on your lower ribs with the elbows resting on the floor. Now three or four times, move your hands and eyes together. What is this like now? Pause. How are you fitting the floor? Sense your hands. How much tension do you feel in them? Check yourself for areas of tension compared to when we began. Slowly roll to your side and sit up. Can you do so without tightening your hands? Then stand. Notice what this is like. Walk around and see what this feels like.

THE MOUTH

As with the interrelationship of the head, neck, shoulders, jaw, and tongue, undue tension or inappropriate manipulation of the muscles that circle the mouth can have an adverse effect on one's sound. This is true even if you are not a woodwind/brass instrumentalist, as noted about the important connection of the tongue with the hands. The following lesson focuses on the mouth.

ATM: SOFTENING THE MOUTH

0. This lesson may be done on the floor or in a chair. The version here is for a chair to facilitate its usage in many places. To do it on the floor, lie with your legs bent and feet on the floor when doing the movements and with the legs stretched out when resting. Throughout the lesson, remember to take a breath after every one or two movements. Because you catch your lips with your hands in the second module, it is advisable to wash your hands thoroughly before doing that part of the lesson.

1. Move forward to the front of the chair. Have both feet firmly and evenly on the floor.

    Turn your head left and right. Notice how it turns. Pause.

    Notice how your face feels. How much tension is there in your neck? How are you breathing? Make a low "Ah" sound two or three times. **Now push your lips forward and allow them to come back.** Repeat fifteen to twenty times, taking a breath after every one or two times. See if you can reduce your "allowing" effort. Notice what your jaw does as you push your lips forward. Pause briefly.

2. **Push your lips forward and bring them back.** How is this different from allowing the lips to come back? Repeat eight to ten times. Again, take a breath after every one or two times your lips return. What does your tongue do as you push your lips forward? Pause for a moment.

    Push your lips forward and allow them to come back once or twice. Stop and rest for a minute.

    Sit back in your chair if you feel the need. Notice what has changed.

3. If you sat back in the chair, move forward. **Lift the corners of your lips toward your ears.** This will feel like pulling back, and will create a wide "grin." **Then let the lips relax and return to normal.** Repeat ten to fifteen times. See if this can be made to feel easier. Pause a moment.

4. **Pull your lips back and keep them there for a moment. With your right index finger, hold the right corner of your mouth. Then let the left return to neutral. Continue to hold the right corner of your mouth while the left corner of your mouth goes toward the ear and back to neutral.** Repeat eight to ten times, taking a breath between each iteration. Release the right corner of your mouth and pause for a moment. What differences do you notice between your left and right sides? Make the "Ah" sound. What differences do you notice?

5. **Pull your lips back and keep them there for a moment. With your left index finger, hold the left corner of your mouth. Then let the right return to neutral. Continue to hold the left corner of your mouth while the right corner goes toward the ear and back to neutral.** Repeat seven to nine times. Pause for a moment after releasing the left corner of your mouth.

    Now move both sides toward the ears a couple of times. What changes did you notice? Pause a moment.

Push your lips forward and allow them to come back twice. How is this different from before? Stop and rest a moment.

Turn your head left and right. What is that like now?

This is the end of this module. It is a logical place to stop if you cannot do the lesson in one sitting. Resume at **step 6**. If you stop here, walk around for a moment or two before going to another activity.

6. **With your palm facing away from you, catch your upper lip with the index finger and second finger of your dominant hand.** The first knuckle is in the middle of the lip. **Gently move your lip up and down several times.** Does it move more easily in one direction than the other? Remember to breathe between movements. Repeat this six or seven more times.

   Now move your lip left and right. Again, see if it moves more easily one way or the other. Does this have anything to do with the hand you are using? Repeat eight to ten times. See if you can make the movement more gently each time.

   Then play with your upper lip as the fancy strikes you. Continue this for about half a minute. Pause and rest.

   Push your lips out and allow them to come back twice. What changes do you notice? Pause for a minute. Notice what, if anything, feels different.

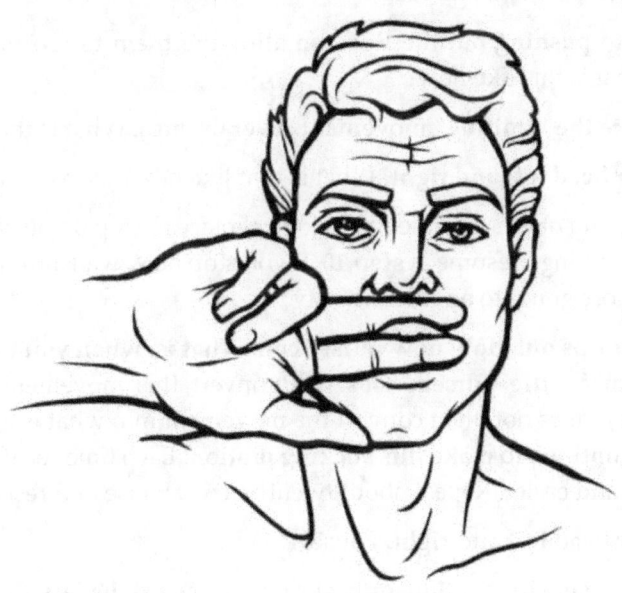

7. **With your thumb on the bottom, catch your lower lip between your thumb and your index finger. Gently move your lips up and down.** Repeat this seven or eight times. Pause while holding on to your lip.

   Now move your lip left several times and then right several times. Pause for a moment. **Then resume by going left and right.** Repeat several times. Then pause.

Finally, play with taking your lower lip up and down, right and left, and on diagonals and any other direction that appeals to you. Stop, put your hand down, and rest for a minute.

8. **With your thumb and the back of your index finger and second finger, grasp both your lips.** The index finger will be between the two lips with the first knuckle in the middle of the lips. **Gently move your lips up and down.** Notice where you feel restrictions as you do this. Repeat this seven or eight times. Pause while holding on to your lips.

    Move your lips left and right several times. Notice which direction is easier. **Then move your lips only from the center to the easier side three or four times.** Pause briefly. **Move your lips from the center to the more difficult side several times. Then move your lips left and right three or four more times.** Pause a moment. Was the movement left and right more even the second time you made it?

    Now move your lips in a circle. Keep doing this for about a minute. What else can you feel moving? Does your head move? How about your ribs? Is there anything happening in the pelvis?

    Reverse the direction and go this way for a little while. What changes when you go in this direction? Pause.

    Finally play with your lips in any way that pleases you for a short time. Stop, take your hand away, and rest.

9. **Go back to pushing out the lips and allowing them to return.** Repeat several times. What is this like now?

    Then make the "smiling" movement several times. What is this like?

    Turn your head left and right. What is that like now? Stop and rest.

    This is the end of this module. It is a logical place to stop if you cannot do the lesson in one sitting. Resume at **step 10**. If you stop here, walk around for a moment or two before going to another activity.

10. **Push your lips out, only now purse them. That is, when you bring them back, keep them a little pursed.** This will convert this movement into a sucking motion. If it does not, then convert the movement into what is a sucking motion for you. **Continue to make this sucking motion.** Each time see if you can make it smoother and easier. Repeat about twenty times. Pause and rest a moment.

11. **Turn your head left and right.** Pause.

    Resume the sucking motion, only suck over toward the left. Repeat eight to ten times and pause.

    Now suck over toward the right. Repeat seven or eight times. Pause.

    Alternate sucking left and right. After three or four repetitions, see which direction you like better. Go that way twice and then resume going left and right another four times. Pause and rest.

12. **Turn your head a little to the right and resume sucking.** Repeat eight to ten times. Do you find yourself sucking slightly off to the right when your head is turned right? Pause and rest.

    Turn your head a little to the left and suck gently. Repeat seven or eight times. Pause.

    Turn your head in the position you prefer and suck off to that side. Repeat four or five times. Pause.

    Turn your head the other way and suck in that direction four or five times. Pause.

    Suck a few times with your head in the middle. Pause and then turn your head left and right. How well can you turn now? Pause and rest a moment.

13. **Make the smiling movement with your lips three or four times.** What is it like now? Pause.

    Make the "Ah" sound. What changes do you notice?

    Push your lips forward and allow them to return two or three times. How easy was the return? What do you notice about your mouth? How does your neck feel?

    Turn your head left and right. What is that like now?

    Stand up, sense your balance, and walk around for a minute. Note how you walk and how upright you are standing.

End of lesson

NOTES

1. You may find that, as the fingers lengthen, you'll sense a consequent lengthening in the shoulder and the back. If you do, enjoy.
2. Pennisi, Elizabeth. 2023. "Tales of the Tongue." *Science* 380 (6646): 786–91.

CHAPTER 13

The Eyes

ROLE OF THE EYES IN MOVEMENT

Like other primates, we humans rely on our eyes as our dominant external sensory system for guiding movement. When we are moving, we want to see where we are going. And when we are stationary, we want to see what is around us and what is moving. This is true even when we have our eyes closed. If you close your eyes and lift your left foot, your eyes will track down and to the left. Wait until you've read the next two sentences to try this. It may be a very small movement in the eyes, so you may need to lift your foot several times to be sure you notice this eye movement. Then if you raise your right leg, the eyes will track right. This happens with no conscious thought or direction on our part. It seems to be hardwired.

The way we use our eyes, however, is learned. A newborn baby has difficulty focusing their eyes. Watching people who are blind is very revealing. People who are blind from birth do not orient using the eyes. They will not necessarily face you to listen to you, nor will they necessarily turn toward the source of a noise. This is primarily because they have never learned to do these things and feel no necessity to do so. They may also move their head in very eccentric patterns when playing or listening to music. Those who have lost their vision, even those who have no eyes, will orient themselves much more like a sighted person. This is because these movement patterns were developed when they were sighted. Once in place, the patterns will, to a great extent, persist, simply because there is no impetus to change and because the eyes also play an important role in balance. Individuals who are blind from birth never develop this aspect of balance. They rely solely on the vestibular system (which is in the ears) and touch. Those who lose their sight, however, have incorporated visual cues into their balance. Even though the eyes are not there, they will move the eye muscles as if they were. Accordingly, eccentric movements of the head will be disconcerting to them.

The role the eyes play in our learning movement is extremely important. It is how we learn to orient in space. Watching a young infant learn to roll over from its back to its front the first time or two is very instructive. Typically, there is no intent to roll. Rather, the infant is trying to track something overhead. At a certain point, the turning of the head, which is proportionately much larger in infants than adults, goes past the point of no return, and all of a sudden the baby is over on their belly. One can also watch the extreme frustration when the eyes focus the head in one direction and the baby attempts to go the other way. Thus we learn to lead with our eyes. Indeed, athletes, such as football players, make use of this by watching their opponents' eyes, which can tell them where the ball is going. Or the eyes can be used to mislead, as when a basketball player looks one way while passing another. As command of the eyes develops, we may actively use them to help us learn movement. For example, using a computer keyboard requires knowing what keys are where. Most people have to look at the keyboard as they use it, but with training, you can learn to use the keyboard while keeping your eyes on the screen.

The eyes also play an important role in maintaining balance. The main balance organ is the vestibular system. When this system is functioning properly, it is easy to maintain your balance. But if you stand up and close your eyes, you will probably feel minor oscillations forward and back—oscillations that were not present before you closed your eyes. Damage to the vestibular system makes the role of the eyes in balance vital. This can be demonstrated with a balance board, a device consisting of a board on top of five inches of heavy-duty foam. When you stand on the balance board, it is as if the ground sways. After a while, you get your balance and can stand comfortably. However, when you close your eyes, you can really feel yourself sway.

Dr. Nelson once worked with a woman, Alma, who lost the vestibular system in her right ear to surgery for a brain tumor. When Alma stood on the balance board with her eyes open, she did as well as a normal person. However, it was impossible for her to retain her balance when she closed her eyes. Her undamaged left vestibular system was insufficient for her to maintain any sense of balance.

Another way to experience the role vision plays in balance is to walk slowly across an empty space in the dark. Because you know the space is clear, you will not have to worry about bumping into anything. Thus you will become aware that some of the trepidation we feel about walking in the dark comes from feeling slightly unsteady.

Loss of the use of one eye (even if only temporary) requires important reorganization in our movement. A person using only one eye (cyclopean vision) moves the head somewhat toward the other side so that the single eye is more centrally located. There is also more turning of the head and neck to make up for the restricted field of vision. Because the hand and arm on the other side are not seen as well, there is a tendency to use them less than if both eyes were working. A one-eyed individual will also position themselves to see other people in a room, taking care to put themselves where they can see the most important person(s). When they are with one person, they will try to keep that person on the side of the seeing eye.

RELEASING MINOR NECK CRICKS

We can take advantage of the way we use our eyes to relieve minor neck cricks. As noted earlier, people with cyclopean vision keep the head turned slightly to get that eye into the center of the visual field. This stretches the neck muscles on the side of the good eye and releases the muscles on the opposite side. Typically, a crick in the neck, or minor neck pain, is caused by strained or stretched muscles on that side of the neck. If you notice this happening, close the eye on the side that pains you. If you cannot close only this eye, cover it with a patch. Then walk around for a couple of minutes, if possible. If you cannot walk, look out into the distance as if you were driving a car. Simply closing the eye usually relieves the pain in the neck because when we close just one eye, we turn our head slightly in that direction. This puts our open eye more in the center. This position also reduces the effort of the neck muscles on the side of the closed eye. As these muscles release, the pain slowly goes away.

VISUAL TENSION

Everyone has experienced some visual tension. When mild, it may result in a squint; when severe, a headache. Prolonged visual tension is believed by some to result in myopia (nearsightedness). One source of strain is bright light, particularly from the sun. Unless your eyes are truly relaxed, you will notice that you squint when you encounter bright sunlight. This is uncomfortable, so many people wear sunglasses. Aging can result in eyestrain. As we age, the lens of our eyes hardens. This makes the lens more difficult for the muscles to move. As a result, our ability to accommodate changes in focal length is drastically reduced; in particular, near vision becomes difficult. As this process progresses, people need reading glasses or bifocals, or they will very rapidly feel eyestrain.

Another source of strain is keeping the eyes focused at one distance for too long, particularly if we are focused in close. This is common in our culture, because we spend so much time viewing things at near distances. Until very recently, humans spent much of their time outside looking at the horizon. This involves keeping the head up level and open, a good position for performing. In close work, we tend to have our head down (reading as you are now is an example) or level (looking at computer monitors). While we can do this, our evolutionary development was rooted in looking out at the horizon for prolonged periods. Curiously, when we are focused out at the horizon, we feel most within ourselves. This is a well-known phenomenon among equestrians, who use a technique known as centered riding; they refer to this as "soft eyes."

The eyes are a key component of the nervous system. Indeed, we receive about 90 percent of our external sensory input from the eyes. Thus, keeping the eyes relaxed can be expected to relax our entire nervous system. Indeed, when we are visually relaxed, we feel very centered, and all the muscles in the head and jaw relax as well. As a result, our sound is open, clear, flexible, and resonant. The following lesson will allow you to feel what it is like to have relaxed eyes and what it does for your sound and sense of well-being.

ATM: RELEASING THE EYES

An audio lesson is available at https://on.soundcloud.com/NouE4.

0. Palming is a great way to reduce eye and systemic tension. It is a key technique of the Bates method, which was created in the early twentieth century to help reverse nearsightedness. It consists of closing your eyes and placing your hands on your face such that the top of the palm is on the brow ridgeline, the hands cross above the nose, and the rest of the palm encapsulates the eye socket. When

the system is truly calm, you will see a velvet black darkness without any pyrotechnics. The preferred way to come out of palming is to slowly open your eyes, and then open your hands by lifting the thumbs first then the index finger, etc. It is like opening a book.

1. Sit in a chair with a straight seat and no arms. Can you sit straight comfortably without relying on the back rest? **Now sit toward the edge of your chair. Turn your head left and right.** Did you notice that your eyes move in the same direction as your head at the same time? **Now turn your head left and right leading with the movement of the eyes.** Repeat this five or six times. Each time, look for any strain in the eyes and eye muscles. Let go of this strain as you move, if you can. Palm your eyes for a minute. Then turn your head left and right one more time and see if there is any difference.

2. **Look at the wall straight ahead of you. Fix your eyes on a point or picture straight in front of you. Now turn your head to the left about two to three inches and back. Go slowly.** Turning the head without the eyes is difficult and can be disconcerting. Repeat this three or four times. Each time, go slow and see if there is any strain in the eyes you can let go of. **Pause for a moment, close your eyes, and put your palms over them (palming). Open your eyes, then put your hands down, by opening like a book (see 0), and fix them on the same point. Now slowly turn your head to the right and back about two to three inches; do this four or five times. Pause for a moment, and palm your eyes.**

3. **Look at the wall straight ahead of you.** (Read this entire direction now as it asks you to close your eyes.) **Focus on a point or an image and close your eyes. With your eyes closed keep this image directly in front of you. Now slowly turn your head to the right about two inches. Keep the image in front of you as you do so. That is, the image moves with you so that your eyes do not move relative to your head. Then return to the center. Repeat this three or four times and pause for as long as it takes to do two movements. Now do the same thing to the left. Move about two inches and return, keeping the eyes on an image that is moving with you.** Repeat this three or four times and pause for as long as two movements. **Moving in this same fashion, move your head left and right three or four times.** Pause for two movements, and slowly open your eyes.

4. **Turn your head left and right.** Pause. How far did you go? How easy was it? What do you notice about your breathing? Where do you feel your center? Has there been any change in your sense of yourself? **Now turn your head left and right leading with the eyes.** What changes do you notice? **Sit back in your chair and rest.**

This is the end of this module. It is a logical place to stop if you cannot do the lesson in one sitting. Resume at **step 5**.

5. **Sit on the edge of your chair. Put your right hand on your right knee. Move your right knee forward without moving your foot. Allow the head and eyes to turn with this movement. Repeat three or four times and then put your right hand by your side.** Pause and notice any differences.

Now put your left hand on your left knee and move your knee forward. Again, let the head and eyes move with the movement of the knee. Do you feel any up and down movement? Repeat three or four more times and see if you feel any up or down movement. Pause and rest for a moment.

6. **Put your left hand on your left knee and your right hand on your right knee and slowly move first the left and then the right knee forward.** Repeat this five or six times. Notice differences between the way you go to the left and to the right. Does being aware of these differences, no matter how slight, change anything? Stop and rest for a moment.

7. Read this entire direction before you begin it. **Close your eyes. Slowly move your right knee forward about one or two inches. Let your eyes move with the head and knee. Return the knee to the starting point and repeat three or four times**. Pause with your eyes closed for two cycles of movement.

   Now slowly move your left knee forward about one or two inches. Do this pattern three or four times. Pause, keeping your eyes closed for two cycles of movement. Finally, alternate moving the left and right knee forward three or four times. **Stop and palm your eyes.** After you open your eyes, notice how you are breathing. Where do you sense your center? What is the quality of noise you perceive?

8. **Put your hands on your knees and once again alternately move your knees forward three or four times.** Pause. How easy is this now? How do you feel your eyes moving? What else do you notice? **Then turn your head left and right.** Has this changed? Sit back in your chair and rest awhile. **Now turn your head left and right, leading with the eyes**. What changes do you notice? Sit back in your chair and rest.

   This is the end of this module. It is a logical place to stop if you cannot do the lesson in one sitting. Resume at **step 9**.

9. **Sit forward on your chair. Put your hand (whichever hand you prefer) in front of you about one foot from your face with the palm toward your face. Move your hand toward your face and then away to full extension of the arm. At some point, as you move away from your face, turn your hand so your palm

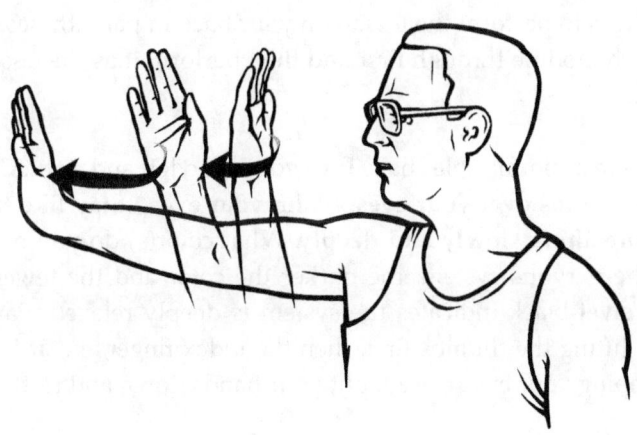

faces outward. You will sense where a good place to turn is for you. Repeat this movement three or four times, following it with your eyes. Perform the movement gracefully, like a Balinese dancer. **Put your hand down and pause for a moment with your eyes closed.**

10. Read both steps 10 and 11 before you do them. **Again place your hand a foot from your face, palm inward. Close your eyes. Move your hand toward your face slowly. Then slowly move it away. Feel where you want to turn your hand to get a more complete extension of the arm. Turn your hand at that place. Then bring your hand toward your face, turning at the appropriate place. Follow this movement with your (closed) eyes.** Repeat five or six times. Go slowly, gently, and with a sense of grace. **Pause with your hand about a foot from your face.**

11. **Continue to follow the movement with your closed eyes. Now move your hand about a foot to the outside and back to the middle.** Slowly and gently repeat this four or five times.

    Then carefully cross your midline and move your hand about a foot in the other direction and back to the middle four or five times. Finally, move your hand all the way left and right attentively four or five times. Follow the hand with your eyes. Pause for a minute and palm your eyes.

    Softly open your eyes. Put your arms down and rest.

12. **Raise your hand and follow it once or twice as it moves away from and toward your face. Turn your head left and right.** Pause. **Now turn your head left and right leading with the eyes.** Notice how you move. Where do you feel your center? How alert are you? How tense do you feel? What is your breathing like? Rest for a minute then stand and see what walking is like.

End of lesson

ATM: DARK EYES

An audio lesson is available at https://on.soundcloud.com/NouE4.

This lesson may be done either seated or lying on your back. This version will be for seated with changes to perform the lesson on your back in parentheses. It is suggested that you read each module through first and then perform it as the lesson is best done with eyes closed.

1. Sit upright in a comfortable chair. Turn your head left and right. **Close your eyes. Place your palms over your eyes. (Palm your eyes.) Stay like this for about a minute, breathing slowly and deeply.** What color(s) do you notice? The more relaxed the nervous system, the darker the color and the fewer colored areas appear. Velvet black indicates the system is deeply relaxed. Pause, open your hands by lifting the thumbs first, then the index finger, etc. It is like opening a book. Keeping your eyes closed, put your hands down and rest.

2. **Look at the bridge of your nose. Then look over as if to see your right ear, and then back to the bridge of your nose.** This movement is partially imaginary; however, you will feel your eyes moving. When you return to the middle, release your eyes and stay there briefly. *Slowly* move your eyes back and forth six or seven times. Endeavor to make the movement as smooth and continuous as possible. Do not worry if you feel the movement is somewhat erratic with smooth areas followed by jumps. This is normal. It takes considerable training and practice to make smooth continuous eye movements throughout the range. Pause and rest a moment.

   Palm your eyes. Stay like this for a short while, breathing slowly. Do you notice any changes from before? Put your hands down and rest a moment.

3. **Now look from the bridge of your nose over to the left ear and back.** *Slowly* move your eyes back and forth six or seven times. Again, move slowly while intending to make the movement smooth and continuous. How does the movement on this side compare with that on the right? **Pause, palm your eyes, and rest a moment.**

4. **Put your hands down. Then look from the bridge of your nose to the right ear back to the bridge and then over to the left ear and back. Make this movement slowly and carefully, breathing comfortably all the while.** Repeat this movement seven or eight times. Can you find ways to make this movement easier? Pause and rest a minute.

   Palm your eyes. Stay like this while breathing slowly. What changes do you notice from before?

   Slowly open your eyes. Wait a moment, open your hands like a book, and then put your hands down. Just notice what you see.

   Turn your head left and right. Take note of any changes.

   This is the end of this module. It is a logical place to stop if you cannot do the lesson in one sitting. Resume at **step 5**.

5. **Look to the horizon. This is the wall in front of you (the ceiling above you). Then look back to the bridge of your nose.** Repeat three or four times. Pause and rest a moment.

   Close your eyes. Again, look from the horizon to the bridge of your nose. Repeat six to seven times. Pause a moment.

   Palm your eyes for a minute. Open your hands like a book, put your hands down, and rest.

6. **Open your eyes. Look to the right at eye level until you reach the wall. Then look back to the bridge of your nose.** Repeat three or four times. Pause and rest a moment.

   Close your eyes. Again, look from the bridge of your nose to the right. Repeat five or six times. Can you allow this movement to feel smoother each time you make it? Pause a moment.

Now look from the bridge of your nose to the horizon, over to the right, back to the point on the right you were looking at a moment ago, and back to the bridge of your nose. Repeat this quadrilateral pattern six or seven times. Pause and rest a moment.

Palm your eyes for a minute. How do your two sides compare? **Then open your eyes, remember to open your hands like a book, then put your hands down, and rest briefly.**

7. **Look to the left at eye level until you reach the wall. Then look back to the bridge of your nose.** Repeat three or four times. Pause and rest a moment.

   Close your eyes. Again, look from the bridge of your nose to the left. Repeat four or five times. Do you feel any weight shifts as you make this movement? **Pause a moment and palm your eyes for a minute before putting your hands down.**

8. **Look from the bridge of your nose to the horizon then over to the left then back to the point on the left you were looking at before and back to the bridge of your nose.** Repeat this four-corner pattern six or seven times. Can you make this pattern more whole each time you try it? That is, can you improve your ability to make the corners square and not need to round them? Pause and rest briefly.

   Palm your eyes. Stay like this while breathing slowly. How evenly are you sitting now? What changes do you notice in the color before you?

   Slowly open your eyes. Wait a moment, open your hands like a book, and then put them down. Just notice what you see. Then turn your head left and right.

   This is the end of this module. It is a logical place to stop if you cannot do the lesson in one sitting. Resume at **step 9**.

9. **Put your thumb (choose your favorite one to look at) at a distance from your eyes about equal to the length of your arm from shoulder to elbow. Look from your thumb to the bridge of your nose and back.** Repeat this four or five times. Pause.

   Close your eyes and look from the bridge of your nose to the thumb and back. Repeat six or seven times. Put your thumb down and pause. **Palm your eyes for a minute.**

   Slowly open your eyes, open your hands like a book, and put them down. Once again, put your thumb up. Look from your thumb to the horizon and back to your thumb. Repeat four or five times. Pause.

   Close your eyes and look from your thumb to the horizon and back. Repeat six or seven times. Do you notice any change in the way you sit as you move your eyes out and back? Pause and put your thumb down.

   Palm your eyes for a minute. Slowly open your eyes, open your hands, and put them down.

10. **Once more, put your thumb at a distance from your eyes about equal to the length of your arm from shoulder to elbow. Now look from the bridge of your**

nose to your thumb then beyond to the horizon and then back to the bridge of your nose by way of your thumb. Repeat three or four times. Pause.

Close your eyes and repeat this movement four or five times. Pause and put your thumb down.

Palm your eyes for a minute.

11. **Put your hands down. Imagine that there is a ping-pong ball on your forehead. (If you are seated, imagine you are lying on your back so that you don't have to worry about gravity dropping your ball.) Now imagine the ball rolling down your forehead, over the bridge of your nose, down across the chin, along your neck and torso to your belly button, and then rolling back up. Follow the ball as it moves with your eyes.** Repeat this seven or eight times, each time allowing the ball to roll smoothly. Pause and rest for a moment.

    Palm your eyes for a minute.

12. **Put your hands down. This time, imagine that there is a pea on your forehead. Let this pea follow the same path as the ping-pong ball.** Repeat seven or eight times. Is this movement as easy to follow as the ping-pong ball? Stop.

    Palm your eyes for as long as you feel like, breathing slowly. How dark is the color in front of you now? Is the image before you solid or are there specks of light or flashes, etc.?

    Slowly open your eyes. Wait a moment before opening your hands, then put them down. How clear is everything now?

    Turn your head left and right. What do you notice?

End of lesson

OCULAR MUSCLES AND THE SINUSES

The six muscles that move the eyes are located within the eye socket. Four of these muscles are straight, each attaching to one of the four quadrants of the eye. They connect to a common tendon. The other two are oblique, that is, they attach at an angle. One of the oblique muscles attaches to the maxilla. The other five muscles attach to the sphenoid. Both the maxilla and the sphenoid bones have sinuses.

The muscles of the eyelids and brow are also important to visual function. They both control the amount of light into the eye and are responsible for blinking. The muscles of the eyelids are over the sphenoid sinuses, and the muscles of the eyebrows are over the frontal sinus.

When we use our eyes, all these muscle groups—all of them intimately related to the sinus cavities—are involved. Thus excessive tension in the eyes will directly reduce resonance by creating pressure on the sinuses. This effect is in addition to the impact of the eyes on the entire nervous system mentioned earlier. Clearly, it is important to keep the eyes soft and relaxed.

CHAPTER 14

Bonus Lessons

The lessons included in this chapter either fit a need or were too interesting to leave out. They also tend to be a bit more difficult than the earlier lessons. This can be because of position, such as the lesson having you on your stomach, or the nature of the movements themselves. Accordingly, we suggest that you do not try these until you have done at least a half dozen or so of the earlier lessons.

A great many people suffer from knee stiffness and/or pain, but the knees do not work in isolation. They work in conjunction with the hips and ankles. A problem in one joint will therefore compromise the others. Thus, most of the time there are knee issues, even though the person does not realize it, the ankles are stiff. Freeing the ankles has usually resulted in a dramatic lessening of minor knee problems. It also often provides temporary relief when the knees have deteriorated to bone on bone—thus, the following lesson.

ATM: ANKLE CIRCLES

An audio lesson is available at https://on.soundcloud.com/NouE4.

This lesson is included for those who have knee problems. When a leg is functioning well, the three leg joints—hip, knee, and ankle—work together in unison. When they don't, the stress can occur in any of the three. In this case, the other two will be impacted. In particular, with knee problems the ankles are usually stiff. By learning how to release this stiffness, a great deal of knee pain can be alleviated.

Unfortunately, we have not been able to figure out any other way to do this lesson except lying on your stomach. If need be, use a bolster underneath your midsection and one for your head to be comfortable. If you cannot lie on your stomach, try using kinesthetic imagination.

1. **Lie on your back and scan how you fit the floor, your breathing, and any area that draws your interest.**

    Roll onto your stomach. Position your head symmetrically. Aim for comfort.

    Alternate bending your knees, slowly. Repeat three or four times. Determine which knee is moving better. We'll designate that the freer knee.

Slowly bend the freer knee until it is at approximately ninety degrees (for this lesson, bend your knee will mean to about ninety degrees, or your best approximation thereof), put the leg down, and repeat several times. On the last time, leave the knee bent. Then gently flex and extend the ankle. Repeat four to six times, put down your leg, and rest.

2. **Now slowly bend the other knee, put the leg down, and repeat several times. With the knee bent, gently flex and extend the ankle.** Can you sense any difference between the way this ankle flexes from the way the prior ankle flexed? Repeat four to six times, put down your leg, and rest.

3. **Slowly bend the freer knee until it is at approximately ninety degrees. With your ankle in neutral, gently flex and extend your toes, extending them and curling them with a light easy motion.** Repeat six to eight times going slowly and gently. Do you move all your toes together? Is there any toe that feels noticeably different from the others in moving? **Pause, put your leg down slowly, and rest for a moment.**

4. **Bend your other knee. With your ankle in neutral flex, extend your toes.** Repeat six to eight times. Allow the movement to become easier and lighter as you proceed. Is the toe movement as easy on this leg? Stop, put your knee down, and pause.

Alternate bending your knees, slowly. What, if anything, has changed?

Roll onto your back. Gently move your feet toward each other and away from each other, keeping your heels in place. Repeat six or seven times. What happens in your head and back as your feet move toward each other and away? Rest with legs long or feet on the floor, whichever is more comfortable.

This is the end of this module. It is a logical place to stop if you cannot do the lesson in one sitting. Resume at **step 5**.

5. **Roll onto your stomach. Make yourself comfortable. If possible, position your head symmetrically.** Pause a moment.

Slowly bend the freer knee. Flex your ankle so that the toes point toward the ceiling. Now in this position, gently flex your toes curling them and then straightening as far back as you can easily. Repeat this seven or eight times. Pause, put your leg down, and rest.

Slowly bend the freer knee. Now extend your heel toward the ceiling as far as is comfortable and leave it there. Once more, gently flex and extend your toes. Repeat six or seven times. Did the toes move more easily than when the toes pointed at the ceiling? Pause, put your leg down, and rest.

6. **Slowly bend the other knee. Flex your ankle so that the toes point toward the ceiling. Gently flex your toes, curling them and then straightening as far back as you can easily.** Repeat this seven or eight times. Pause, put your leg down, and rest.

Slowly bend the other knee. Now extend your heel toward the ceiling as far as is comfortable and leave it there. Once more, gently flex and extend your toes. Repeat six or seven times. Pause, put your leg down, and rest.

7. **Slowly bend the freer knee. Extend your ankle and stay extended as you flex and extend your toes. Go back through neutral and flex your ankle. Stay there and flex and extend your toes.**

    Repeat this sequence six to eight times, pausing in the middle for a short while after every other sequence. Then put your knee down and rest.

8. **Slowly bend the other knee. Extend your ankle and stay extended as you flex and extend your toes. Go back through neutral and flex your ankle. Stay there and flex and extend your toes.**

    Repeat this sequence six to eight times, pausing in the middle for a short while after every other sequence. How freely do you breathe on this side as you make this movement? Then put your knee down and rest.

    Alternate bending your knees, slowly. What, if anything, has changed?

    Then bend both knees and alternate bending and flexing the ankles. Repeat several times. How different is this movement between your two legs? Does the difference correspond to the way the knees bend? Stop.

    Roll onto your back. Gently move your feet left and right simultaneously, keeping them about the same distance apart, and with your heels in place. Repeat three or four times. What happens with your head and back as you make this movement? Pause, and rest a minute.

    This is the end of this module. It is a logical place to stop if you cannot do the lesson in one sitting. Resume at **step 9**.

9. **Roll onto your stomach. Make yourself comfortable. If possible, position your head symmetrically.** Pause a moment.

    Slowly bend the freer knee. Rotate the ankle such that the outer edge of your foot is closer to the ceiling. And return to neutral. Repeat this movement four to six times. Be very gentle. Remember that you are interested in the how of doing not in achieving any external goal, such as how far. Pause.

    Now rotate the ankle so that the inner edge of your foot is closer to the ceiling. Return to neutral. Repeat this movement four to six times. Go slowly; this is apt to be more difficult than the previous movement. Pause, put your knee down, and rest.

10. **Slowly bend the freer knee until it is at approximately ninety degrees. Now alternately rotate the outer and inner edges of your foot toward the ceiling.** Repeat five to seven times. After every two sequences, pause and take a couple of breaths, then resume. Each time, see if you can make this movement smoother

and gentler. What do you feel your leg doing as you make this movement? Pause, put your leg down, and rest a moment.

11. **Slowly bend the other knee. Rotate the ankle such that the outer edge of your foot is closer to the ceiling. And return to neutral.** Repeat this movement four to six times. Be very gentle. Pause.

    Now rotate the ankle so that the inner edge of your foot is closer to the ceiling. And return to neutral. Repeat this movement four to six times. Attend carefully to the quality of this movement. How much of yourself do you feel is involved in this movement? Pause, put your knee down, and rest.

12. **Slowly bend the other knee. Now alternately rotate the outer and inner edges of your foot toward the ceiling.** Repeat five to seven times. Periodically pause and take a breath and then resume. Pause, put your leg down, and rest.

    Alternate bending your knees, slowly. What, if anything, has changed?

    Then bend both knees and alternate bending and flexing the ankles. Repeat several times. How different is this movement between your two legs? Does the difference correspond to the way the knees bend?

    Roll onto your back. Rotate your ankles together and apart several times. Rest with legs long or feet on the floor, whichever is more comfortable.

    This is the end of this module. It is a logical place to stop if you cannot do the lesson in one sitting. Resume at **step 13**.

13. **Roll onto your stomach. Make yourself comfortable. If possible, position your head symmetrically.** Pause a moment.

    Alternate bending your knees, slowly. How do they compare now?

    Then bend both knees and alternate bending and flexing the ankles. Repeat several times. How different is this movement between your legs now? Does the difference correspond to the way the knees bend? Pause in place.

    Now alternate moving the outer edge and inner edge of first your freer knee and then the other knee. Repeat three or four times. Notice how this movement differs between legs. Pause, put your legs down, and rest.

14. **Bend the freer knee. Having moved the foot in all four directions, toes up and down and inner and outer edge up and down, make a circle with the foot.** Repeat three or four times. **Pause, take a breath, and continue in the same direction but make the circle with your ankle.** Repeat three or four times. **Pause and reverse the direction.** Make four to six circles in this direction. See if each time you can make the movement smoother or easier. Pause, put your leg down, and rest.

15. **Bend the other knee. Make a circle with the foot.** Repeat three or four times. Aim for ease. **Then pause briefly and continue in the same direction but make the circle with your ankle.** Repeat three or four times. **Now reverse the direction.** Make four to six circles in this direction. Pause, put your leg down, and rest.

    Alternate bending your knees, slowly. What, if anything, has changed?

Then bend both knees and alternate bending and flexing the ankles. Repeat several times. How different is this movement between your two legs? Does the difference correspond to the way the knees bend? Stop and put your legs down.

Roll onto your back. Bend your knees and put your feet on the floor. Lift your right heel from the floor. Imagine that there is a bar between your right big toe and second toe. Rotate your right heel around this bar. Repeat four or five times. Pause and put your right heel down.

Lift your left heel from the floor. Move the imaginary bar to be between your left big toe and the second toe. Rotate your left heel around this bar. Repeat four or five times. Pause, and put your left heel down.

When you are ready, stand up. Notice what standing feels like now. Then walk around and notice what this feels like.

End of lesson

In performing a movement, does one push or pull? And do you move from an internal feel or from external impulses? These questions, and the opportunity to use a cool name from the Doctor Dolittle stories, sparked this lesson.

ATM: PUSH ME, PULL YOU

This lesson is unusual in that it has aspects that feel the opposite when you do it lying on the floor from when you are sitting in a chair. You are encouraged, therefore, to try the lesson both ways. It is written for the seated version in the expectation that you can lie down flat on the floor with your feet up (down when at rest) and adapt it.

Throughout the lesson, unless otherwise noted, try and keep the pauses about as long as the movement.

1. **Sit erect in your chair.** How are you breathing? How evenly are you breathing between your two sides? How easy is it for you to breathe into your belly? How easy is it to breathe into your ribs, your sternum? **Pushing (internally not with your hands) through the ribs on your left moves your ribs to the right.** Repeat eight to ten times. Go gently each time, seeing how much more plastic you can feel your ribs and spine. Be aware of how long your pauses are. Remember to keep the pauses about as long as the movement. Stop and rest.

2. **Pulling with the ribs on your right moves your ribs to the right.** Repeat ten to twelve times. Again, take long pauses and see if you can allow your ribs to become freer, more fluid. Be very gentle. The muscles you are using, the intercostals, are not commonly used this way. If you pull very hard, you will be sore tomorrow and the lesson will not be helpful. Stop and rest. Take a few breaths and compare your right and left sides.

3. **Now push with your right ribs, moving your ribs to the left.** Repeat seven to nine times. Notice how this differs from the movement to the right. If you have

scoliosis, this could feel very different. Again, allow the spine and ribs to move freer and freer each time you make this movement. Stop and rest.

4. **Pull with your ribs on the left to move your ribs to the left.** Repeat ten to twelve times. Remember to be very gentle. If you can't smile while making this movement, you are working too hard. Stop and rest.

   Notice how evenly you are sitting now. How are you breathing? What differences do you notice?

   This is the end of this module. It is a logical place to stop if you cannot do the lesson in one sitting. Resume at **step 5**.

5. Notice how you are breathing. **Move your ribs gently back and forth between left and right, going only so far as is easy and comfortable.** Repeat this ten to twelve times. Please pause after every other movement for the length of a movement. In which direction do you go more easily? Do the two sides become more even as you continue this movement? Can you find ways to make the movement softer? Do you feel you move more by pushing from the opposite side or pulling from the direction you are going? Stop and rest.

   After a minute, notice how you are breathing.

6. **Tilt your head to the right. As you do so, you will feel the ribs opening on the left and closing on the right. Allow this to happen.** Repeat this nine to twelve times, always pausing in between movements for as long as it takes to make a movement. Pause.

   Take three or four slow complete breaths. Stop. How did your two sides feel? How easy was the breathing. Luxuriate in sitting for a moment.

7. **Tilt your head to the left. Notice the ribs opening on the right and closing on the left. As you return to the center, let there be a passive feeling, a gentle returning to homebase.** Repeat ten or eleven times, again pausing as long between movements as moving. Pause.

8. **Move your ribs gently back and forth between left and right going only so far as is easy and comfortable.** Repeat eight to ten times, pausing between movements. How even is this now compared to the last time? Stop.

   Take three or four slow complete breaths. Stop. How even did your two sides feel now? Rest quietly for a moment.

   This is the end of this module. It is a logical place to stop if you cannot do the lesson in one sitting. Resume at **step 9**.

9. **Lift your right hip slightly from the chair. Allow the weight to go down through the left hip as you make this movement. Make this movement without strain.** Repeat four or five times. Remember to pause as long as it takes to make this movement between movements. Notice which ribs open when you make this movement and which ones "close." Pause.

Repeat the movement of lifting the right hip. As you do so, inhale. Repeat three or four times. Pause.

Again, lift the right hip, exhale as you do so. Repeat three or four times. Pause. Which way of breathing makes it easier for you to lift your hip?

Now lift your hip three or four times while breathing in a way that makes this movement easiest. Stop and rest a moment.

10. **Lift your left hip from the chair. Push upward toward your shoulder through your left foot.** Repeat five to seven times. Remember the between-movement pauses. Notice which ribs open when you make this movement. Pause.

    Again, lift the left hip. As you do, exhale. Repeat three or four times. Pause.

    Now lift your left hip as you inhale while letting the weight go down through your right hip. Repeat three or four times. Pause. Which way of breathing makes it easier to lift this hip?

    Now lift your left hip two or three times while breathing in the way that makes this movement easiest. Stop and rest.

11. **Push the floor through your left foot.** Repeat four to six times. Notice what happens in the ribs as you push. Pause.

    Now as you push through your left foot, deliberately pull your ribs to the right. Repeat four to six times without any sense of strain. Remember to pause as long as it takes to make this movement between movements. Does this make it easier to push through the foot? Do your ribs move further than before? Pause.

12. **Push through your right foot.** Repeat four to six times. What happens in the ribs when you push with this foot? Pause.

    Now as you push through the right foot, deliberately push your ribs to the left. Repeat four to six times. Do the foot and the ribs move more easily when you push than when you pull? Pause.

    Move your ribs gently back and forth between left and right going only so far as is easy and comfortable. Repeat six to eight times. How even is this now compared to the last time? Stop.

    Notice how you are breathing now.

    This is the end of this module. It is a logical place to stop if you cannot do the lesson in one sitting. Resume at **step 13**.

13. **Lower your right arm directly downward without moving your torso. (Slide your arm along your side.) Go only as far down as you can move comfortably and easily and then return to the starting position.** Repeat this slow movement four to six times. Remember to pause as long as it takes to make this movement between movements. Pause and rest.

    Lift your right shoulder, pulling the arm up with it. Again, you'll feel the arm slide along your side. Keep the movement smooth and steady. If you feel any jerking as you raise your shoulder, stop and go back down to neutral. Repeat four to six times. What do you notice on your left side when you make this movement? Can you keep this movement smooth? Pause and rest.

Now raise and lower your right shoulder five to seven times, slowly. What happens to your ribs as you do this? What happens to your left shoulder as you make this movement? Stop and rest.

14. **Raise your left shoulder.** Repeat four to six times. Compare how this shoulder moves with the right. Is it easier? Is it smoother? Does it track up and down better? Pause and rest.

    Now lower your left shoulder with great gentleness. Repeat four to six times. Pause and rest.

    Lower and then raise your left shoulder. Repeat this sequence seven to nine times. Stop and rest.

15. **Raise your left shoulder while you tilt your head to the right. As your head returns effortlessly to neutral, the left shoulder drops back to neutral.** Repeat this movement seven to nine times. Remember to pause as long between movements as it takes to make a movement. Pause and rest a moment. Notice how you are breathing now. Compare your two sides.

16. **Raise your right shoulder while you tilt your head to the left. Let the return to neutral be free and easy.** Repeat this movement seven to nine times. Pause and rest a moment.

    How is your breathing now? How even is it between left and right? How well can you feel your back open as you breathe? Do you feel your vertebrae separate with the breath?

    Move your ribs gently back and forth between left and right going only so far as is easy and comfortable. Use aspects of all the movements we explored in this lesson so far to make this movement easier and easier. Repeat six to eight times. How even is this now compared to the last time? Stop.

    What is your breathing like now? How erect (or straight) do you feel? Stand up, walk around for a minute, and notice any changes.

End of lesson

Tightness in the sternum impedes the ribs which, because of the way they tie in with the thoracic spine, can also lead to back discomfort, as well as with breathing and the shoulders. In North American culture, the sternum tends to be held rigidly, but it need not be so—just watch videos of the Carnival in Rio de Janeiro to see mobile sternums. The following lesson's title is self-explanatory.

ATM: MOVING THE STERNUM

1. Sit squarely in a chair with a flat seat and no arms. **Slowly turn your head left and right several times. Stay in your comfort range as you turn your head.** Pause for a moment. How far were you able to turn your head? How much of your back could you feel participating in the movement?

2. **Arch and round your back, again staying in your comfort range.** Do this four or five times. Each time, see if you can find a way to make it easier or have more of your back participate in the movement. Rest for a minute.

3. Put the fingers of both hands on your sternum (breastbone). Notice how it moves both up and down and in and out as you breathe. **Now guide it with your fingers to move downward and in a little more as you exhale. Use very gentle pressure to enhance whatever movement you can feel.** Repeat this eight or nine times. See if you can sense this movement becoming clearer or bigger. Pause, and put your hands down. Notice how your sternum is moving as you breathe.

4. **Move your sternum forward and back to neutral. Breathe in as you make this movement forward.** Actually, all of your back has to move to make this movement, but there is no movement of the pelvis. That is, you will not feel movement in the hips. Repeat this movement eight to ten times. Each time, try to make the movement easier. Can you feel the movement of the sternum more clearly? Stop and rest for a minute.

   Slowly turn your head left and right several times. Do you notice any changes?

   Stand up and walk around for a minute. Notice how erect you feel while walking.

This is the end of this module. It is a logical place to stop if you cannot do the lesson in one sitting. Resume at **step 5**.

5. Place your hands on your legs. **Move your sternum forward and back to neutral. Breathe in as you make this movement forward.** Repeat this seven or eight times. Can you feel movement of your shoulder blades over your ribs as you make this movement? This may not be clear or apparent at first, but see what happens as you repeat the movement. Clarity often comes with repetition. Rest for a minute without changing the position of your hands.

6. **Move your sternum backward and then return it to neutral. Breathe as you make this movement.** Repeat this seven or eight times. Do you find yourself inhaling or exhaling as you move your sternum backward? Pause for a moment.

    Now move your sternum forward and back. Repeat this six to eight times, pausing every other breath. See how lightly you can make this movement. What movement do you sense in your shoulder blades? Stop and rest for a minute with your hands at your sides.

7. **With your hands at your sides, move your sternum forward and back.** Repeat six or seven times. How is this different from when you have your hands on your knees? Stop and rest for a minute.

8. Place both your hands on your sternum. **Gently move your sternum to the left. This is a small movement.** Repeat four or five times, making each movement gentler. **Pause, put your hands down, and take a few breaths.**

    Place your hands on your sternum and gently move it to the right. Repeat five or six times. Pause and put your hands down. Rest a moment.

    With your hands on your legs, move your sternum forward and back. Repeat five or six times.

    Did it change from the last time you did this? If so, how? Stop and rest a minute.

    Slowly turn your head left and right several times. What is that like now?

    This is the end of this module. It is a logical place to stop if you cannot do the lesson in one sitting. Resume at **step 9**.

9. **Interlace your fingers and put your hands on top of your head. Move your sternum forward and back to neutral.** If this hand position causes a strain, try it without interlacing the fingers. Repeat this eight to ten times. What does this position of the hands allow you to feel in your ribs and shoulder blades? Put your hands down and rest for a minute. Notice how you breathe.

10. **Again, interlace your fingers and put your hands on top of your head. Move your sternum backward and return to neutral.** Repeat seven to nine times. Does this hand position make it easier or harder to move the sternum backward? What do you notice about your breathing as you make this movement? Put your hands down and rest.

11. **Again, interlace your fingers and put your hands on top of your head. Move your sternum forward and backward.** Repeat this six to eight times. Put your hands down and rest.

    Spend a minute or so just breathing gently.

12. **With your hands on your legs, move your sternum forward and back.** Repeat six or seven times. What is this like now? What do you notice that has changed since the last time you did this movement? Stop and rest.

    Slowly turn your head left and right several times. What is that like now?

    This is the end of this module. It is a logical place to stop if you cannot do the lesson in one sitting. Resume at **step 13**.

13. **Place your right hand on your left shoulder. Grasp your right elbow with your left hand. Raise and lower your right elbow using a slow smooth movement of your left arm.**

    Repeat this five or six times. Pause and rest.

    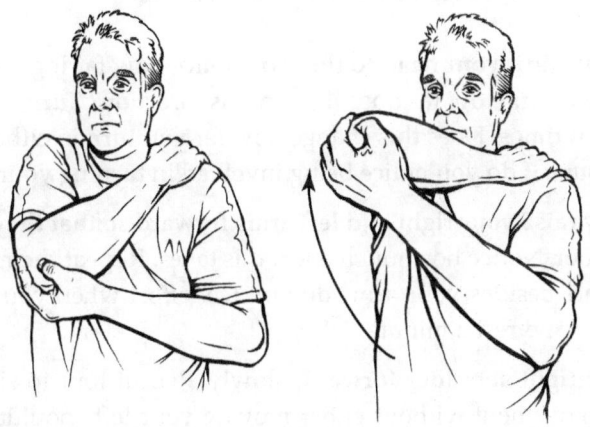

    Now place your left hand on your right shoulder. Grasp your left elbow with your right hand. Raise and lower your left elbow using a gentle even motion of your right arm. Repeat this five or six times. Stop and rest for a minute. Notice the sensation in your shoulders. What is your breathing like now?

14. **Place your left hand on your right shoulder and right hand on your left shoulder. Raise your elbows toward your head. Do not move your head as you do this. You need not raise your elbows any higher than is sufficient for the top arm to caress your chin.** Repeat this six or seven times. Put your arms down and rest for a moment.
    Now reverse the positions you had your arms in and repeat this movement. Do this five or six times. Put your arms down and rest.

15. **Place your left hand on your right shoulder and right hand on your left shoulder. Now move your sternum forward and back.** Repeat this five or six times.

Reverse the position of your arms. Move your sternum forward and back. Repeat six or seven times. Put your arms down and rest. Notice how you are breathing now.

16. **With your hands on your legs, move your sternum forward and back.** Repeat six or seven times. What is this like now? What do you notice that has changed since the last time you did this movement? Stop.

    Slowly turn your head left and right several times. What is that like now?

    Slowly stand up. Notice how you feel standing. Walk a little and notice how this feels.

End of lesson

We've already explored neck and shoulder freedom. The following lesson combines the two.

ATM: RELEASING THE NECK AND ARMS

1. Sit in a chair. **Turn your head to the left.** Notice how far it goes. **Then turn your head to the right.** How far does it go in this direction? **Turn your head left and right several times.** Does this change how far you turn in either direction? How much of yourself do you notice being involved in turning your head? Pause.

   Alternately raise your right and left arms forward so that they would be parallel to the floor. Notice how much effort this takes. **Repeat the movement several times.** Where besides your arms do you feel effort when you make this movement? Pause and rest a minute.

2. **Move your right shoulder forward, slowly.** Repeat four to six times. Can you make this movement without either moving your left shoulder or raising your right shoulder as you move it forward? Do you breathe in or out as you make this movement? Pause. Rest for a minute.

   Move your left shoulder forward gently. Repeat four to six times. Again, see if you can make this movement without raising your shoulder. Do you sense yourself growing a little taller as your shoulder moves forward? Pause.

   Alternately move your left and right shoulder forward. Repeat five to seven times. Does the effort seem the same on the left as on the right? How does your weight against the chair change as you move your shoulders? Stop and rest for a minute.

3. **As you slowly move your right shoulder forward, turn your head to the left.** Repeat seven to nine times. Allow your shoulder to suggest that your head move to the left. Can you tell if you are leading with the head instead? **One time only, deliberately lead the movement of the shoulder with the head. Pause. And again move the right shoulder forward leading the head to move to the left.** Repeat two times. Pause and rest.

As you slowly move your left shoulder forward, let it lead your head in turning to the right.

Repeat seven to nine times. Pause and rest.

Alternately lead your head left and right by moving first one shoulder and then the other forward. Pause after each two back and forth movements for at least as long as it takes to make the movement. Then resume, starting with the direction you did last. Repeat this cycle four to six times. Can you make the movement smoother as you repeat it? Pause and rest a minute.

4. **Turn your head to the left.** Notice how far it goes now. What changes, if any, do you notice? **Then turn your head to the right.** How far does it go in this direction? Is it any easier to move? Do you feel taller or shorter? Pause.

   Alternately raise your right and left arms forward so that they would be parallel to the floor. Notice how much effort this takes now. **Repeat the movement several times.** Where besides your arms do you feel effort when you make this movement? Is more of you involved than before? Pause and rest a minute.

   This is the end of this module. It is a logical place to stop if you cannot do the lesson in one sitting. Resume at **step 5**.

5. **Put your hands on your legs. Gently move your right shoulder backward.** Repeat two or three times. Did you allow your hand to move along your leg as you made this movement? **Gently move your right shoulder backward as your right hand slides up your leg.** Repeat two or three times. **Now move your right shoulder back without moving your hand or arm several times.** Pause and rest a minute.

   Slide your left shoulder backward, allowing your hand to come with it. Repeat three or four times. Can you make this movement without either raising or lowering your shoulder? Pause.

   Now move your left shoulder backward without moving your hand or arm. Repeat three or four times. Does this change your ability to keep your shoulder level? If so, how? Pause and rest a minute.

6. **Lightly move your right shoulder forward as you move your left shoulder backward.** Repeat six to eight times, sometimes allowing the hands to move and sometimes not. Pause and rest a minute.

   Move your left shoulder back as your head turns to the left. Repeat five to seven times. Do you lead the movement with your shoulder or your head? See if you can lead the movement with your shoulder. Do you feel yourself growing taller and shorter? Pause and rest a minute.

7. **Slowly move your left shoulder forward as you move your right shoulder backward.** Repeat six to eight times. Sometimes allow your hands to move while others hold them still. Which use of the hands makes the movement easier for you? Pause and rest a minute.

Move your right shoulder back as your head turns to the right. Repeat five to seven times. Do you lead the movement with your shoulder or your head? See if you can lead the movement with your shoulder. Pause and rest a minute.

8. **Slowly move your left shoulder forward as you move your right shoulder backward. Once you return to neutral, move your right shoulder forward as you move your left shoulder backward. Leave your head stationary as you make this movement.** Repeat this movement softly seven or eight times. What do you notice in your back as you make this movement? Pause and rest. What do you notice in your back as you are resting?

   Alternately raise your right and left arms forward so that they would be parallel to the floor. Notice how much effort this takes now. **Repeat the movement several times.** How has where you feel effort when you make this movement changed? Is more of you involved than before?

   Turn your head to the left. Notice how far it goes now. What changes, if any, do you notice? **Then turn your head to the right.** How far does it go in this direction? How much of yourself do you involve in this turning? Has that changed? Pause and rest a minute.

   This is the end of this module. It is a logical place to stop if you cannot do the lesson in one sitting. Resume at **step 9**.

9. **Slowly move your left shoulder forward as you move your right shoulder backward. Once you return to neutral, move your right shoulder forward as you move your left shoulder backward.** Repeat this movement pattern gently two or three times.

   Cross your arms on your chest (hug yourself). Now turn your head left and right, slowly and gently. Repeat four to six times. Pause. **Uncross your arms, reverse their position, and turn your head left and right.** Repeat four to six times. Pause and put your arms down.

10. **Raise your right arm and move it forward** (the direction your nose points). Repeat five to seven times. Remember to take a breath between each movement. How much do you use your shoulder when you make this movement? Pause and lower your arm.

    Raise your left arm and move it forward. Repeat four to six times. How much of your back participates? Pause and lower your arm.

    Raise both your arms and alternately move one and then the other forward. Repeat four to six times. Can you use equal effort between the sides as you make this motion? Pause, lower both your arms, and rest.

11. **Turn your head to the left as you move your left shoulder forward.** Repeat four to six times.

    Pause and rest.

Gently turn your head to the right as you move your right shoulder forward. Repeat four to six times. Pause and rest.

Alternately lead your head left and right by moving first one shoulder and then the other forward. Pause after each two back and forth motions for at least as long as it takes to make the movement. Then resume, starting with the direction you did last. Repeat this cycle two to three times. How much of you is involved in the movement now? Pause and rest.

12. **Turn your head slowly to the left as you move your right shoulder forward. Leave your head to the left as you take your shoulder back to neutral. Then move your right shoulder forward and notice what your head does.** Repeat this movement of the shoulder only four or five times. Return to neutral and pause.

    Again, turn your head slowly to the left as you move your right shoulder forward. What is it like now? Pause and rest a minute.

    Turn your head slowly to the right as you move your left shoulder forward. Leave your head to the right as you take your shoulder back to neutral. Then move your left shoulder forward and notice what your head does. Repeat this movement of the shoulder only three or four times and pause.

    Now turn your head slowly to the left as you move your right shoulder forward. What is it like now? Pause and rest a minute.

    Alternately raise your right and left arms forward so that they would be parallel to the floor. Notice how much effort this takes now. **Repeat the movement several times.** Where besides your arms do you feel effort when you make this movement? Is more of you involved than before? Pause and rest.

    Turn your head to the left. Notice how far it goes now. What changes, if any, do you notice? **Then turn your head to the right.** How far does it go in this direction? How much of yourself do you feel is involved in this movement now? Pause and rest.

    This is the end of this module. It is a logical place to stop if you cannot do the lesson in one sitting. Resume at **step 13**.

13. **Shift your weight onto your right sit bone. Then shift it to your left sit bone. Go back and forth between the two.** Repeat this four or five times. Pause.

    Raise your right arm forward as you shift your weight onto your left sit bone and then return to neutral. Repeat this movement five to seven times. Can you improve the connection between the two movement components as you repeat the movement? Pause and rest a minute. Where do you feel your weight is now?

14. **Raise your left arm forward as you shift your weight onto your right sit bone and then return to neutral.** Repeat this movement five to seven times. Is this movement as easy as on the other side? What do you notice as you continue to make the movement? Pause and rest a minute.

15. **Turn your head to the right as you raise your left arm.** Repeat this movement eight or nine times. Does it feel natural? If so, why? Pause and rest a minute.

    Turn your head to the left as you raise your right arm. Repeat seven or eight times. How does this compare to the previous movement? What do you do with your weight on your sit bones? Pause and rest a minute.

16. **Alternately move your left and right shoulder forward.** Repeat five to seven times. Does the effort seem the same on the left as on the right? How does your weight against the chair change as you move your shoulders? Stop and rest for a minute.

    Turn your head to the left. Notice how far it goes now. What changes, if any, do you notice? **Then turn your head to the right.** How far does it go in this direction? Compare the ease and quality of this movement with what it was like when you began. Pause.

    Alternately raise your right and left arms forward so that they would be parallel to the floor. Notice how much effort this takes now. **Repeat the movement several times.** How heavy do your arms feel now? What changes, if any, do you notice since you began? Pause and rest.

    Stand up and walk around for a minute or so. Notice how your arms move as you walk. What are your head and eyes doing as you walk? How tall do you feel?

End of lesson

CHAPTER 15

Perspectives from Instrumentalists

PREAMBLE

From Sam Nelson:

Ever since I began working with musicians at the Eastman School of Music over thirty years ago, I've felt that these were a specialized class of athletes. So, I want to stress harpist (and our illustrator) Amy Walts's point that you should "resign yourself to thinking of your body as the tool of an elite athlete and treat it accordingly." Add to this the critical proviso that you never think of yourself as *having* a body, but rather of being *embodied*.

This chapter presents a group of such athletes: expert professional instrumentalists. They were asked, and answered, four questions.

1. When in position to play your instrument, what is typically the main area (or areas) where tension may be problematic?
2. Regarding performance injuries, what are the most frequent to occur with your instrument? Have you ever encountered such injury or know of a musician/student who has?
3. If so, what kind of remedies have you/they sought? How effective were those remedies?
4. How do you prevent such injuries? If you teach, what advice do you give to your students to help them from becoming injured while at the same time preserving the integrity and functionality of their performance position? How do you encourage your students (and yourself) to play without strain?

The respondents include a broad range of backgrounds, some at the beginning of their professional careers, some in mid-career, and those with decades of experience. All are still actively performing and, in many cases, teaching.

We have organized the responses by instrumental families. While it is tempting to immediately find your specific instrument and only read that one response, we strongly recommend you read them *all*. Your experiences may not necessarily be cited by your instrumental associate, but could very well be discussed elsewhere. Lastly, in some instances, there are non-musical "occupational hazards" (such as transporting heavy, bulky instruments and/or equipment) shared across instrumental groupings.

At the conclusion of each instrumental group, Sam provides valuable recommendations including suggested Feldenkrais Awareness Through Movement lessons found in this book.

RESPONSES

Strings: Primarily Bowed

VIOLIN: ANNE RARDIN

1. Right and left elbow tendons. Right wrist carpal tunnel; left shoulder blade/upper trapezius/levator. Left sternocleidomastoid; upper occipital neuralgia. Temporomandibular joint (TMJ) syndrome. Right ulnar nerve entrapment, mid-thoracic back.
2. In addition to my own multiple playing-related injuries, I have worked with many students (eighteen to twenty over the course of my thirty years of teaching) who have experienced various injuries, including elbow tendonitis, carpal tunnel, chronic neck pain, headaches, and TMJ syndrome. These common injuries have ranged from a few months to several years, and I have become a specialist in guiding high school– and college-level string students through performance injuries. Occasionally, I will have younger students who require attention due to chronic pain, but in this age group it is more rare and seems to focus on upper extremities and neck.
3. I have found that a combination of allopathic and alternative techniques is most effective. The most helpful is regular Feldenkrais training and treatments, along with physical therapy that focuses on releasing trigger points and soft-tissue work. Careful analysis by an experienced teacher of how a student is incurring muscle imbalance and using excess tension is essential. Swimming or other strength training that corrects muscular imbalances can be highly effective once these prior steps have effected change.
4. Injury prevention is a big topic in lessons while setting up flexible and body-friendly technique, healthy warm-ups, and proper stretching routines. It is important that students are taught to listen carefully to discomfort, tension, and pain. Understanding how to (1) play while sitting or standing with balanced support, (2) leverage weight and create flexible movement, (3) take frequent breaks, (4) stretch to undo held positions, and (5) create healthy practice limits are all crucial learning for young musicians. Each one of these elements is a regular part of my teaching and ethos. When your instrument is your body, you must develop highly sensitive body awareness. Feldenkrais is especially valuable, as it both corrects muscular imbalance and teaches exquisite awareness.

Dr. Anne Rardin teaches high school orchestra in Pasadena, California, and Baroque violin for the Historical Performance Practice Department at Claremont Graduate

University. She is a member of the American String Teachers Association's National Health and Wellness Committee Leadership.

VIOLA: JOHN ROXBURGH

Mid-back, upper-back, neck, jaw, shoulders, all the way down the arms to the hands.

1. Overuse injuries related to the hand/arms/shoulders.
2. Physical therapy; a teacher that has experience dealing with excess tension.
3. a. Warm-up, stretching (spine mobilization stretches in particular), strengthening.
   b. On the instrument, I dedicate a good portion of my practice to figuring out how to play with more ease: general warm-ups as well as focused work on difficult sections. It is typical for me to tense up when there is something difficult to play, or musically tense, so I work on playing the sections focusing on physical ease, while still bringing out the musical tension, etc.
   c. The Broken Wing Feldenkrais ATM (see chapter 2).

John D. Roxburgh, DMA, is a violist and music educator originally from New Zealand, currently residing in State College, Pennsylvania.

CELLO: TERESA KUBIAK

1. The trapezius muscle group is a common area of pain and dysfunction for many cellists. This would cover the mid-back, shoulder, and neck areas. Over the years, my tension has manifested most prominently in the upper back along the spine, between the shoulder blades. This may have been due in part to a compression fracture I sustained from a car accident and the protective measures my body developed in response to that injury. There are issues that have cascaded down my right (bow) arm as well. At one point, my elbow had become stiff and would not open to the full extent necessary. As I get older, my right deltoid succumbs to pain during prolonged A-string melodies. This is something that can affect cellists at any age, even children. However, focusing on the exact point of injury will often not eliminate the pain, unless you are able to find the source of a contracting reflex, such as a squeezing thumb or flying fingers.
2. Most performance injuries are related to tension. Even if one works diligently to eliminate sources of strain in one's technique while practicing, during performance, a body can revert to fight or flight (sympathetic) patterning. This same sympathetic response can also affect the brain's ability to process images, such as when reading music.
3. I have found that the best remedies are those that focus on maintaining a relationship with our parasympathetic neural state—one of coherency and ease. Feldenkrais uses movement to encourage awareness and embodiment, which transform the "emergency response system" into a state of safety, knowing your body from within. The more we practice this awareness, the more readily it will be available to us in times of stress. For example, our skeletal system responds to stress by

contracting. Your pelvis (or one side of your pelvis) can be contracted in response to a situation that may have occurred many years ago. When the body experiences safety on a regular basis, these patterns reverse: a pelvis can widen, a sacrum can rest properly at the bottom of the spine, letting the lower lumbar straighten and relax, pulling the tailbone out of the pelvis. Even the hard palate of the mouth can expand and relieve tension in the jaw. These physical responses communicate with our entire system. A parasympathetic neural state also encourages fluidity of tissues, resulting in facial releases. For areas of the body with stubborn fascial adhesions, I have found a deep pressure method called Block Therapy is very helpful in liquifying and releasing the adhesions, but if the sympathetic/parasympathetic states are not addressed, these releases will be temporary, much like going to a chiropractor.

4. The most important aspect of my teaching is instilling a sense of safety, which includes developing a better relationship with one's inner critic. I also coach students to develop a sense of the vertical, otherwise known as posture, but you want it to come from a place of natural ease and expansion. This can cue the parasympathetic state, which will enable systems in the body such as muscular, skeletal, fascial, and circulatory to allow a fluid and facile technique to emerge. Sympathetic holding (protective) patterns are our worst enemy, but they need to be respected and gently encouraged to release. All great technique comes from a place of ease and this prevents injury. The more we clean up our holding patterns, the more easily we can access a system of levers, applying weight and force where needed without straining.

Teresa Kubiak began playing the cello at the age of eighteen, moved to New York City after attending Ithaca College, and pursued a career as a freelance musician where she held the position of principal cellist with the Bronx Opera Company and The Orchestra of The Bronx, as well as substitute for the New York City Ballet. She has been teaching cello to children and adults for over twenty-five years and now teaches online from her home in Rochester, New York.

CELLO: LISA TERRY

1. Right shoulder, right side of neck. This is the bow arm, which has to do a lot!
2. Tendonitis in the right shoulder, overuse injury. I have rotator cuff tears and had to have a lot of physical therapy to rebuild other muscles to take over for the two tears (which cannot be repaired). I also have to play cello with a modified bow grip now.
3. Body awareness has been crucial, and I'm still working on new ways to sit, to practice, to use my body well in practice, rehearsal and performance. I continue with my physical therapy exercises to keep my muscles supportive.
4. All musicians should do body work to become very mindful of their bodies while practicing. They should be trained to build in breaks in rehearsal and practice sessions to stand, walk, and move around. They should be exquisitely aware of pain and get help instead of pushing through.

No amount of pressure to learn a piece should make a person play with pain.

Lisa Terry is a professional cellist and viola da gamba player in New York City, with Parthenia Viol Consort and Tempesta di Mare Baroque Orchestra. She teaches privately and at workshops for adult amateur musicians and is the past-president of Viola da Gamba Society of America.

DOUBLE BASS: JACOB PEMBELTON

1. For players who stand, calves/hamstrings; many have lower back and shoulder tension as well. Forearms, elbows, and finder/hand tension. For players who bow, they may have elbow tension in the right elbow and right arm/hand due to the bow.
2. The lower back and shoulder can have chronic pain. Elbow issues include tennis elbow and wrist and forearm overuse (carpal tunnel is very common). I have had mostly overuse injuries in my back and arms/wrists. However, I know many bass players with injuries all over.
3. Some have had to go as far as surgeries, but commonly use braces and wraps for arm/wrist as well as use inserts for shoes to help problems with the legs. The back is really the killer—some people move to sitting or using an angled endpin to help reposition the instrument. Unfortunately, the best remedy is to always stretch before practicing/playing.
4. Always stretch! If problems continue, adjusting your instrument setup (i.e., lower strings, lower tension strings, angled endpin, sitting while playing) and being mindful of tension while you're playing is key to a continued career playing the bass. It is such a large instrument that even moving the double bass, you can injure yourself. Treating the bass as a dance partner and working with it to find a neutral and stress-free playing position is important to longevity and injury-free playing.

Settled in The Plains, Virginia, Jacob S. Pembelton is a freelance jazz bassist and musical instrument maker serving Northern Virginia. When not playing, he can be found at Thomas Andres Double Bass Makers, where he specializes in the setup, repair, restoration, and new construction of the double bass.

SAM'S RECOMMENDATIONS

It appears that shoulders are a common problem. Because a lot of attention has been paid to them by teachers, therapists, etc., an excellent place to start is with breathing and the ribs.

The shoulder blade sits directly over the ribs. Accordingly, tightness in the shoulders impedes breathing and rib movement; conversely, freeing up the ribs and breathing frees up the shoulders. ATM: The Broken Wing (chapter 2) is also very useful as it clarifies the relationship between the shoulder and arm to the torso. In addition, the lesson includes the use of kinesthetic imagination, an excellent way to explore this powerful tool.

For those who have issues with the mid-back, try ATM: Circling the Legs (chapter 9).

If you're concerned about the *possibility* of carpal tunnel syndrome, then the ATM: Mobile Wrists (chapter 12) can be useful. *However*, avoid that lesson if you are *actually dealing* with carpal tunnel issues; instead, focus on lessons for the back and shoulders (see appendix B). Typically, carpal tunnel issues arise from using weak muscles in the wrist because of a disconnect to the stronger muscles of the shoulders and back.

For TMJ, try the ATM: Softening the Mouth (chapter 12) as well as those lessons for the eyes (chapter 13).

As for help with the lower back, read chapter 6 and also explore these ATMs: The Pelvic Clock (chapter 7), Relating Head and Pelvis (chapter 11), and Balance in Standing (chapter 6).

Strings: Primarily Plucked

ACOUSTIC GUITAR: CRAIG LINCOLN

1. When I play my guitar, tension in the left hand (which can radiate all up the arm to the shoulder) is an issue. To chord the guitar, especially the steel-string acoustic, a lot of finger and hand strength is required, often in awkward positions, both sustained and changed quickly. When standing, the shoulder strap rides in the notch of my left shoulder and presses uncomfortably after a while. It may be affecting circulation or nerve activity.
2. I have never experienced significant injury as a result of playing. Most of the physical discomfort of blisters and tender fingertips goes away at the beginner level, although it can be easy to strain the hand and/or fingers by learning a new chord progression and overworking it: too much too soon.
3. I'm not aware of specific remedies other than consciously taking time to periodically relax my hands, arms, and shoulders, and working chord by chord to eliminate any unnecessary tension.
4. For me, the best way to prevent injuries is to continue to focus on relaxing as I play, take frequent breaks to stretch and relax my hands, and work on minimizing the pressure I use to fret the strings, even finger-by-finger in chordal playing. I believe I picked up the notion from guitar teacher Jamie Andreas that the only reason I make mistakes in my playing is that there is somewhere in my body where there is too much tension. I hope to make every mistake an opportunity to find the tension.

Craig Lincoln is a performing songwriter, musician, and actor living in Los Angeles. Largely self-taught, Lincoln has been playing and/or performing acoustic steel-string guitar for six decades.

ELECTRIC BASS: HELENA GOLDBERG

1. When in position to play electric bass, tension is located in my back (lumbar spine), back of the neck (cervical spine), and left forearm.
2. I believe that the particular history I've had with the piano may have affected the physical results of my bass playing and performance injuries that occur. In order to fully answer this question, there are several pieces of information to share that are significant. I have not met another musician or student with all of the specific set of challenges I have in the present day.

I began piano lessons at the age of four (I'm now thirty-eight); soon thereafter I began increasing practice time for the purpose of competitive playing, and from ages eleven to twenty-one I was practicing an average of four to six hours daily. I developed tendonitis in both of my forearms as a teenager, and this seemed to "crossover" in a way to my left forearm when I began touring extensively while playing bass with my band Akris in my early twenties.

The tendonitis at its most extreme example resurfaced during my first tour with Akris playing bass, and resulted in my fingers actually turning blueish-white toward the end of a forty-minute set. I experienced a stiffening in the fingers to the point where I was unable to move them until about thirty minutes later. Many other bassists I have met experience similar tightening in the forearm while playing, although I can't say with certainty it's a result of tendonitis.

It is also significant to mention that I play a heavier weighted electric bass with my band, an Epiphone Thunderbird. The extra weight of the instrument, combined with the fact that I am an extremely physically active performer, has undoubtedly exacerbated and maybe even been a leading cause of my performance injuries. Directly after performances and for about twenty-four hours afterwards, my neck will be extremely stiff and in pain.

The genre of music has to be discussed marginally here; it's difficult to define due to the diffusion of musical genres in the last twenty-five years (the impact of technology and the internet on music in this way is a fascinating topic of discussion best left for another time)—however, in the world of "heavy music," my band has been most often described as sludge/doom/progressive metal. Sound crafting with speakers, amplifiers, and various other equipment is an intrinsic and defining part of this style of music.

My band has been a two piece for most of its sixteen-year history (myself on bass and vocals with drummer), and so I have been the one loading in, setting up, and immediately after playing, breaking down and loading off my own bass equipment. In most cases, until a band has the financial backing to support a crew, band members must be the ones loading in extremely heavy equipment, amplifiers, and speaker cabinets.

As noted, I play an unusually heavy instrument and additionally also use a rig for Akris comprised of an Ampeg 8/10E speaker cabinet (the heavier 165-pound model), a 2/15 speaker cabinet, and at times additionally a 4/10 cabinet.

When you consider the amount of exertion needed for this type of weight lifting, increased by the number of consecutive nights on a tour, and factor in a performance each night that is extremely physically active, you absolutely have a situation that has led many colleagues of mine to having herniated disks and other spinal injuries.

At this time, after having played bass with my band, touring and performing consistently for about sixteen years, I do have pain in my lower back that is almost constantly present.

I also tend to break out in excruciatingly painful, burning itching hives when practice hours run significantly long in one session. I have studied, journaled, and chronicled these hives for twenty years since the issue first emerged, and it has gotten worse as I've gotten older. I've seen doctors, allergists, even been to the emergency room for them before, and I have yet to find an effective remedy or treatment. What I have noticed that is interesting is that they do seem to be linked to some kind of inflammation and heat, which seems to happen in my hands and wrists when I am practicing virtuosic and technical piano pieces for long periods of time. They also appear on my neck where my bass strap lies after practice or a show. They will usually also appear on my head, palms, and feet during and after a performance.

3. Tendonitis has always been relieved for me by massaging the specific areas in the forearm that are feeling "tight." It's most important for me to do this before a performance and also afterwards.

A lacrosse ball behind my back against a flat wall or on the floor behind my back has worked absolute miracles for controlling the direction and pressure by which I can "work out" knots on my own the day after a performance.

In 2015, before I knew about the lacrosse ball, for a span of about six months after every show I would notice the inside of my right wrist (on the pinky side) would have a bleeding circle the size of a nickel rubbed off by my bass. These were, interestingly, the first shows and tours after taking almost a year off during the time in which I had my daughter, and I do think my body changed in a way—suddenly the same Thunderbird bass I had since 2010 was making my wrist bleed!

At the suggestion of my drummer, who implemented the lacrosse ball for muscle knots in his back, I started doing the lacrosse ball on my upper back and shoulders every night to help with the knots I was getting. After just a couple weeks of consistent lacrosse balling on my *upper back*, my wrist was totally completely unaffected at the end of every show and it has never happened again. I still lacrosse ball my back every now and then when I need to, but the issue has not returned. My conjecture is that I was out of alignment in some way after the pregnancy and birth of my daughter, and that lacrosse ball shifted my wrist up or down maybe just a centimeter back to where it wouldn't get hurt!

In terms of the pain in different regions of the spine, many of my colleagues have needed surgical procedures for performance-related spinal injuries that were a result of years of playing, touring, and loading heavy equipment in extreme metal bands.

As far as the hives go, again, there are no allergy, herbal, over-the-counter, or prescribed medications or treatments I have ever tried in twenty years that have "cured" me of them and there is only one thing I have ever found that alleviates them slightly: CBD mentholated roll-on gel. I feel it deeply penetrates the hive, which does get to the intense burning when they are flaring up; however, when the hives are on my palms it is an absolutely miserable time because we use our hands constantly. Any gel I put on them usually comes off, gets washed off, wiped off, or my hands are just too aggravated for even that one working treatment.

I have never known any other person to get hives of this specific nature, and I really wish I did! They just simply do not seem to be only allergy or stress related and the way they pop up, they look almost like something you'd see related to poison ivy, and then they leave as quickly as they came with no marks.

4. In terms of the specific injuries mentioned for myself and prevention, massaging my forearms, using the lacrosse ball, and stretching my whole entire body before a long practice or show will usually significantly reduce symptoms of tendonitis as well as soreness in my back, neck, and shoulders.

Limiting my practice time to shorter segments has also been somewhat effective, as has ensuring that I properly warm-up by playing slowly and easily for between five to ten minutes. I have been teaching piano and voice for twenty years. I am so lucky to be able to put into practice what I teach my students as a professional musician who still strives for and seeks opportunities to perform. I believe I will always have a deep need to perform, and I will always continue to do it, even though I understand the risks of pain and possible injury. The most important starting point for me to impart to my students on this subject is that all technical practice strategies should be practiced during specifically categorized "practice time." This aligns with the other important method of isolation; I deeply believe that we, as musicians, must practice each new facet of learning on its own in order to deeply imprint into our bodies, muscle memory, subconscious, and conscious awareness. For this reason, injury prevention practices like stretching, relaxing while playing, and the particular way we warm up must be isolated in the same way. This preserves our integrity of performance because we will then separate the potentially mentally distracting elements of proper technique into their own designated category for ourselves. Thoughts like, "have I stretched enough?" and "am I holding my bass the right way/sitting at my piano the right way?" even, "am I going to make a mistake?" will, ideally, have already been addressed in the practice room during practice time. When we walk out onstage for a performance, we can then be liberated by the fact that we have isolated the techniques already, we have already strengthened our foundation, we have done our stretches, and our correct way of playing is already in our muscle memory—the functionality will be in place and all we have to do is relax and enjoy expressing music and being the individual, wonderful, unique performers that we are. In this way, I am able to play without strain during a performance because mentally I am free. In particular, with Akris, again, the nature of how free this performance is for me indeed may be one of the contributing factors to injury. With Akris, when playing bass in performances, I am propelled into a spiritual and transcendental state. I do not ever want to lose this because it is absolutely part of my spirituality and part of how I feel close to something beyond this world.

In summation, while I have seen the successful results of implementing isolation, relaxation, and balance in my teaching and practice methods, I do have concerns for the longevity of my career in Akris independent of major financial backing that would finance a road crew to load in and load out around three hundred pounds of equipment twice a night for me if I am ever unable to do so! I also feel that having new body strengthening systems and stretches in place as I get older could potentially help me avoid inflammation that may be a trigger of a hive condition, as well as a path that might lead to spinal surgeries.

Helena Goldberg is a piano/voice/composition instructor, classical pianist, bassist and vocalist of metal group Akris, owner of The Goldberg School of Music, LLC, in

Berryville, Virginia, and co-founder/chief executive officer of Green Sloth Records, Inc., a student-led nonprofit record label.

LUTE: DEBORAH FOX

1. Shoulders, left upper arm, right forearm and wrist, lower back.
2. I don't know. I had De Quervain tenosynovitis in my right wrist, whether from playing my instrument is unclear.
3. I had tendon release surgery. Sessions with Sam Nelson (Feldenkrais practitioner) helped the pain but did not alleviate the problem.
4. Allow the weight of the body (arms, shoulders) to initiate the sound and the movement. Be aware of back and shoulders, as well as tension and stability in legs.

Deborah Fox is a professional lute player. She is the founder and director of Pegasus Early Music in Rochester, New York.

HARP: AMY WALTS

1. It should be noted that harps come in very different sizes and configurations, so the physical requirements of the harpist will vary accordingly, relevant to the size of the instrument. (Naturally, potential overuse injuries apply to both.) A lever/folk harp allows the harpist to sit with both feet on the floor, and its smaller size usually requires less of a reach for the arms. The left arm does "double duty," as it's used not only to play, but to quickly reach up to the neck of the harp to flip the sharpening levers, which can be a very abrupt action and is not necessarily ergonomic. This sort of harpist's injuries or discomfort happens mostly in the neck, shoulders, and arms. A harpist on a concert/orchestra/pedal harp, however, has more of a "full body" experience and injury potential, as the legs and feet are involved in working the pedals. Due to the size, shape, and weight of the instrument, more extreme arm and shoulder positions are required and physical stress is likewise increased.

    For either type of harpist to maintain the most ergonomic position while playing, the elbows are slightly raised, with the forearms more or less parallel to the floor. Over long periods, this can really tire the trapezius and deltoid muscles as well as the supraspinatus and infraspinatus muscles. To achieve the arm reach required in the lower registers of the instrument by the harpist's cheek/ear, the left shoulder blade is generally slid *forward* of a neutral "vertical midline" position; this can be very hard on the subscapularis (this is the prime location for trigger points). To achieve the reach required of the uppermost registers, with the elbow raised, the right shoulder is often considerably *behind* a neutral "vertical midline" position, with the hand near face height. Again, it's tough on the trapezius, deltoid, and supra-/infraspinatus muscles. The slight combination of left-shoulder-slid-forward and right-shoulder-slid-back can create a subtle twist/tension in the back. The harp physically rests on the right shoulder, with the music stand to the left of the harpist, so while all of this is going on, the head is turned slightly to the left, which can aggravate that twist and create fatigue in the descending part of the trapezius, the splenius capitis, and semispinalis muscles (again, prime spots for trigger points). Aside from needing to move the arms freely while playing, pedal harpists will also be moving the legs and feet. This means often sitting balanced on the ischial tuberosities with feet off the floor and can be tiring.

2. Repetitive strain injuries. Lifting and moving injuries to the back. I have had overuse injuries to my hand/wrist. I have pesky trigger points in my left shoulder and the base of my skull. I think these are all pretty typical of harpists.

3. I've done chiropractic/osteopathic work to keep my back aligned and my neck loose. Osteopathic work is a lifesaver and is absolutely worth tracking down a doctor of osteopathy (they are few and far between)! Eventually, I had tendon release surgeries on my left wrist and elbow. Regular massage therapy tackles those pesky trigger points. For chronic pain, especially back pain, a TENS unit really helps. *The importance of careful stretching before playing really can't be overstated*, nor can icing after a long musical workout. There are companies that make customized ice packs for hands and arms and shoulders, and they are amazing (and can be warmed for heat therapy, too). And speaking of workouts, having a trainer or physical therapist design exercises to help you is money well spent. I actually brought my pedal harp into my physical therapist's office and had all the therapists try the instrument so they could see the innate problems and what I was trying to achieve or avoid (and now they can help all the other harpists they encounter in the future). They had a whole new appreciation for musicians! It's much better to do that as preventative medicine rather than injury recovery. Resign yourself to thinking of your body as the tool of an elite athlete, and treat it accordingly.

4. I don't teach, but I've learned a lot about ergonomics over the years. Never underestimate the importance of proper seating! The height is important for good arm and hand positioning, but so too is being able to tilt the angle of the seat, freeing the legs for pedaling. It also keeps good blood supply to the legs, as the chair edge doesn't dig into muscles and nerves, restricting circulation. There are several companies making performance chairs for particular types of instrumentalists, and they are worth every penny. Once again, from a physical perspective, stretching before and after playing is critical for the whole body, as well as "warming up" and repeating the process during breaks. Insist on reasonable breaks! When I first started performing at restaurants or events, I felt guilty for it. People think playing the harp is just a graceful thing you do sitting down—it never even occurs to most people that you had to get the instrument out of your house, in and out of the car, setup, and then have to do it all in reverse at the end (the only other musicians who feel your pain are double bassists)—so clients can really be nasty about building in your break time. It was tempting for me to just power through without breaks to keep people happy, but was the source of a lot of my problems. When you're exhausted, you're not holding your back and shoulders well or your arms in good position, so you're not playing with good form, thereby stressing your body and ultimately causing injury. The tension on those wires requires real strength! Beginner students should have their playing posture evaluated and perfected from the very start to build good ergonomic habits, and experienced harpists should have their technique evaluated every few years to retain good form. It's far easier to learn correctly than

undo bad habits! Keeping hands and wrists warm helps—I sometimes play with fingerless gloves in colder environments.

Amy Matson Walts has been a performing harpist for twenty-five years; she plays pedal harp, lever harp, and electric harp. She is also a medical illustrator whose brilliant drawings grace the pages of this book as well as both editions of *Singing With Your Whole Self: A Singer's Guide to Feldenkrais Awareness Through Movement*.

SAM'S RECOMMENDATIONS

There seems to be a common theme of both back issues and the need to sit in a balanced way. ATM: Sitting to Standing (chapter 3) would be a good place to start. When you learn how to sit and stand with ease, and the reverse, you also learn how to position yourself to sit with greater ease. You don't jar yourself by falling into a chair, nor do you strain your back (as well as other areas of your body) in coming to standing. Furthermore, you lengthen your back going both up and down.

Regarding shoulder issues, read the recommendations for strings, primarily bowed, as the same information applies here.

For dealing with back issues, work with ATM: The Pelvic Clock (chapter 7). In addition, ATM: The Connection of the Feet Through to the Head (chapter 6) and ATM: The Role of the Pelvis in Sitting Erect (chapter 7) may also prove fruitful.

With neck problems, ATM: Neck Turned Passively and ATM: Relating Head and Pelvis (both in chapter 11) are a good place to start. One can check out ATM: Moving the Sternum (chapter 14) as well, but only after you have a good sense of how to do these lessons.

Wind Instruments

WOODWINDS

FLUTE: GLENNDA DOVE PELLITO

1. The problematic areas for flutists are the neck, hands, and jaw.
2. Flutists can experience neck pain, carpal tunnel, tendonitis, arthritic thumbs, and jaw pain from the TMJ.
3. I have encountered all of these injuries over many years of teaching. I have taught students of all ages from eight to eighty, and the injuries can be age related and require different solutions. My personal experience with one issue in particular involved the neck. I am also careful at my age now to be very aware of tension in my hands and to avoid long hours of practicing without a break.

    Players with neck pain must learn to correct their posture and strive to play without tension in their arms, upper back, and neck. In my case, I had gotten bifocal glasses for the first time. In trying to utilize the lower part of the prescription, I was tipping my head up. After a short time, this caused extreme neck pain. The solution was to get a pair of single prescription glasses specifically for reading music. It worked like a charm because then I could keep my posture in the correct position and alleviate the awkward pressure on my upper neck. This drove home the importance of a relaxed and tension-free approach.

For flutists with hand problems, many times the solution is correcting their hand position. Not only does this fix hand discomfort and prevent injury, it also releases tension in the upper body and embouchure. This also improves tone and breathing. Players who had problems become severe and who develop carpal tunnel syndrome may require surgery, which can provide tremendous relief.

Some hand problems require creative solutions. For older players experiencing arthritic hands, often just plugging the open holes or playing a closed hole flute will solve the problem. For extreme hand problems due to arthritis or previous injury to the fingers, there are attachments that snap on the flute to facilitate better balance and positioning of the right hand thumb and left hand index finger. These often help tremendously and are worth a try as they allow some players to play more comfortably.

I have had a few students who played with so much tension in their embouchure and jaw that it caused jaw pain, in the TMJ. If the player pushes into the flute with the left arm, it presses the head joint into the chin, causing pressure on the jaw and misshapes the embouchure, resulting in tightness along with tonal and pitch problems. Long hours of playing this way will cause severe jaw pain and fatigue of the embouchure. Correcting the posture regarding the hands and relaxing the pressure and tension on the chin almost always fixes the problem.

4. One of the most rewarding aspects of teaching has been helping players perform more comfortably and efficiently. Most problems that flutists experience are directly related to how they hold the flute and the unnecessary tension in the upper body. These factors affect every aspect of playing: from being pain free to having better tonal quality, pitch, breathing, and technique.

The first step is to hold, or as I like to say, "float the flute" correctly. It is suspended or "floated" between the right hand thumb, left hand joint of the index finger, and the chin. To do this, the player needs to align the head joint so that the body of the flute rests gently in the left hand and the right hand reaches over the keys in a gentle arch. The flute should not be rolled back into the right hand, causing the wrist to bend backwards. I refer to this incorrect position as "the claw." The left hand should not push the flute firmly into the chin. The flute should float with no fingers on it at all, just resting on the right hand thumb and left hand. This avoids all tension in the hands and forearms, and enables the embouchure to be flexible.

Because the flute is held off to the right, the left hand crosses over the body and causes a slight twist and tilt of the neck. If this becomes too extreme, neck problems will develop. The player should turn the body slightly to the right, shortening the reach of the left arm. The only arm movement required to bring the flute up to the embouchure is bending the elbows. Shoulders should not be involved at all, and the right arm should not pull the flute back, but rather push the end of the flute gently forward. I tell my students to feel all of their weight going down to their feet. We should not feel like we are trying to levitate off the ground. I recommend standing while practicing as you can be more aware of muscle tension throughout the body.

Once the flute is assembled and held correctly, playing can be effortless and pain free. The worst thing you can do, and I have seen many advanced students and young professionals make this mistake, is to practice with tension for long, intense hours. This almost always results in injury, so much that it can be career ending. Playing relaxed for shorter periods and taking breaks to stretch the body is essential. Stretch the arms, shoulders, neck, back, and hips, and give your embouchure a rest. Take a break, go for a walk, have a cup of tea, and you will love playing the flute for your entire life.

Glennda Dove Pellito earned degrees from the Eastman School of Music and the Royal College of Music and studied with Joseph Mariano, John Francis, Jean-Pierre Rampal, and Marcel Moyse. She resides in Rochester, New York, and is retired after nearly forty years from the Hochstein School of Music and Dance, and State University of New York, Geneseo.

OBOE: GEOFFREY BURGESS

1. The weight of the instrument is on the right thumb, so that can cause problems in that hand; the left arm has to be held higher to operate the tone holes and keys on the upper section of the instrument. This unbalanced posture can create tension resulting from the compensatory work done between left and right sides of the upper back. Tension also tends to concentrate in the jaw and neck, for me particularly the left side of the neck.

    The tension and repetition injury involved in reed making should not be underestimated. This is very close, detailed work that also requires strained hand positions and can involve many hours for professional oboists.

    Playing the oboe requires sustained breath work; the biggest danger is that the player forgets to exhale, because it is easy to play extremely long phrases, but this also results in significant tension in the intercostal muscles.
2. Right thumb, shoulder, and neck. I am lucky that I have not experienced injuries of this type, although I would say that I suffer chronic pain from repetitive and habitual postural abnormalities.
3. The most effective is regular yoga combined with corrective structural physical therapy, re-education. Feldenkrais has also been useful for getting over serious difficulties and breaking patterns.
4. Number 1 advice is to breathe with the music. Number 2 is conscious exhalation to allow a release of tension. Build awareness of tension and inhibiting habits. Practice as much without the strictures of the instrument as applying that mental work to active practice.

Geoffrey Burgess combines a career playing historical oboes with scholarship in the field of early music. He has taught at the Eastman School of Music in Rochester, New York, and has given masterclasses at Curtis Institute, the Juilliard School, the Mozarteum in Salzburg, and the Royal Conservatory in The Hague. He is the oboe editor for the International Double Reed Society, the co-author of *The Oboe*, and the author of *The*

Thorn of the Honey Locust, a work of historical fiction based on the life of a musician who worked with Johann Sebastian Bach.

CLARINET: ZACHARY THOMAS

1. I commonly get pain or tension in my right hand, specifically in the wrist. This tends to happen if my hand is not at the right position on the lower joint of the clarinet to reach all of the notes, thus having it rest at an odd angle can cause problems.
2. Tendonitis is unfortunately a common issue for woodwinds in both arms and hands. Hand position is an important part to playing and getting it right early on can prevent injuries in the future. Another place that can be a concern is the jaw. TMJ dysfunction is another common problem encountered by both woodwind and brass players which can lead to tooth and jaw discomfort. Thankfully, I have not run into tendonitis, but I do suffer from TMJ.
3. Correcting the hand position so there aren't any weird angles in the hands is a good way to prevent any injuries. One clarinet technician I know has a right hand thumb rest relocation service where they re-drill the screw holes further up the lower joint in order to align the thumb with the index finger. That way, the two fingers are parallel, whereas the default position for some people puts their hand into a position similar to how you would represent the number "4." For TMJ, taking frequent breaks during practice sessions helps my case, but everybody's situation is different. Luckily, in most cases, TMJ is treatable without surgery.
4. Teaching proper position is always the first step to prevent complications in the future. The earlier you set good habits, the better. Back when I was teaching full time, I always made it a point to make sure the index finger and thumb on both hands were aligned as best as the keywork allowed. Relaxed muscles are also paramount not only for comfort but ease of technique. One professor I know has what she calls the "turtle and giraffe" technique where she instructs the students to tense up their shoulders up to their ears in a "turtle shell." Then she says to drop the shoulders as far down as they can go to stretch the neck up like a "giraffe." This helps to relieve any tension in the shoulders and upper body. The most relaxed you can be on any instrument, the less risk of problems years later.

Zachary Thomas has been passionate about music for as long as he can remember. When he is not repairing instruments, he can be seen performing at various theme parks and in the pit for musicals.

SAXOPHONE: NICHOLAS DAVIS

1. Breathing and embouchure can be problematic. Fortunately, there's less of a tension problem with alto saxophone because they are not as heavy as some instruments. Also, this smaller instrument is hanging from a neck chain.
2. In all the many years I've played, I've never known of anyone, including myself, being injured.

3. Unknown regarding injuries, but I would think physical therapy would be appropriate for possibilities.
4. How do I prevent injuries? I always observe general caution for myself and my saxophone.

Nicholas K. Davis, OD, started performing on the trombone at age twelve, adding the alto and tenor saxophone at age fifteen. Seven decades later, he continues to perform as a singer and instrumentalist.

BASSOON: JON BEEBE

1. Trapezius, hips, lower legs, ankles.
2. Left arm/wrist tendonitis, TMJ.
3. I have a few students with the former and one with the latter. I am very proactive (see answer to question 4) so my students have stayed safe, for the most part.
4. Changing the angle of the bassoon across the body has always been effective in combating/preventing tendonitis. The TMJ case required time away from the bassoon, appropriate care from a medical professional, then rebuilding the embouchure correctly. The result was a complete recovery.
5. Since the bassoon is quite ergonomically friendly, especially when compared to some other instruments (such as the flute), during forty-five years of teaching, I have encountered very few serious issues, as noted in question 2. If the student's hand and wrist placement is correct, and if the embouchure is properly formed, there will be no problems.

   Focusing on question 1 above, *the chair is critical*. While it has become quite common for the bassoon to be played standing up in solo situations, which is usually better for posture (unless the player leans forward) and breathing, most of the time it is played while seated, and most chairs are designed more for resting than working. Furthermore, they are not well suited to the bassoon because it is usually supported by a seat strap.

   While this is an improvement over a neck strap that tends to pull the right shoulder back, it does require the player to maintain sufficient thigh weight on the strap to keep it from sliding. A low and/or shallow chair necessitates crossing the ankles and/or leaning forward, creating the potential for tension in any or all the locations noted in question 1. Additionally, the buttocks-friendly contours of most chairs contribute to the collapsing of the spine into an "S." Using a wedge-shaped cushion to elevate the back legs of the chair can somewhat help to re-align the head/neck/shoulders and prevent or alleviate the tension in the trapezius, but these can also exacerbate the issues with the lower body. Raising and leveling the chair can be effective in preventing/alleviating all the issues.

Dr. Jon Beebe is professor emeritus of bassoon and music theory in the Mariam Cannon Hayes School of Music at Appalachian State University in Boone, North Carolina.

SAM'S RECOMMENDATIONS

Provided one is breathing properly, playing most of these instruments is relatively benign. A common complaint is TMJ. For that, ATM: Softening the Mouth (chapter 12) may help free the jaw without directly trying to move it. Likewise, the two eye lessons in chapter 13 could be helpful, as eye tension constricts the face. They can also help those instrumentalists who work on their reeds (making and/or fine-tuning them), as the close, intimate work involved can strain the eyes. Further, *palming* (see ATM: Releasing the Eyes, chapter 13) also softens the hands. The Mini-ATM: Clarifying the Hands (chapter 12) can also alleviate the strained feeling of intense, close hand work.

BRASS

TRUMPET: JOHN OWEN

1. In playing position, the most likely area for tension is in both forearms, between the wrist and elbow, since that is where the weight of the instrument is supported. This might also lead to tension in the shoulder blades, as weight can be transferred there through the forearms. This is especially true if the performer attempts to hold the trumpet with the bell of the instrument high (as is frequently done in marching bands). Tension in the hands and fingers is also common, especially among younger players. During performance, the most problematic area for tension is in the neck/throat and the lower jaw. Finally, tension in the diaphragm is common (the Valsalva maneuver).
2. Primarily, performance injuries for trumpet players are to the muscles of the lips, due to excess pressure of the mouthpiece against the lips and teeth. These can range from muscle fatigue, necessitating recovery time with no playing, to damage to the lip muscles, especially to the upper lip. In rare instances, this can result in puncturing the upper lip with the teeth. I have known two players who experienced this injury. Both resulted in lengthy recovery times away from the instrument. Improper playing position can also cause injury to the forearms and elbows, although these are generally not serious injuries. However, playing position can be a contributing factor in elbow tendonitis. I experienced this myself, requiring the assistance of a physician and a massage therapist.
3. I haven't experienced injury to the lip muscles. For my elbow tendonitis, I used a doctor-prescribed elbow support. My massage therapist demonstrated a range of stretching and preventative exercises which have been very helpful, and I continue to use them regularly.
4. Prevention is dependent upon proper playing technique, which I always stressed with my students. A key component of this is to be aware of, and to prevent, overuse. Overuse can occur when performers practice for extended periods of time without a break for rest. It is crucial to alternate periods of practice with periods of rest to allow adequate recovery of stressed muscles and joints. There is an adage among trumpet players to "rest as much as you play" (although this is difficult to do, for various reasons). To avoid overuse and excess fatigue to the lips, it is important to use proper speed and compression of the air, rather than pressing the mouthpiece

against the lips. Daily work on breathing exercises is helpful, and there are some devices which can be used to develop air compression while not using the trumpet. I regularly use a device called the compression training system for that purpose and have found it to be highly effective.

John E. Owen is professor emeritus of trumpet and bands at Heidelberg University, where he was also associate dean and director of the School of Music and Theater. He holds a PhD in music education and trumpet from The Ohio State University.

TROMBONE: AUSTIN FAIRLEY

1. Main areas of tension are shoulders (mostly rotator cuff) and the left wrist.
2. Tendonitis, shoulder injuries/alignment; "trigger finger." I have experienced chronic shoulder pain in the past.
3. Strength training, physical warm-up before playing, stretching.
4. The most essential advice is that the best care is preventative care: stretching, regular light exercise, not pushing through the pain. Most importantly, I teach them to always video themselves in lessons and practice so they can see the physical changes.

Austin Fairley, a Stafford, Virginia, native, currently holds the position of adjunct professor of trombone at the College of Southern Maryland. Fairley is a frequently requested freelancer and clinician in the District of Columbia area.

FRENCH HORN: ANNA LORENZEN

1. There are a few areas that tension may be problematic, such as my left wrist, elbow, shoulder, and neck. That is the side that holds up and plays the instrument. Typically, if a higher area on that side of my body has tension, then it trickles down into the lower parts of the arm as well.
2. The most frequent injuries for horn are tendonitis or carpal tunnel on the left side, or something centralized to the face such as focal dystonia, nerve damage, or TMJ. I have known a horn player who got tendonitis in their shoulder, another who has painful TMJ, and someone else who was diagnosed with focal dystonia.
3. Those people have sought help from medical professionals. A massage therapist for the tendonitis in their shoulder helped a lot, and a night guard for the TMJ has helped a little with pain, but hasn't necessarily improved the overall condition. Unfortunately, the student who was diagnosed with focal dystonia was not able to keep playing their instrument.
4. There are moments where I can realize that I am overdoing it, like when I feel tension, my face gets tired so I can tell I've been playing too long, or I am getting frustrated with something so I keep repeating it, trying to solve the problem. When those moments occur, I either take a break or I stop for the day. Playing your instrument is not supposed to be painful, so if there is pain, you shouldn't keep going. There are also many ways to practice without having to actually play your instrument, such as taking a day just to listen to recordings of yourself and professionals,

singing through the music, and score study. Those practice sessions are just as beneficial as time on your instrument.

Anna Lorenzen is a freelance horn player based out of Baltimore, Maryland. She holds degrees from Shenandoah University and Ball State University, and a graduate performance diploma from the Peabody Institute of Johns Hopkins University.

TUBA: BRENDAN MCCROWELL

1. Unnecessary tension is a frequent problem for young brass players and can hinder their tone quality and complicate air flow. Common areas of tension include lower back, shoulders, neck, abdominal muscles, hips, and upper thighs. Engaging these muscles while trying to play can prevent the player from taking in an efficient amount of air when breathing in.
2. Some brass players will exert themselves by playing intensely for too long. The embouchure is made by engaging the corners of the lips around the edge of the mouthpiece and vibrating the inner lips. Like all muscles, the corners of the lips can be overworked and even injured.
3. Improper posture can lead to engaging these general muscle areas from question 1 and can cause short- and long-term problems for the musician. The student can remedy this by practicing proper posture. When playing the tuba, usually in a chair, you want to sit upright, neither leaning back nor forward to the point of strain. Always bring the tuba to your face, instead of bringing your face to the tuba. If the player has to use an unnecessary amount of strength to hold the tuba in their lap, then the player should invest in a tuba stand, which holds the tuba in place at a chosen height. The stand can be adjusted to a height that is neither too high nor too low to let the player sit with proper posture with no unnecessary tension.
4. Never practice intensely for more than about four hours, even if you are a professional player. Take frequent breaks. After working a muscle intensely, the muscle needs time to heal, and the embouchure is no different. For beginner to intermediate players, it would be wise to build endurance in a healthy way. For middle schoolers or those who just started, an hour of practice is a reasonable limit. For high school to early university students, two hours is enough, and so on and so forth.

Brendan McCrowell, a tuba player from Richmond, Virginia, is a graduate of Shenandoah University in music performance, currently completing a graduate degree in music performance at the University of North Carolina at Greensboro.

SAM'S RECOMMENDATIONS

Brass players cite shoulders and arms as potential problem areas. Unlike string players, they are well aware of their breathing. Therefore, the shoulder lessons in chapter 10 would all be very useful, especially Reach and Drop. This is best done lying on the floor. In addition, Winging It is beneficial. Drop Your Elbow is more difficult, but it can help clarify the elbow-shoulder relationship.

KEYBOARD

PIANO: BRIAN WOODS

1. Pianists most often experience tension in their shoulders, wrists, elbows, neck, and forearms.
2. The most frequent performance injuries for pianists are tendonitis/tendinosis of the wrist, tennis elbow and golfer's elbow, shoulder bursitis, and nerve injuries like carpal tunnel and cubital tunnel. Many musicians face the potential for injury; in fact, I would argue that it is rare for a musician seriously pursuing performance to never encounter any physical problems.
3. Many musicians unfortunately tend to mask physical issues with non-steroidal anti-inflammatory drugs or short periods of rest before returning to the same habits and schedules. I have regularly consulted physical therapists to stay in good shape at the instrument and have found great success in working with such specialists to increase my physical awareness. Acupuncture has been effective for some, although admittedly can be another temporary fix for a larger issue.
4. I do not teach, but as a touring concert pianist I stay in the best shape I can to help with an often taxing schedule on the road. This means conscious weight lifting and regular cardio to make sure my body is ready to face the challenges of what many musicians are afraid to admit is a physically demanding line of work. I am also very tall, and rarely do piano benches go low enough to accommodate my height at the instrument. I have to be extra careful when touring to be especially aware of my physical approach to the piano when performing conditions are less than ideal.

   I take time with every practice session to approach each new piece with the least amount of strain, and I focus as much as possible on slow practice to avoid repeating the same phrase at tempo over and over. In the end, many physical injuries come from other sources, such as general anxiety, being overworked in school, relationship issues, stage fright, etc. I find that conscious work on these areas of my life can be helpful in preventing physical issues as well.

Brian Woods is a touring concert pianist and music director for classical programming at the World Chess Hall of Fame in St. Louis. Learn more at www.brianwoodspianist.com or follow Brian on Instagram @brianwoodspianist.

ORGAN: PETER DUBOIS

1. For organists, in my experience primary areas of tension tend to be in the shoulders/neck, forearm, and lower back. Because we often play on instruments with three or more keyboards, our physical orientation changes depending on which keyboard (manual) we are playing, sometimes leading to shoulder/neck tension. With keyboards of varying heights, forearm tension also can enter the equation. And lower back tension results from the fact that it becomes our center of gravity as we pivot, side to side, playing with both hands and feet.
2. The most common injuries of which I am aware have been tendonitis in the forearms/elbows, resulting from prolonged tension such as that mentioned earlier. I

personally have experienced shoulder pain from time to time, from a combination of a necessary posture of "reaching" forward to play on multiple keyboards, without periodic correction to a more "open" upper body posture. I believe it is compounded somewhat by choral conducting with elevated arm position. The combination of the two has resulted in periodic inflammation of the muscles comprising the rotator cuff.

3. For the shoulder pain/injury referenced in question 2, I have in the past sought out physical therapy to both retrain my awareness of upper body posture, while engaging in resistance exercises to strengthen the various muscles in the shoulder. For tendonitis (which I have not experienced), I believe I have known people to undergo various relaxation therapies and/or ultrasound therapy. I have not followed this enough to have extensive knowledge of the effectiveness of these.

4. Injury prevention is largely dependent on continued awareness of motions or positions that are likely tension generators. For forearm tension, as soon as one becomes aware of it, it is important to stop playing and totally relax the arms and hands, shaking out tension, and resuming a relaxed hand position before proceeding. It is something of a "trained response" to be able to identify it before the tension becomes an issue. For shoulder/neck tension, it is important to do stretches before and after practice or performance (and sometimes during a practice session) to restore a proper upper body posture. Again, it takes awareness and training oneself to recognize when posture or tension are beginning to create physical problems while in a practice session. Slow practice often gives the opportunity to be more observant of potential strain. *Gradually* increasing tempo to performance speed can help integrate that continued physical awareness into a relaxed playing even in performance.

Peter DuBois recently retired as director of music/organist at Third Presbyterian Church, Rochester, New York (thirty-two years). He combined a career as full-time church musician (forty-two years) with part-time work as assistant professor of sacred music (Eastman School of Music, fourteen years), concert artist (more than forty years), and broadcaster ("With Heart and Voice," WXXI Public Broadcasting since 2009).

ACCORDION: DOUG MCCONNELL

1. The accordion is a heavy instrument, weighing between fifteen to twenty pounds, depending on the make and model. Shoulder straps take some of the burden off the performer; some players also use a third strap that connects the two larger straps. I never liked this option, mostly as it is harder to attach by yourself! This does provide additional support, however. Strolling accordionists are romantic, of course, but even at an early age, I found it difficult to stay upright, walk, play, etc., without some back discomfort after a short time. At my current age (sixty-eight), I won't do this.

    The right hand needs to be placed extending out from the keyboard; do not let your hand or arm droop down. This is important both for dexterity for challenging passages (runs, etc.) but also to avoid difficulties physically. The left hand is

a different issue due to the use of the hand strap, but even here, one must be conscious of the placement of the left hand itself.
2. I have been fortunate not to have experienced issues with my arms, hands, and fingers while playing the accordion; using proper technique probably helps. My biggest issue has always been with my back and the weight of the instrument. As I grow older, I have to be more careful.
3. I have not attempted any particular remedies for back comfort issues. I suspect that more regular use of that third back strap would go a long way to increasing my comfort, but I have to be willing to put up with the inconvenience of attaching it myself. It is also important to sit up straight at all times, and not allow your body to sag. Distributing the weight of the instrument is very important.
4. I have not had many opportunities to teach my instrument to others. When I do, I am very aware of the positioning of their arms, hands, and fingers, to make sure that beginning players begin their studies with good physical support. If I see the body relaxing or drooping over too much, I point this out to the player.

Doug McConnell, DMA, is professor emeritus of composition and music at Heidelberg University, Tiffin, Ohio. His compositions have been performed in the United States and abroad.

SAM'S RECOMMENDATIONS

There is agreement among those who play these instruments that a straight back is essential. The key to sitting with a straight back is having the pelvis properly supporting the lower back and the lower back under the mid-spine. ATM: The Role of the Pelvis in Sitting Erect (chapter 7) can teach this in half an hour, unless there is a physiological injury that prevents it. Keep in mind that this must be reinforced over a period of about three months so that the new posture becomes habitual. Once that happens, it is set, barring a serious injury.

Beyond that, we have the two most athletically demanding instruments: the organ (because both hands and feet can be moving simultaneously) and the accordion (because of the weight of the instrument). All three keyboard instruments require delivering the weight through the fingers. It is essential that the back-shoulder-wrist-finger connection be solid. If not, the risk of carpal tunnel problems increases. ATM: Moving Back to Reach Forward (chapter 3) and ATM: Reach and Drop (chapter 10) can help.

PERCUSSION

SPECIALTY—TIMPANI: CHARLES ROSS

1. For me, issues have arisen in my forearms when playing too tense or not breathing fully. Also, sitting on a stool sometimes causes strain in my lower back and sacral area.

2. Tendonitis in the wrist and forearm, as well as carpal tunnel are probably the most common ailments for percussionists. I had an issue with this in my twenties. Much less since then.
3. I have done acupuncture, chiropractic, Rolfing, and some Feldenkrais. In addition, certain essential oils and creams have helped when I feel a flare-up; wintergreen is especially effective.
4. Definitely playing with less tension, while not compromising technique and control. I also meditate regularly and encourage my students to do the same. Creating a more balanced schedule between their music endeavors, rest, and other life-affirming activities that they enjoy greatly improves their performance level.

Charles Ross is the principal timpanist of the Rochester Philharmonic Orchestra, and assistant professor of timpani at the Eastman School of Music, Rochester, New York.

SPECIALTY—MARIMBA: BILL YOUHAS

1. Unwanted tension can occur in the wrist, forearms, and upper arms.
2. The most frequent injuries are probably tendonitis in the forearms and wrist. I have personally never had any such injuries because my first teacher understood the body very well and taught us from the beginning, starting at the age of twelve! I was lucky. I know of percussionists who have had tendonitis, but never my students.
3. Not applicable.
4. Such injuries can be prevented by first of all understanding what the dangers and mistakes in use of the body are: important proper posture, correct and "EFFORTLESS" MOTION. One word I remember my teacher always repeating over and over was "effortlessly." Always use as little effort as possible—tension may be necessary, but only when done with intention—and release should occur the instant the tension is no longer required, from the fingers to the wrists to the forearms, to the upper arms to the shoulders, to the back and hips. Only the intentional ("in tension"), necessary use of muscles. When I was teaching, I stressed this every minute with every student. For me, a lot of it is natural by now, but I still must watch and observe when unneeded tension arises; and then, let go.

Percussionist Bill Youhas, college teacher (1968–1985) is the founder and owner of Fall Creek Marimbas, a percussion repair service (1973–2015) in Victor, New York.

SAM'S RECOMMENDATIONS

Both percussionists mention tendonitis in the forearms and wrists. ATM: Mobile Wrists (chapter 12) is a good preventative. However, it is not advisable to do this lesson if there is an active problem of inflammation.

Those who stand to play their instruments may find ATM: Balance in Standing (chapter 6) useful.

Also explore the lessons which involve shoulders/hands (see appendix B).

FINAL THOUGHTS FOR EVERYONE

1. Because all instrumentalists need finger mobility, Mini-ATM: Fast Finger Release (chapter 12) is a great warm-up for everyone. It incorporates an area of concern cited by almost all of our representatives, the shoulders. When done with attention and care, it releases the shoulders, relaxes the fingers, slows down the breath, and provides calm.
2. Performance anxiety, aka "stage nerves." Anyone who has bouts of performance anxiety (an occupational hazard for nearly all performers) might find the third module of ATM: Releasing the Eyes (steps 9 through 12) of great interest. Dr. Blades has taught this mini-lesson all over the globe, with great success. Calming the eyes calms the entire system, thereby enhancing the performance experience.
3. Anna's (French horn) and Helena's (electric bass, but also a pianist) issues, while very different, both mention physical challenges that arise with practicing—or overpracticing!

Helena, regarding breakout of hives: "What I have noticed that is interesting is that they do seem to be linked to some kind of inflammation and heat, which seems to happen in my hands and wrists when I am practicing virtuosic and technical piano pieces for long periods of time."

Sam: This is a classic example of where practicing using kinesthetic imagination could help. It's likely that she gets stuck and repeatedly goes over difficult passages. If she got unstuck using kinesthetic imagination, then she might not have to practice for such a long period of time . . . or the difficult passages wouldn't be so difficult. Also, the human system is usually only good for about forty-five minutes before a rest time is needed; to work longer brings diminishing returns and stress increases.

Anna: "There are moments where I can realize that I am overworking it, like when I feel tension, or my face gets tired so I can tell I've been playing too long, or I am getting frustrated with something, so I keep repeating it, trying to solve the problem. When those moments occur, I either take a break or I stop for the day. Playing your instrument is not supposed to be painful, so if there is pain, you shouldn't keep going. There are also many ways to practice without having to actually play your instrument, such as taking a day just to listen to recordings of yourself and professionals, singing through the music, and score study. Those practice sessions are just as beneficial as time on your instrument."

Sam: Does this sound familiar? "I am getting frustrated with something, so I keep repeating it, trying to solve the problem." The real problem is that the more you repeat the problem area without progress, the more you reinforce doing it badly. If this applies to you, check out the chapter on kinesthetic imagination. Not only is there another way to deal with this issue beyond the three Anna mentions, but it gets at the root of the problem: that your internal program for playing this section is faulty and does not match the sound you desire.

1. According to Bill Youhas, percussionist: "One word I remember my teacher always repeating over and over was 'effortlessly.' Always use as little effort as possible—tension may be necessary, but only when done with intention, and release should occur the instant the tension is no longer required, from the fingers to the wrists to the forearms, to the upper arms to the shoulders, to the back and hips."

This sage advice applies not only to all instruments, but really, to all our activities. Certainly, this applies to all Feldenkrais work, not only doing the Awareness Through Movement lessons, but also being able to provide hands-on Functional Integration. It is a curious phenomenon that the less effort we expend, not only is our sensitivity greater, but it is much easier to be "in the moment." If only it were as easy to approximate as it is to say . . . which is why it is good to remind ourselves of this!

Lastly, the following story is attributed to Ikkyu, a fifteenth-century Japanese zen master about the meaning of attention:

A student said to Master Ikkyu, "Please write for me something of great wisdom."
Ikkyu picked up his brush and wrote one word: "Attention."
The student said, "Is that all?
The master wrote, "Attention. Attention."
The student became irritated. "That doesn't seem profound or subtle to me!"
In response, Master Ikkyu wrote simply, "Attention. Attention. Attention."
In frustration, the student demanded, "What does this word, attention, mean?"
Ikkyu replied, "Attention means attention."

APPENDIX A
Functional Integration

Functional Integration is one-on-one learning where the practitioner uses gentle touch to guide the students through a lesson. Typically, the student lies on a firm table built expressly for this purpose. Each lesson is crafted for the particular student, although the practitioner may use an Awareness Through Movement (ATM) lesson as a template. The course of any lesson depends mostly on the student's response to the work and on the practitioner's knowledge and sensitivity, rather than to a predetermined plan. There are three ingredients to a lesson: the lesson content, the performance style (or touch), and the organization of the practitioner.

The lesson content of Functional Integration often resembles that of an ATM lesson in that it revolves around a function such as breathing, spinal rotation, or the relationship of the pelvis to the head. However, in Functional Integration, the practitioner is free to explore many more diverse options, some of which would not be available to the student without assistance. The peculiarities of the individual are also more able to be taken into account. Finally the pacing, range, and variety of options are dictated by the student's response. Thus, even when using the same ATM as the template, the lesson will always look and feel somewhat different. Indeed, there are times when the lesson that evolves is so radically different from the original plan that a different function is evoked from the one originally expected.

Touch is absolutely critical to the success of a lesson. It must be gentle, noninvasive, and directionally clear. A harsh touch will tighten the student's system, causing them to resist the lesson content. The touch must not invade the person's sense of self or it will be rejected. Thus, if an area "doesn't want to move," that must be respected. This noninvasiveness allows the nervous system to accept the lesson as its own rather than something that has been imposed on it.

Finally, the directions must be clear; otherwise, instead of a lesson, it becomes an unintelligible series of sensations.

When two organisms are linked by touch, they become, in a real sense, one interconnected system. Thus, the student is constantly aware of the practitioner's organization even if they are not conscious of this. The practitioner is also constantly aware of the student's organization. Much of this awareness is at levels below conceptual consciousness, hence, the ability, at times, to infer the student's needs without quite "knowing" how or why. As a result of this interconnection there is an implicit information flow from the better to the less organized system. In most cases, this is from practitioner to student. Thus, there can be improvement in the student's functioning that is, to some extent, separate from the content of the lesson.

A successful lesson results in the student integrating the changes into their life. This means that some of what the student desires, be it more mobility, less pain, or being able to perform a given task better, becomes part of their life. Some successful lessons may not be immediately realized by the student. It may take several days to process fully the information received and feel the changes.

APPENDIX B

ATM Lessons and Areas of Major Impact

The following list is alphabetized by the name of the Awareness Through Movement lessons throughout the book. Where the lesson title does not indicate all the areas where significant change can happen, these are listed following the title in order of greatest impact.

ATM LESSONS (MAIN) AND ADDITIONAL AREAS OF IMPACT   PAGE

Ankle Circles
Knees

Attending to the Back of the Head   21
   Kinesthetic Imagination
   Neck
   Back

Balance in Standing   54
   Grounding
   Hip Joints

The Broken Wing   14
   Spinal Rotation
   Kinesthetic Imagination
   Shoulders
   Back

Circling the Legs   92
   Mid-back
   Hip Joints

Clarifying the Hands   127
  Hands

The Connection of the Feet Through to the Head   58
  Feet and Ankles
  Hip Joints
  Knees
  Sitting in a Chair
  Back

Dark Eyes   142
  Eyes

Drop Your Elbow   105
  Shoulders

Evening the Sides   91
  Scoliosis
  Leg Length
  Balance

Fast Finger Release   126
  Hands
  Shoulders

Freeing the Neck to Turn Easily   9
  Neck

Freeing the Ribs   78
  Shoulders
  Breathing
  Ribs

Lateral Flexion   88
  Back
  Breathing
  Ribs

Mobile Wrists   121
  Hands
  Shoulders

Moving Back to Reach Forward   28
  Shoulders
  Breathing

Moving the Sternum   **155**
Ribs
Neck
Breathing

Neck Turned Passively   **114**
Neck
Back

Opening the Lungs   **75**
Breathing

The Pelvic Clock   **64**
Back (Especially Lower Back)
Neck
Hip Joints

Push Me, Pull You   **151**
Ribs
Breathing
Back

Reach and Drop   **97**
Shoulders
Breathing

Relating Head and Pelvis   **110**
Sitting in a Chair
Balance
Neck

Releasing the Neck and Arms   **158**
Shoulders

Releasing the Eyes   **139**
Eyes
Centering
Performance Anxiety and Stage Nerves

Releasing the Neck   **119**
Headache

The Role of the Pelvis in Sitting Erect   **70**
Back
Balance

Shoulders: A Thought Experiment   23
    Shoulders

Sitting to Standing   33
    Back
    Balance
    Sitting in a Chair

Softening the Hands for Calm   129
    Hands
    Calm

Softening the Mouth   132
    Jaw
    Temporomandibular Disorder

Spinal Rotation   83
    Back
    Shoulders

Winging It   101
    Shoulders
    Neck

AREAS OF IMPACT (MAIN) AND ATM LESSONS   PAGE

Ankles
Ankle Circles	147
The Connection of the Feet Through to the Head	58

Back
The Pelvic Clock	64
Spinal Rotation	83
Lateral Flexion	88
Circling the Legs	92
Freeing the Ribs	78
The Role of the Pelvis in Sitting Erect	70
Sitting to Standing	33
Neck Turned Passively	114
Attending to the Back of the Head	21
The Connection of the Feet Through to the Head	58
Push Me, Pull You	151

Back, Low
    The Pelvic Clock   64

Back, Mid
    Circling the Legs   92

Balance
    Balance in Standing   54
    Evening the Sides (mini-ATM)   91
    Relating Head and Pelvis   110
    Sitting to Standing   33

Breathing
    Opening the Lungs   75
    Freeing the Ribs   78
    Lateral Flexion   88
    Moving the Sternum   155
    Push Me, Pull You   151

Calm/Centering
    Softening the Hands for Calm (mini-ATM)   129
    Releasing the Eyes   139
    Dark Eyes   142

Eyes
    Dark Eyes   142
    Releasing the Eyes   139

Grounding
    Balance in Standing   54

Hands
    Clarifying the Hands (mini-ATM)   127
    Fast Finger Release (mini-ATM)   126
    Softening the Hands for Calm (mini-ATM)   129

Headaches
    Releasing the Neck (mini-ATM)   119

Hip Joints
    Circling the Legs   92
    Balance in Standing   54
    The Connection of the Feet Through to the Head   58

Kinesthetic Imagination

The Broken Wing	14
Shoulders: A Thought Experiment (mini-ATM)	23
Attending to the Back of the Head	21

Knees

Ankle Circles	147
The Connection of the Feet Through to the Head	58

Jaw

Softening the Mouth	132

Leg Length

Evening the Sides (mini-ATM)	91

Mouth

Softening the Mouth	132

Neck

Freeing the Neck to Turn Easily (mini-ATM)	9
Releasing Neck and Arms	158
Releasing the Neck (mini-ATM)	119
Relating Head and Pelvis	110
The Pelvic Clock	64
Moving the Sternum	155

Pelvis

The Pelvic Clock	64
Relating Head and Pelvis	110

Performance Anxiety and Stage Nerves

Releasing the Eyes	139

Ribs

Freeing the Ribs	78
Lateral flexion	88
Moving the Sternum	155
Push Me, Pull You	151

Scoliosis

Evening the Sides (mini-ATM)	91

Shoulders

Reach and Drop	97
Shoulders: A Thought Experiment (mini-ATM)	23

Winging It	101
The Broken Wing	14
Fast Finger Release (mini-ATM)	126
Releasing Neck and Arms	158
Freeing the Ribs	78
Mobile Wrists	121
Spinal Rotation (mini-ATM)	83

Sitting in a Chair

The Role of the Pelvis in Sitting Erect	70
Relating Head and Pelvis	110
The Connection of the Feet Through to the Head	58
Sitting to Standing	33

Sitting to Standing

Sitting to Standing	33

Spinal Rotation

Spinal Rotation (mini-ATM)	83

Temporomandibular Disorder

Softening the Mouth	132

Wrists

Mobile Wrists	121

Index

accommodation, convergence and, 42, 43
accordion, 181–82
acoustic guitar, 36, 166
actuation, imagination compared with, 14
air, free flow of, 74, 75
Akris (band), 167, 169
Alexander, F. Matthias, 38
alignment, 35, 61
ambidexterity, 22, 88
amblyopia, 43
American String Teachers Association, 163
Andreas, Jamie, 166
ankle, 58, 59, 192; circles, 145–49
anxiety, performance, 184, 194
arch: back, 65, 66, 120, 122, 153; of feet, 58; neck, 108, 109, 110
armpit, 78, 79, 80, 81, 82
arms, 81; bow with, 32–33, 163, 164, 165; circle with, 98, 99; freeing the, 156–60; head with, 86, 99, 100, 101, 102; raised, 120, 121, 122, 123; reach of, 95–99
arthritis, in hands, 173
"associative flow," 40
athlete, instrumentalist as, 1, 2, 161, 171
ATM. *See* Awareness Through Movement
Attending to the Back of the Head, 21–22, 189
attention, 40, 185
audio version, of lessons, 9
autonomic function, 48
Awareness Through Movement (ATM), 2, 4, 6, 38, 42, 187; Ankle Circles, 145–49; Attending to the Back of the Head, 21–22, 189; Balance in Standing, 54–57, 166, 183, 189; Broken Wing, 14–20, 163, 165, 189; Circling the Legs, 90–93, 165, 189; Connection of the Feet Through to the Head, 58–61, 172, 190; Dark Eyes, 140–43, 177, 190; Drop Your Elbow, 103–5, 179, 190; on floor, 111–16, 119–23, 127–29; Freeing the Ribs, 78–82, 83, 190; Lateral Flexion, 86–88, 190; lessons for, 189–92; Mobile Wrists, 119–23, 165, 183, 190; Moving Back to Reach Forward, 28–32, 182, 190–91; Moving the Sternum, 152, 153–56, 172, 191; Neck Turned Passively, 111–16, 172, 191; Opening the Lungs, 75–78, 83, 191; palming, 137–43; Pelvic Clock, 64–68, 166, 172, 191; Push Me, Pull You, 149–52, 191; Reach and Drop, 95–99, 179, 182, 191; Relating Head and Pelvis, 108–11, 166, 172, 191; Releasing Neck and Arms, 156–60, 191; Releasing the Eyes, 137–40, 177, 184, 191; Releasing the Neck, 117–18, 191; Role of the Pelvis in Sitting Erect, 69–72, 172, 182, 192; seated, 28–32, 33–35, 75–78, 125–27; Sitting to Standing, 33–35, 172, 192, 195; Softening the Mouth, 129–33, 166, 177, 192; on stomach, 145–49; Winging It, 99–102, 179, 192. *See also* Mini-ATM
axonal sprouting, 37

Bach-y-Rita, Paul, 39
back, 165, 192–93; arched, 65, 66, 120, 122, 153; pain in, 62, 167; straight, 182
balance, 193; board for, 136; dynamic, 53, 54; impaired, 107, 108; with vision, 135, 136
Balance in Standing, 54–57, 189; for percussionists, 183; for string instrumentalists, 166
ball and heel, 58, 59, 60
Baroque violin, 162
bass: double, 165; electric, 166–70, 184
bassoon, 176
Bates, William Horatio, 37; method by, 41, 42, 137
Beebe, Jon, 176
Bell Hands, 42
Beth Israel Deaconess Medical Center, 20
bilateral differences, 53, 86, 87, 89–90; kinesthetic imagination for, 22, 23, 24
bimodal stimulation, 45
blindness, 41, 42, 43, 135
Block Therapy, 164
board, balance, 136

Bohm, David, 38
bow arm, 32–33, 163, 164, 165
bowed strings, primarily, 161–66
The Boy Who Could Walk but Not Run (Pape), 51
brain, 5, 20, 47, 48, 51; changes in, 40–41; cortex of, 125; localization, 38–39; reorganization of, 37, 38
The Brain's Way of Healing (Doidge), 39
The Brain That Changes Itself (Doidge), 20, 39
Brass instruments, 177–79. *See also specific instruments*
breaks, performance, 171
breathing, 29, 75, 193; difficulty with, 58, 69, 78, 95; integrated, 30, 31; mechanics of, 73, 74
bridge, of nose, 141, 142, 143
Broca, Paul, 38
The Broken Wing, 14–20, 189; for string instrumentalists, 163, 165
Bronx Opera Company, 164
Burgess, Geoffry, 174–75
buttocks, 58, 62; hip joint connection with, 87, 112, 113, 115, 116

calm, 127–29, 192, 193
cane, walking, 43, 44
Carnival, Rio de Janeiro (Brazil), 152
carpal tunnel syndrome, 119, 162, 165, 166, 173
The Case of Nora (Feldenkrais), 5
CBD mentholated gel, 168
cello, 32, 33, 163–65
cerebral palsy, 51
cervical spine, 107, 111
chair exercise. *See* seated exercise
chest, 14, 15, 16, 19, 77, 97
chin, 173; to sternum, 108, 117
circle: with ankle, 145–49; with arms, 98, 99; with elbows, 105; with foot, 61; with pelvis, 66, 67, 68
Circling the Legs, 90–93, 165, 189
Claremont Graduate University, Historical Performance Practice Department, 162–63
Clarifying the Hands, 125–27, 177, 190
Clarify program, 45, 46
clarinet, 175
clarity, of intent, 48, 49
cognitive function, 38
Cole, Kelly, 20
College of Southern Maryland University, 178
comfort, in environment, 7
compression training system, 178
compulsive choice, 5
computer keyboard, 136
confusion, infant, 47

Connecting the Feet Through to the Head, 58–61, 172, 190
consciousness, 48, 174
contractions, imaginary, 20, 21
convergence, accommodation and, 42, 43
cortex, brain, 125
"Covering the Eyes," 42
crossed legs, 83, 84, 85
curiosity, of movement, 5–6
curvature of spine. *See* scoliosis
cyclopean vision, 136

dark, walking in, 136
Dark Eyes, 140–43, 177, 190
Davis, Nicholas, 175–76
desk work, 102
diaphragm, *63*, 74
differentials, leg-length, 53, 61, 62
difficulty, 50; breathing, 58, 69, 78, 95
Doctor Doolittle, 149
Doidge, Norman, 20, 39
dominant hand, 88, 125, 126, 127
doorway, 63
double bass, 165
Drop Your Elbow, 103–5, 179, 190
Dubois, Peter, 180, 181
Duke University, 125
dynamic balance, 53, 54
dynamic posture, 32
dystonia, focal, 178

ears, 77, 86; electronic, 44
Eastman School of Music (Rochester, NY), 13, 161, 174, 183
economic decision, 47, 52
effort, 6, 8; extra, 36, 49, 50; playing without, 185
elbows, 121, 122, 123; circle with, 105; drop your, 103–5, 179, 190; head connection with, 113, 114, 115; shoulder connection with, 155, 179
elbow tendonitis, 162, 165, 177, 180
electric bass, 166–70, 184
Electronic Ear, 44
elevated shoulders, 102, 103
embouchure, 175, 176, 179; tension with, 173
environment, comfort in, 7
Epiphone Thunderbird, 167
equestrian, 11
equipment, heavy, 167, 169
ergonomics, 171
error, pattern of, 12–13, 38
Evening the Sides, 89–90, 190
excess tension, 11, 35, 162, 163

exercise, 20; jaw-clenching, 35, 36; seated, 28–32, 33–35, 75–78
exhalation, 174
extended practice, 12, 174, 178, 179
extra effort, 36, 49, 50
eyes, 41, 42, 193; dark, 140–43, 177, 190; head connection with, 70, 71; neck connection with, 136–37; releasing the, 137–40, 177, 184, 191; squint from, 137
eyestrain, 37, 137, 138

Fall Creek Marimbas, 183
Farley, Austin, 178
Fast Finger Release, 124, 184, 190
faulty function, 3, 4
feet, 51; arch of, 58; ball and heel of, 58–61; on floor, 64, 73, 90–93; head connection with, 58–61, 172, 190; stability of, 53; weight on, 54, 55, 56, 57, 58
Feldenkrais, Moshe, 3, 5, 11, 27, 38; martial arts background of, 35
Feldenkrais Access, 42
Feldenkrais Method. *See specific topics*
fetus, development of, 125
FI. *See* Functional Integration
fingers, 125, 126, 127; freedom of, 124; interlaced, 121, 122, 123, 154, 155; lengthened, 120, 133; pinky, 24, 127, 128; release of, 124, 184, 190
fist, 7, 23, 99, 100, 122, 124
flexibility, upper trunk, 83
flexion, lateral, 86–88, 190
"float the flute," 173
floor: ATM, 111–16, 119–23, 127–29; feet on, 64, 73, 90–93; shoulder blade on, 96, 97, 98, 99; sternum to, 32, 64
flow, 49; of air, 74, 75; information, 48
fluid, in lungs, 78
flute, 172–74
focal dystonia, 178
forcing, habitual, 49
forearms, 121; tendonitis in, 167; tension in, 181, 182, 183
Fox, Deborah, 170
freedom: in fingers, 124; in hand, 119–23; knee and ankle, 145–49; of shoulders, 74–75
Freeing the Neck to Turn Easily, 9, 190
Freeing the Ribs, 78–82, 83, 190
French horn, 178–79, 184
friction, 4, 78
fulcrum, seesaw, 32
Functional Integration (FI), 1, 2, 4, 187; lessons with, 38, 44

Geneseo, State University of New York, 174
Goldberg, Helena, 166–70, 184
Goldberg School of Music (Berryville, Virginia), 169
Gottlieb, Ray, 43
Gould, Glenn, 12
Green Sloth Records, 170
grounding, 193
guitar, 36, 166

habits, 51, 171; of forcing, 49; power of, 50, 52
hand dominance, 88, 125, 126, 127
hands, 193; arthritis in, 173; bell, 42; clarifying the, 125–27, 177, 190; in fist, 7, 23, 99, 100, 122, 124; freedom in, 119–23; shoulder connection with, 124; softening the, 127–29, 192; tongue connection with, 125, 129
Hara, 63
harp, 170–72; strings of, 33
Harris, Marion, 42
head, 32, 107; arms with, 86, 99, 100, 101, 102; back of, 21–22; elbow connection with, 113, 114, 115; eye connection with, 70, 71; feet connection with, 58–61, 172, 190; pelvic connection with, 108–11, 166, 172, 191; positioning of, 108, 109, 110
headaches, 162, 193; tension, 116–17
healing practices, Tibetan Buddhist, 42
hearing, 44, 45
heavy equipment, 167, 169
Hebb, Donald, 39
heel, 89, 112; ball and, 58, 59, 60
Heidelberg University (Tiffin, Ohio), 177, 182
hip joint, 193–94; buttocks connection with, 87, 112, 113, 115, 116; pelvis with, 89, 90; raised, 60, 65, 109, 111, 150, 151; shoulder connection with, 87, 88
Historical Performance Practice Department, Claremont Graduate University, 162–63
hives, 167–68
Hochstein School of Music and Dance, 174
holonomic brain model, 38
homebase, 54, 58
horizon, focus on, 137, 142, 143
horn, French, 178–79, 184
hunt, lion, 73

ideal tension, 36
Ideokinesis, 38
Ikkyu (zen master), 185
illness, recovery from, 78
image, kinesthetic, 11

imagination: actuation compared with, 14; of contractions, 20, 21; kinesthetic, 12, 13, 14–20, 22, 23, 24, 40, 184, 194
impact, areas of, 192–95
impaired balance, 107, 108
inertia, law of, 27
infant: confusion of, 47; roll over of, 135
inflammation, pleural, 78
information flow, 48
injuries, 51; carpal tunnel, 119, 162, 165, 166, 173; knee, 3; of musician, 12, 180; overuse, 163, 164, 165, 177; performance, 1, 161, 167, 168, 169, 180; prevention of, 161, 162; recovery from, 13, 24; shoulder, 163, 170; from tension, 174
integrated breath, 30, 31
intention, 28, 50; clear, 48, 49
interconnection, 187
intercostal muscles, 74
interlaced fingers, 121, 122, 123, 154, 155
internal organization, 24
International Double Reed Society, 174
ischial tuberosities, 63
ischium. *See* sit bone
isolation method, 169

James, William, 47
jaw, 194; exercise for, 35, 36
Joliot-Curie, Frederic, 3
Jones, Marcy, 1
judo, 3

Kaetz, David, 45
Kano, J., 3
keyboard: computer, 136; instrument, 180–82
kinesthetic image, 11
kinesthetic imagination, 12, 13, 40, 194; for bilateral differences, 22, 23, 24; lesson for, 14–20; rest through, 184
kinetic energy, 33
knees, 58, 59, 70, 71, 72, 194; freedom of, 145–49; injuries of, 3
knots, muscle, 168
Kubiak, Teresa, 32, 163–64

lacrosse ball massage, 168
Lasik, 43
Lateral Flexion, 86–88, 190
law of inertia, 27
leg-length differentials, 53, 61; performance with, 62
legs, 55, 194; circling the, 90–93, 165; crossed, 83, 84, 85
lengthening, 120, 133
lesser side, performance of, 24

lesson, 42, 188; ATM, 189–92; audio version of, 9; FI, 38, 44; kinesthetic imagination, 14–20; preparation for, 6–7, 8, 9; "Seeing Clearly," 43; touch with, 187
lever, 32, 33
lift, shoe, 53, 62
Lincoln, Craig, 166
Linere device, 45
lion, hunt of, 73
lips, 130, 131, 132, 133; muscles of, 177
Listening with Your Whole Body (Kaetz), 45
lobes, lung, 76
localization, brain, 38–39
logical development, 5
Lorenzen, Anna, 178–79, 184
lower back, 165, 193
lower ribs, 127, 128, 129
lungs, 73, 76; fluid in, 78; opening of, 75–78, 83, 191; vacuum in, 74
lute, 170

manipulation, tongue, 125
Mariam Cannon Hayes School of Music, Appalachian State University, 176
marimba, 183
martial arts, 35
massage, lacrosse ball, 168
McConnell, Doug, 181–82
McCrowell, Brendan, 179
mechanical choice, 5
mechanics: of breathing, 73, 74; Newtonian, 27, 95
mechanisms, repair, 12
"Mel's Lesson," 119–23
memory, 40
mental practice, 20
mentholated gel, CBD, 168
Merzenich, Michael, 39, 40, 41
mid back, 193
mid-spine, 85
migraines, 116
mind, quiet, 114
Mini-ATM (Awareness Through Movement): Clarifying the Hands, 125–27, 177, 190; Evening the Sides, 89–90, 190; Fast Finger Release, 124, 184, 190; Freeing the Neck to Turn Easily, 9, 190; Releasing Neck and Arms, 156–60, 156–60, 191, 191; Shoulders: A Thought Experiment, 23–24, 192; Softening the Hands for Calm, 127–29, 192; Spinal Rotation, 83, 85, 89–90, 192, 195
misalignment, 1
Mobile Wrists, 119–23, 165, 183, 190
momentum, 33; reversibility and, 35
Montreal Neurological Institute, 39

mouth, 194; softening the, 129–33, 166, 177, 192
movement, 7, 19, 35, 51; curiosity of, 5–6; reaction of, 28; rules of, 8, 119; slow, 103, 104; "smiling," 132, 133; three planes of, 85, 86
Moving Back to Reach Forward, 28–32, 182, 190–91
Moving the Sternum, 152, 153–56, 172, 191
muscles, 20, 166; intercostal, 74; knots in, 168; lip, 177; mouth, 129–33; neck, 32, 107, 136; ocular, 143–44; shoulder, 95; tension of, 4, 49, 50, 54, 116–17; trapezius, 163, 170
musician, injuries of, 12, 180
myopia, 137

National Health and Wellness Committee Leadership, American String Teachers Association, 163
Nazareth College, Rochester, New York, 51
neck, 17, 18, 194; arched, 108, 109, 110; eye connection with, 136–37; muscles of, 32, 107, 136; pain in, 162, 172; releasing the, 9, 117–18, 156–60, 191; strap, 176
Neck Turned Passively, 111–16, 172, 191
negative changes, 41
Neosensory wristband, 45
neurogenesis, 39
neurons, 37, 39, 40
neuroplasticity, 20, 37, 38, 40, 51
Newtonian mechanics, 27, 28, 32, 33, 49, 95
New York City Ballet, 164
nose, bridge of, 141, 142, 143

oboe, 174
occipital region, of skull, 21
ocular muscles, 143–44
Opening the Lungs, 75–78, 83, 191
opera singers, 44
opportunity cost, 47
optometrist, 43
The Orchestra of the Bronx, 164
organ, 180, 181
The Organization of Behavior (Hebb), 39
orientation, in space, 135
"oromanual region," of cortex, 125
osteopathic work, 171
overuse injuries, 163, 164, 165, 177
Ovid, 50
Owen, John, 177–78

pain, 164; back, 62, 167; neck, 162, 172; shoulder, 181; with spine, 85, 89
painting the floor, 90–93
palming, 129, 177; ATM with, 137–43; sunning and, 37, 41
Pape, Karen, 51

parasitic tension, 49, 100
parasympathetic neural state, 163, 164
Parthenia Viol Consort, 165
Pascual Leone, Alvaro, 20
pattern, wiring, 51, 52
pattern of error, 12–13, 38
Pegasus Early Music, 170
Pellito, Glennda Dove, 172–74
The Pelvic Clock, 64–68, 191; for string instrumentalists, 166, 172
pelvis, 63, 64, 194; head connection with, 108–11, 166, 172, 191; hip joint with, 89, 90; lifting of, 34, 65; relaxed, 164; shifting of, 54, 89; in sitting, 69–72, 172, 182, 192
Pembleton, Jacob, 165
Penfield, Wilder, 39
perception, sensory, 48
percussion, 182–83
performance, 103; anxiety, 184, 194; breaks during, 171; injuries from, 1, 161, 167, 168, 169, 180; with leg-length differential, 62; of lesser side, 24; of preferred side, 22, 23, 88, 89; with slouching, 69; suboptimal, 49, 54
physical challenges, of instrument, 1–2
physical practice, 20
piano, 180–81; practice with, 20, 166–67
pinky finger, 24, 127, 128
playing: without effort, 185; stretch before, 165, 169, 171
pleasant movement, 7
pleura, inflammation of, 78
plucked strings, 166–72
positioning, head, 108, 109, 110
Posit Science, 39
posture, 38; dynamic, 32; proper, 69, 179
potential energy, 33
power of habit, 50, 52
practice, 169, 181; extended, 12, 174, 178, 179; physical, 20; piano, 20, 166–67; silent, 13
practitioner, organization of, 187
preferred side, performance of, 22, 23, 88, 89
preparations, lesson, 6–7, 8, 9
prevention, injury, 161, 162
Pribram, Karl, 38
proper posture, 69, 179
pulled feeling, 78
Push Me, Pull You, 149–52, 191

de Quervain tenosynovitis, 170
quiet mind, 114

Rardin, Anne, 162–63
Reach and Drop, 95–99, 191; for brass instrumentalists, 179; for keyboard instrumentalists, 182

reaction, of movement, 28
reading, 44
Read Without Glasses Method, 43
recovery: from illness, 78; from injuries, 13, 24
Relating Head and Pelvis, 108–11, 191; for string instrumentalists, 166, 172
relaxation, 166; of pelvis, 164
Releasing Neck and Arms, 156–60, 191
Releasing the Eyes, 137–40, 177, 184, 191
Releasing the Neck, 9, 117–18, 191
reorganization, brain, 37, 39
repair mechanisms, 12
repetition, 8
representation, of self, 11
rest time, through kinesthetic imagination, 184
"reverse mimicry," 24
reversibility, momentum and, 35
ribs, 64, 74, 194; floating, 73; freeing the, 78–82, 83, 190; lower, 127, 128, 129; open, 58, 150, 151, 152; shoulder blade connection to, 29, 76, 165; tightness in, 95
"right" movement, 7, 8
Rio de Janeiro, Carnival (Brazil), 152
Rochester, New York, 164; Nazareth College, 51
Rochester Philharmonic Orchestra (New York), 183
The Role of the Pelvis in Sitting Erect, 69–72, 172, 182, 192
roll over, infant, 135
Ross, Charles, 182–83
rotation, spinal, 83, 85, 89–90, 192, 195
Roxburgh, John, 163
Royal College of Music, 174
rules, movement, 8, 119
running, after walking, 51

safety, bodily, 164
Sam, audio recordings from, 9
saxophone, 1, 175–76
S.B. (stroke survivor), 43, 44
scapula. *See* shoulder blade
Schneider, Meir, 41, 42
scoliosis, 86, 88–89, 194
seated exercise: Moving Back to Reach Forward, 28–32; Opening the Lungs, 75–78; Sitting to Standing, 33–35
second law of motion, by Newton, 27
"Seeing Clearly" lesson, 43
seesaw, 33; fulcrum of, 32
self representation, 11
sensitivity, 6
sensory perception, 48
shoe lift, 53, 62

shoulder blade, 79, 95, 121, 163, 170; on floor, 96, 97, 98, 99; rib connection to, 29, 76, 165
shoulders, 156, 157, 158, 159, 195; elbow connection to, 155, 179; elevated, 151, 152; freedom of, 74–75; hand connection with, 124; hip connection with, 87, 88; injury of, 163, 170; muscles in, 95; pain in, 181; tendonitis in, 164, 178; tension in, 102–3, 165
Shoulders: A Thought Experiment, 23–24, 192
shoulder strap, 166, 181
silent practice, 13
Simons, David G., 62
singing, 44, 50, 58, 64, 73
Singing With Your Whole Voice, 172
sinuses, 116, 143, 144
sit bone, 63, 159, 160
sitting erect, 69–72, 172, 182, 192
Sitting in a Chair, 195
Sitting to Standing, 33–35, 172, 192, 195
skeleton, 63, 64
skull, occipital region of, 21
sleeping, 127
slouching, 69, 77
slow movement, 103, 104
"smiling" movement, 132, 133
Softening the Hands for Calm, 127–29, 192
Softening the Mouth, 129–33, 166, 177, 192
"soft eyes," 137
Sorbonne, 3, 44
sound, 13, 45
Sound Awareness program, 45
Spinal Rotation, 83, 85, 89–90, 192, 195
spine: cervical, 107, 111; pain in, 85, 89; weight on, 64
sprouting, axonal, 37
squint, eye, 137
stability, of feet, 53
State University of New York, Geneseo, 174
sternum, 73, 107; chin to, 108, 117; to floor, 32, 64; moving the, 152, 153–56, 172, 191
stiffness, ankle, 145
stimulation, bimodal, 45
stomach, ATM on, 145–49
straight back, 182
strap: accordion, 181–82; neck, 176
strength, 20, 58
stretch, before playing, 165, 169, 171
strings: guitar, 36; harp, 33; plucked, 166–72; primarily bowed, 161–66
stroke survivor, 43, 44
structural problems, 3
suboptimal performance, 49, 54
sunning, and palming, 37, 41

surgery, 170, 171
symmetrical alignment, 35

Tempesta di Mare Baroque Orchestra, 165
temporomandibular joint (TMJ), 195; of string instrumentalists, 162, 166; of wind instrumentalists, 173, 175, 176, 177, 178
tendonitis, 175, 176; elbow, 162, 165, 177, 180; forearm, 167; of percussionists, 182–83; shoulder, 164, 178
tennis elbow. *See* elbow tendonitis
tenosynovitis, deQuervain, 170
tensing for action, 73
tension, 1, 5, 161, 166; embouchure, 173; excess, 11, 35, 162, 163; forearm, 181, 182, 183; hand, 129; headaches from, 116–17; ideal, 36; injury from, 174; muscular, 4, 49, 50, 54; parasitic, 49, 100; shoulder, 102–3, 165; visual, 137
TENS unit, 171
Terry, Lisa, 164–65
The Thinking Body (Todd), 64
third law of motion, by Newton, 27, 28, 32
Third Presbyterian Church, 181
Thomas, Zachary, 175
Thomas Andres Double Bass Makers, 165
three planes of movement, 85, 86
Tibetan Buddhist, healing practices of, 42
tightness, 58, 95, 124, 152
time delay, of consciousness, 48
timpani, 182–83
tinnitus, 45
TMJ. *See* temporomandibular joint
Todd, Mabel Ellsworth, 38, 64
Tomatis, Alfred A., 44
tongue, 130; hand connection to, 125, 129
tonus, vision and, 37
touch, in lesson, 187
tour, musician on, 180
training, Feldenkrais, 125
trapezius muscles, 163, 170
Travell, Janet M., 62

"trigger finger," 178
trombone, 178
trumpet, 177–78
tuba, 179
tuberosities, ischial, 63
"turtle and giraffe" technique, 175

upper trunk, flexibility of, 83
upright position, 7
uveitis, 41

vacuum, in lungs, 74
velvet black, 138, 140
"vertical midline," 170
vestibular system, 135, 136
viola, 163
Viola de Gamba Society of America, 165
violin, 13, 51; Baroque, 162
vision, 21, 41–43; balance with, 135, 136; tension of, 137; tonus and, 37
Vision for Life (Schneider), 41

walking: cane for, 43, 44; in dark, 136; running after, 51
Walts, Amy Matson, 161, 170–72
Webber, David, 41, 42, 43
Weber-Fechner's law, 6
Webster, Merriam, 11
weight: applied, 32; on feet, 54, 55, 56, 57, 58; shift, 53, 54, 58; on spine, 64
Wernicke, Carl, 39
wind instrument, 73, 75; brass, 177–79; wood wind, 172–77
Winging It, 99–102, 179, 192
wiring pattern, 51, 52
Woods, Brian, 180–81
wood wind, 172–77
World Chess Hall of Fame, 180
wristband, Neosensory, 45
wrists, 195; mobile, 119–23, 165, 183, 190

Yhe, Guang, 20
Youhas, Bill, 183, 185

About the Authors

Samuel H. Nelson, PhD, is a graduate of the Toronto Professional Feldenkrais Training Program (1987) and has offered Awareness Through Movement classes to the public since 1985. He taught a seminar of the Feldenkrais Method at the Eastman School of Music (Rochester, New York) for many years, as well as seminars at music schools in Ohio, Rhode Island, Indiana, and Virginia. He has a private practice in Rochester, New York, where he has worked with professional instrumentalists, instrumental teachers, and students for decades. In addition to providing Functional Integration to clients in person, he currently teaches online classes. Nelson is the author (with Elizabeth Blades) of *Singing With Your Whole Self: A Singer's Guide to Feldenkrais Awareness Through Movement* (Rowman & Littlefield, 2018).

Elizabeth L. Blades, DMA, is a vocal performance specialist, pianist, clarinetist, and guitarist who also studied and performed harp for many years. For over four decades, she has taught in higher education, serving on music faculties including Shenandoah University (Virginia), Heidelberg University (Ohio), the Eastman School of Music, Nazareth College, and Alfred University (New York). She holds advanced degrees from University of Kansas (MS) and the Eastman School (MM, DMA). Blades is the author of *A Spectrum of Voices: Prominent American Voice Teachers Discuss the Teaching of Singing* (2018), as well as coauthor (with Samuel Nelson) of *Singing With Your Whole Self: A Singer's Guide to Feldenkrais Awareness Through Movement* (2018), both published by Rowman & Littlefield. Blades is also a Certified Core-Singing™ teacher and is founder/director of Harmony House Online Music Studio.

www.ingramcontent.com/pod-product-compliance
Lightning Source LLC
Chambersburg PA
CBHW080937300426
44115CB00017B/2850